THE POLITICS
OF
RIGHT TO WORK

Recent Titles in
Contributions in Labor Studies

THE POLITICS
OF
RIGHT TO WORK

The Labor Federations as Special Interests, 1943–1979

GILBERT J. GALL

Contributions in Labor Studies, Number 24

GREENWOOD PRESS

New York • Westport, Connecticut • London

Library of Congress Cataloging-in-Publication Data

Gall, Gilbert J.
   The politics of right to work.

   (Contributions in labor studies, ISSN 0886–8239 ;
no. 24)
   Bibliography: p.
   Includes index.
   1. Right to labor—Political aspects—United States.
2. Trade-unions—United States—Political activity.
I. Title. II. Series.
HD4903.5.U58G34   1988   331.88′92   87–29564
ISBN 0–313–24910–5 (lib. bdg. : alk. paper)

British Library Cataloguing in Publication Data is available.

Library of Congress Catalog Card Number: 87–29564

ISBN: 0–313–24910–5
ISSN: 0886–8239

First published in 1988

Greenwood Press, Inc.
88 Post Road West, Westport, Connecticut 06881

Printed in the United States of America

The paper used in this book complies with the
Permanent Paper Standard issued by the National
Information Standards Organization (Z39.48–1984).

10 9 8 7 6 5 4 3 2 1

Contents

Tables

Preface

Ever since Florida and Arkansas passed the first right-to-work laws in November 1944, state legislation restricting union security—the requirement that a worker must become a member of a union as a condition of employment—has become one of the foremost legislative issues occupying the time and minds of labor's political leaders. This work strives to be both a comprehensive history of organized labor's response to the challenges posed by the right-to-work movement, and an in-depth examination of the partisan political dimensions of that challenge. The first goal—a chronological account of the right-to-work phenomenon from the perspective of the labor movement—is important because to date there has been no full-length treatment of the issue from the early 1940s through the late 1970s. The second aim—an inquiry into the implications of the politics of right to work—is even more significant because the controversy over union security, admittedly a "special interest" issue of the first rank, lends itself well to generalizations about labor's political alliance with the Democratic party. This subject, of course, has tremendous currency in the 1980s as unions struggle to cope with powerful conservative forces, even as they seek to prod the Democratic party into being more committed to its pro-labor policy positions.

To carry out these two tasks, the following pages employ both a qualitative and quantitative analysis. The qualitative aspect is based on traditional historical research in the archives of labor organizations, the manuscripts of crucial political figures, and, to a lesser extent, the records of pro–right-to-work individuals and business groups. From these materials emerges a picture of the strategic and tactical gambits of the parties to the dispute, as well as a general account of their successes and failures. The quantitative research buttresses the qualitative materials and, more importantly, provides

a means to measure and evaluate the relative effectiveness of union executives' attempts to influence the political power structure.

In fact, because of the generally poor historical quality of the manuscript
collections of lawmakers below the executive level, a broad-scale quantitative methodology was necessary to identify supporters of the labor lobby
on right-to-work measures at the state and national levels. Since a key feature
of labor's politics in the post-war years was its almost programmatic alliance
with the Democratic party, a statistical technique of legislative roll call
analysis that would indicate how strongly Democrats supported labor on
this question by comparing their response with Republicans would be particularly appropriate. The method applied, the Rice Index of Cohesion, fit
these specifications. By analyzing the concept of cohesion (how strongly a
group solidifies) across the variables of party, region, and time, an empirically grounded evaluation can be made of the ability of organized labor to
influence political parties on special interest questions, and hence of the
utility of the labor-Democratic alliance. In addition to the indexes of cohesion for both the state and national levels, tables with descriptive statistics
on those right-to-work laws passed by referendums help put the actions of
state legislators, where appropriate, in a constitutent context.

The structure of the study follows a general chronology; however, some
themes internal to several chapters are less time-bound in their discussion
of certain topics. Chapter 1 serves as an introduction, combining a short
history of the antecedents of the right-to-work movement, a review of the
industrial relations literature on the impact of right-to-work laws, and a
discussion of the overall thesis of the work. Chapter 2 outlines the genesis
of the right-to-work movement in the early 1940s, and the response of the
AFL and CIO to the increasing popularity of right-to-work legislation up
to 1949. Chapter 3 picks up the story in 1950 and carries it forward to
1956, shortly after the merger of the federations, examining right-to-work
developments on both national and state levels and organized labor's varied
reactions. Chapter 4 charts the largely unsuccessful efforts of the National
Right to Work Committee to pass laws through referendums in six states
during the 1958 elections. Chapter 5 traces, through 1963, the AFL-CIO's
failed attempts to capitalize on its 1958 victory over right-to-work forces.
Chapter 6 presents organized labor at the apogee of its influence within the
Democratic party during the reformist Eighty-ninth Congress of 1965–1966,
when it finally succeeded in pressuring the factionalized congressional party
into seriously pursuing change. Chapter 7 extends the chronology into the
late 1970s at both state and national levels, concluding shortly after organized labor's last attempt to favorably amend national labor law. And
finally, Chapter 8 presents conclusions based on indexes of cohesion derived
from aggregate legislative roll call statistics over 36 years. For those interested in the technical side of the quantitative research, Appendix A discusses
the derivation and interpretation of the Rice Index of Cohesion, includes a

comprehensive table of state legislative votes on right-to-work measures from 1943 through 1979, and provides the sources for the roll calls at both the state and national levels. Appendix B briefly explains the statistical items and the documentation for the tables on public right-to-work voting. The last section is a selected bibliographical essay on sources for the study of labor politics and right-to-work legislation.

Every author has a multitude of debts, and so do I. My dissertation committee at Wayne State University, and particularly my adviser, Robert H. Zieger, provided many helpful comments during the writing of an earlier version of this study. Also, rather than impose an extensive listing on the reader, let me say that virtually without exception all research institutions listed in the notes rendered the highest professional assistance. A few, how-ever, deserve special mention: the staffs of the Archives of Labor History and Urban Affairs at Wayne State University, the Tennessee State Library, and the Dwight D. Eisenhower and Lyndon B. Johnson presidential libraries all went beyond the call of duty. I would also like to thank the AFL-CIO for making a number of the collections in the George Meany Memorial Archives available for research, and the *Labor Studies Journal* for allowing earlier published portions of my research to appear in this book. Lastly, and above all, I thank my family—my wife Beth, and sons Ryan and Kevin—for their love and support, and for the sacrifices they made during the years of work on this project.

THE POLITICS OF RIGHT TO WORK

1

The Politics of Right to Work

"But," said Mr. Hennessey, "these open shop min ye menshun say they are f'r unions if properly conducted."

"Sure," said Mr. Dooley, "*if properly conducted....* No strikes, no contracts... hardly iny wages and 'dam few members."
—Irish Newspaper Humorist Finley Peter Dunne, on the Second Open Shop Campaign, 1920[1]

Like Mr. Hennessey's bartender Mr. Dooley, American labor leaders have always expressed a heavy dose of skepticism about the true motives of supporters of the open shop. In the early part of the century, the open shop was ostensibly the philosophical position that employers should be free to hire whomever they pleased, regardless of whether the worker was a union member or not. In fact, it was over just this question of union membership—or rather how it was being applied by employers—that American business and the labor movement engaged in two power struggles of significant proportions in the first third of the twentieth century. Union leaders' experiences during these contests indicated that while some employers may have legitimately believed that important issues of individual liberty were involved, in practice business used the idea of the open shop to weaken, and in some cases to destroy, union organizations. Thus, by the time that right-to-work legislation arrived on the industrial relations scene in the early 1940s—in essence enshrining the open shop principle in the statute books of eventually some twenty states—labor leaders with any memory at all took a jaundiced view of the ultimate objectives of the proposals. Right-to-work laws, their experience told them, aimed at removing effective unions from the workplace, not protecting individuals' rights to refrain from union activity.

The following study, however, does not focus on the historical antecedents of the right-to-work issue, or what industrial relations scholars have found regarding labor's dire predictions about the consequences of this legislation on unions. Because of the politically charged nature of the problem, it instead aspires to be a history of organized labor's response to the *political* challenges posed by the right-to-work movement from its inception through the late 1970s, and an analysis and evaluation of the unions' abilities to influence party structures on questions of a special interest nature. It is hoped that providing a fairly comprehensive chronology will also yield a useful survey of labor politics in the post–World War II era, and that the analysis and evaluation of labor's special interest influence will enable empirically based generalizations to be made about the effectiveness of union political activity, and particularly organized labor's partisan alliance with the Democratic party. Before going into more detail about the underlying rationale and thesis of the work, it would be helpful to set the discussion in context by briefly reviewing the open shop controversies of the early twentieth century, and the current industrial relations literature on the effect of state right-to-work laws.

THE OPEN SHOP AND ORGANIZED LABOR

On a brisk March evening in 1921, a crowd of people filed into the Lexington Theater in New York City to hear a debate on one of the most contentious public issues of the day—the benefits of the open shop as an industrial policy. The audience, containing many labor sympathizers, considered the points of Walter Gordon Merritt, a renowned employers' attorney, and Andrew Furuseth, legendary founder of the Seafarers Union and at that time chief lobbyist for the American Federation of Labor (AFL). Furuseth, after listening patiently to Merritt argue that union leaders' preference for closed shop conditions violated the principles of freedom, finally reached a point where he could no longer contain his anger. After mocking the attorney, the aged unionist recalled his early years in the labor movement for the audience. "Isn't it too bad my distinguished opponent was not in public life some forty years ago?" Furuseth asked rhetorically. "He could have perhaps made company with me when I had to deny my name, when I had to deny everything in order to get employment; when I had to say, 'No I am not a union man; don't want to be one.' Why? Because I was hungry." All the open shop defenders of human freedom were conspicuously absent back then, Furuseth observed sarcastically. The attorney had nothing, absolutely nothing, to teach him or any trade unionist about freedom. "God knows," he closed, "if anybody understands the meaning of liberty it is men of my kind, because you denied it to us when you gave it to everybody else."[2]

Furuseth's outburst was revealing. Perhaps no union leader has better expressed the visceral reaction, often bordering on rage, that trade unionists feel when appeals for the open shop are made on the basis of individual freedom. And this was especially true of those like Furuseth, who had struggled long and hard to build stable unions in an era that lacked the state's protection of the right to unionize, a struggle often made even more difficult by blatant employer discrimination against union members. Juxtaposed to the pleas for freedom was the reality of trade union leaders' working lives, when employer blacklisting forced them to deny their very names in order to get employment. Unionists' experiences had taught them only too well that what open shop advocates wanted was not individual choice on union membership, but unrestricted power over workers.

And more than anything else, it was the question of power that lay at the heart of the debate about union security.[3] Labor activists have always believed that union security prevents non-members from benefiting unfairly from the sacrifices they make to obtain fair wages and conditions. But union security has always had an even greater relevance for labor leaders because union building in the United States—with its extremely dynamic economy, its divided working class, and its business interests seemingly intransigently opposed to unionization—has made leaders all the more aware of the insecure nature of their organizations. For union officers, the ability to achieve some form of union security protected against employers or non-members undermining wage and labor standards. It also enhanced organizational stability, particularly financial stability; and most importantly, it made the threat of a strike much more potent. By freeing union leaders from these bedeviling problems, union security practices aimed to establish a stable power base for their organizations.

Grounded as it was in a power relationship, the controversy over union security could easily assume expansive connotations. When it did so, the discussion was not really over individual freedom—or the ethics of labor solidarity for that matter. The dispute instead resembled something akin to a debate about the desirable extent of union power in American society. When viewed from this perspective, the volatility of the subject and its keen concern to both unions and employers is easier to understand.

Nevertheless, in the labor movement's formative years, unions did not always have the power to enforce their preference for union security, and most often haphazardly achieved closed shop conditions on a local basis. With the growth of national unions in the late nineteenth century, though, organized labor improved its record, occasionally excluding non-members from entire trades by refusing to work with anyone who did not carry a union card. This success provoked a counterreaction from employers, who became ever more fearful that the closed shop gave too much strength to their unionized workers. Regarding this growing employer opposition as a serious threat, union leaders began to shed their previous informal arrangements on union security and insisted on written provisions in contracts whenever possible.[4]

As well they should have, for by 1901 three interrelated factors convinced employers to undertake an *organized* campaign against union security. Both an explosive growth in union membership and an increasing militancy among workers fighting erosion of their craft skills supplied a sufficient rationale for employers to launch such a drive. And the development and expansion of nationwide employers' associations enabled business leaders to coordinate an industry-wide challenge for the first time. This first open shop drive, as it came to be known, started in the metal trades with a coalition of employers' groups marketing a form of industrial warfare under the rubric of the "open shop." Refusing to deal with unions where possible, more and more of these business associations joined in a concerted effort to weaken labor organizations where they existed by firing or locking out union workers, and using spies, strikebreakers, and court injunctions to break the union in the resulting disputes. Also, these associations functioned well as clearinghouses for the dissemination of information on successful anti-labor techniques to other employers, and as propaganda mills seeking to create general anti-labor feeling in the community at large.[5]

For the most part, mainstream union leaders denounced the organized employer campaign and resolved to join the battle at the point of production. Most of organized labor in America consisted of the skilled trades, and AFL chiefs such as Gompers confidently believed that the economic power of their skills would ultimately force business to drop the campaign. Despite this optimism, the first open shop drive, which continued until 1907, substantially hampered union growth. In some sectors of the economy, such as the steel industry, unions were virtually put out of business; in some cities, such as Detroit, Dayton, and Los Angeles, the open shop philosophy reigned supreme. Still, unions in industries that had as yet experienced little skill dilution fought employers to a standoff, while strong labor cities like Chicago and San Francisco maintained a vital labor movement despite losses to the open shoppers. Overall, however, the first campaign seriously impeded further expansion of organized labor's power.[6]

Though the *organized* nature of the open shop struggle abated during the Progressive era, it continued on in several industries. During this period of violent labor struggles, the determination of many employers to avoid unions created a festering sense of grievance in labor leaders. Explicit struggles over the issue of union security could break out, and often did, whenever labor conflict appeared.[7]

It took another period of expanding labor power, however, to convince business leaders that another open shop campaign was in order. The federal government's industrial relations regulations during World War I, fostered by the need for uninterrupted industrial production, led in short order to a quasi-collective bargaining system in many segments of the economy formerly operating on an open shop basis. Organized labor's membership swelled to 5 million by the war's end; and its key challenge after the armistice in November 1918 was whether it could consolidate its gains and keep its toehold in the previously open shop areas. Therefore, in many industries unions struck for recognition under peacetime conditions.

The most notable of these industrial conflicts, of course, was the Great Steel Strike of 1919. The strike, called by an AFL organizing committee, provoked a response from steel magnates that signaled American employers wished nothing more earnestly than a return to the pre-war system. Led by United States Steel, the companies used private police, strikebreakers, and manipulation of public police authority to break the strike and return to open shop conditions. Moreover, their sentiments were ratified by prominent business leaders at President Wilson's first post-war industrial conference, convened to find an answer to widespread labor unrest. The conference failed because of the unwillingess of business members to endorse the concepts of union representation and collective bargaining. Once again, labor leaders could clearly see that to American management the open shop and individual bargaining were one and the same. And that, of course, left little room for unions.[8]

In short order, the National Association of Manufacturers (NAM) tapped into the desire of local employers' associations to launch a second coordinated assault on union security. Through an open shop department and publications program, NAM led American business into an even more energetic assault against unionism than the first open shop drive, including a strident effort to associate mainstream American unionism with "radical" elements fomenting social unrest. In addition, business experienced rising prosperity during the 1920s, allowing companies to match or better union-scale wages. Another popular innovation was the installation of employee representation plans, designed to give workers an organized way to express any non-pecuniary grievances to management without having to consider forming a union.

The combination of welfare capitalism, growing business prestige, conservative-minded Republicans' control of government, and vicious attacks against organized labor for "radicalism" left union leaders with few workable alternatives. The AFL executive council met in 1921 and tried to organize an anti–open shop publicity effort. Many unions clutched at the last-gasp effort of the progressive movement by supporting Senator Robert LaFollette's (R) independent presidential campaign in 1924. Unfortunately, there was little labor could do against the onslaught. In many industries—steel, maritime, meatpacking, railroad, building—open shop employers pushed back labor's wartime gains. The second open shop campaign removed established trade unions from many workplaces, sometimes almost from entire industries. Such virulent opposition contributed to a decline in union membership of nearly two million. Open shop employers had practiced union avoidance at any cost, and the circumstances of the 1920s gave particular effectiveness to their efforts. The multitude of options open to them could make insecure organizations out of what were once strong unions in a relatively short time.[9]

For trade union leaders, the economic insecurity resulting from the open shop drives produced a mind-set that evaluated all criticisms of union security practices in the light of what they saw happen in the first three decades of the twentieth century. More than anything else, it was for this reason that organized labor responded to the post–New Deal campaigns for right-to-work laws in the way that it did. Now, however, the battlefield would be the political and legislative arenas instead of private contests of economic strength. "The labor history of America shows clearly that for many years the chief activity of unions was to engage in constant struggle to remain in existence," announced new AFL-CIO president George Meany in 1956. While some things had changed, "we find there are those who still lovingly embrace the idea that unions can be eliminated from the American scene by adverse and punitive legislation like . . . so-called 'right-to-work' laws," he contended. Clearly, the fear that the open shop would be used to destroy unionism dominated, and would continue to dominate, organized labor's reaction to the spread of state anti–union security legislation.[10]

INDUSTRIAL RELATIONS RESEARCH ON THE IMPACT OF RIGHT-TO-WORK LAWS

Perhaps some of the uneasiness with which labor executives contemplated right-to-work laws would have lessened had they had a good idea of how the legislation would affect their unions. Despite a research literature dating from the mid–1950s, industrial relations scholars have as yet failed to reach a consensus on the economic effects of right-to-work legislation. Essentially, as William J. Moore and Robert J. Newman, the authors of the leading review article on the literature, have put it, industrial relations researchers have primarily focused on trying to determine if state right-to-work laws have hampered union growth and the ability to bargain, and if so, to what degree. A second, and more distant objective, has been an effort to study the legislation's relationship to industrial location decisions.[11] Two types of studies have emerged over the last three decades. In the mid–1950s through late 1960s, articles and reports based on survey research or deductive reasoning argued along two lines. One group of these impressionistic investigators contended that the economic impact of the laws was minimal and that their significance was largely symbolic, at most operating as psychological impediments to increased unionization. Other scholars contested that interpretation, insisting that right-to-work legislation did have a negative effect on union growth and bargaining power.[12]

The second and more recent line of industrial relations inquiry, dominant since the 1970s, has taken the symbolic versus substantive debate and subjected these questions to empirical analysis using statistical modeling techniques. These economists have attempted to specify demand and supply models determining the level of union membership as a function of several variables, among them the cost (dues and initiation) of becoming a union member, the levels of income in an area, the relative union wage effect, the non-pecuniary benefits of unionism, and the preferences or attitudes toward unionism found in an area. By isolating and controlling for these other factors as the right-to-work variable is introduced into the equation, it is believed that the economic effects of right-to-work legislation are amenable to more precise specification.

Unfortunately, the studies differ in their evaluations. With regard to the negative correlation between right-to-work laws and the extent of union membership, several researchers affirmed that connection while several others, using different assumptions in their treatment of the right-to-work variable, found no significant impact on the level of unionism. A more recent investigation adopted a different method of analysis, examining the changes in the flow of workers into unions before and after the passage of restrictions, rather than the general level of unionization, and only afterward translated those findings into general terms. This study concluded that there was a reduction in union organizing following the inauguration of a right-to-work law amounting, after a decade, to a level of unionization approximately 5 percent lower than it would have been had the legislation not been passed.

Similarly, econometricians' investigations on other impacts of right-to-work laws are at this point inconclusive. For example, only three quantitative studies have dealt directly with the impact on bargaining by examining the effect of right-to-work statutes on wages: two of these inquiries found no statistically significant relationship between union security restrictions and wage levels while the third one did. And of the two studies concerned with the connection between right-to-work legislation and industry location decisions, the earliest suggested that the laws did not result in increased industrial employment. A much more recent endeavor to answer the same question discovered a significant positive correlation between the statutes and increases in industry-specific, labor-intensive employment. Over a fairly substantial period of time, though, relocations due to anti–union security legislation subsided into insignificance.

Thus, to date little of a definitive nature can be said about the macroeconomic impact of right-to-work legislation on unions, bargaining, and industrial location. It is somewhat surprising that with all the sound and fury surrounding the issue since it first appeared in the early 1940s, no one can say with assurance exactly how important the laws have been in economic terms. In the realm of politics, however, much more can be said about their significance.

THE POLITICS OF RIGHT TO WORK

Even though the jury is still out concerning the industrial relations effects of right-to-work legislation, there is no question that this issue has had a

heavy impact on post–World War II politics. As a standard reader on labor
in American politics points out, anti–union security agitation since the
1940s—and particularly the referendum battles—has been of tremendous
"long-run significance." These "campaigns, even more than election campaigns," the editors declare, "created a need for substantial political machinery, demonstrated the gains to be made from its use, and forced the
education of union members on a whole range of political and social issues."
From these seemingly never-ending contests, labor's political directors
learned that to win in lobbying you had to win at the ballot box. Thus, the
education of union families could not be avoided. And for "issue" education
to make a difference, effective voter registration strategies had to be pursued
with vigor; indeed, in right-to-work struggles scores of labor activists learned
that all political activity required "skill, practical support, money, and day-
in, day-out attention and work."[13]

It was with this in mind that this study undertook an examination of the
politics of right to work. A subject of such import and continuity, it was
hoped, if analyzed in sufficient depth and with appropriate quantitative
techniques, would provide more than an opportunity to chronicle the right-
to-work story. It would also assist in making empirical evaluations about
labor's ability to deal with special interest issues since the culmination of
the restructuring of organized labor's political alliances during the 1930s
and early 1940s. No other trade-union-related issue boiled down so clearly
into a pro-union/anti-union choice for the labor movement, the legislators
it tried to influence, and the public at large. No other issue crossed the
decades and involved electoral and legislative politics at both the state and
national levels in virtually all regions of the country. Hence, organized
labor's attempts to influence the political structure on the question were
cast in sharp relief across a broad landscape, as was its ability to do so.

And what, in fact, does this examination of organized labor's response
to the right-to-work challenge tell us about special interest labor politics in
the last four decades? And even more specifically, what does an investigation
into the quantitative dimension of party reactions reveal about the efficacy
and wisdom of labor's political ties to the Democratic party from the perspective of organizational self-interest?

The answer to the first question is perhaps better handled by attempting
a broader perspective. When reviewing the intense amount of political energy that unionists have put into efforts to cope with union security attacks,
one is left with a distinct impression that the chief rationale for partisan
political activity in the post-war years has been an overarching desire to
protect trade unionism from legislative restrictions, and that a partisan
alliance with moderate and liberal Democrats was the best way to do so.
This very practical motivation underlay both an increasing solidification of
the labor-Democratic alliance at the state level and laborites' crucial participation in trying to build a broad liberal coalition. After a somewhat slow

start in the early 1940s, organized labor responded to the anti–union security agitation in a realistic way, seeking to exercise power and influence in that part of the political structure where it perceived it had power and influence, and from that position attempting to expand its abilities to achieve legislative goals by working to reshape party structures in its favor. Labor relations legislation at the national level (often involving union security questions) and the threat of right-to-work measures at the state level prodded union leaders into seeking the legislative protection that a closer relationship with non-conservative Democrats would bring. From that base, union political operatives then tried to achieve offensive strength by removing non-progressive elements from the Democratic party through rank-and-file electoral activism and union organizing in conservative-dominated Democratic areas. When this strategy, for a number of reasons, proved insufficient to accomplish the goal of ideological restructuring, trade unionists sought other social allies—within the civil rights movement, for example—who could aid labor electorally, in both right-to-work elections and ultimately in breaking through the legislative obstructionism of conservatives in Congress. Although labor was never completely successful in that endeavor from a narrow trade union standpoint, it was not due to any defect in the labor-Democratic partnership that was not recognized at the outset; and through the influence that labor *did* wield in the party, it often prevented legislative constraints from becoming worse. Thus, over four decades the union security issue in many ways served as a catalyst that turned labor's Democratic affinities into a much more structured partisan alliance and helped bring together a progressive political coalition that did accomplish important social-welfare reforms.

The answer to the second question on the utility and wisdom of partisan politics as a technique for special interest influence can only be dealt with by referring to the quantitative dimension of party responses. Based upon a fairly extensive legislative roll call analysis of party cohesion, the conclusion is that organized labor received a favorable and cohesive party-oriented response from Democrats in every region of the country except the South. Moreover, this support was generally consistent at both the national and state levels, and in fact increased over time. It seems that in most instances the Democrats labor had identified as allies performed dependably as just that. The main defections always occurred in the South, and though there were indeed problems and limitations inherent in the relationship of organized labor to the party leadership (often stemming from the fact that party leaders themselves were from the South), most failures in legislative policy making on labor law issues were, in one way or another, tied to the fact that the Democratic party had a large block of tenacious conservatives willing to make common cause with the solidly conservative Republicans, and in combination they could defeat most offensive legislative forays because the tactical advantage of inertia was on their side. Thus the most accurate portrayal of the wisdom of the labor-Democratic alliance, from the perspective of narrow special interest issues, is that it has been a fruitful partnership, particularly for defensive protection. Labor's seeming inability, despite its activism, to initiate favorable changes in labor relations legislation lay not in an exploitive relationship with moderate and liberal Democratic forces, but in the final analysis in macroeconomic issues such as the extent and distribution of unionization and the particular historical development of political parties in America.[14]

NOTES

1. Dunne's satirical observation is presented in H.S. Brown, "Ten Years of Folly: Compulsory Open Shop in Texas" (Texas AFL-CIO, [1957?]), copy in Charles Baker Collection, Box 2, Archives of Labor History and Urban Affairs, Walter P. Reuther Library, Wayne State University, Detroit, Michigan (hereafter WPRL). Emphasis added.

2. League for Industrial Rights, *The Open Shop: A Debate Between Andrew Furuseth and Walter G. Merritt* (New York: League for Industrial Rights, 1921), p. 35.

3. I use the term *union security* to mean the general desire of labor organizations to form some sort of institutional attachment between the union and the workers in a given workplace, company, or industry. This attachment can be entirely voluntary, of course, but where this fails it often becomes coercive, usually through the unwillingness of union workers to work beside non-members or through written contract provisions requiring membership. The strongest form of union security is the closed shop (now illegal under the Taft-Hartley Act), where a worker had to be a member of the union before obtaining employment. The weakest type is the agency shop, which requires employees to pay a fee somewhat less than normal dues levels to the union for its collective bargaining services. The most common form of union security practiced today is the union shop, where workers must become members within a certain time period after being hired by an employer. When a state passes a right-to-work law, any form of union security is generally illegal within that state's legal jurisdiction.

The open shop, on the other hand, has traditionally had two meanings. By definition, employers asserted that it meant they would be completely impartial in their treatment of union and non-union employees, and that it was wrong to coerce workers to associate with a union if they did not wish to do so. Historically, however, business leaders regarded union security of any type as threatening because they believed it infused strength into the union, and that demands for union security inevitably flowed from engaging in collective bargaining. Hence, the aim of the open shop employers often came to be a hard-line refusal to recognize and deal with unions as agents of their employees. In the post–New Deal years, when national labor policy mandated collective bargaining if a union represented a majority of employees, employers could no longer refuse to bargain. But a right-to-work law, which put the previous private economic struggle over union security into the arena of politics and government action, could accomplish through legislation at least part of what anti-union open shop employers had desired previously. For an examination of the open shop from an historical perspective, see Philip Taft, *Organized Labor in American History* (New York: Harper and Row, 1964), chapters 17 and 27.

4. Frank T. Stockton, *The Closed Shop in American Trade Unions* (Lancaster, Pa.: New Era Printing, 1911), pp. 30–32; Jerome L. Toner, *The Closed Shop in the American Labor Movement* (Washington, D.C.: Catholic University Press, 1941), pp. 186–187.

5. For an example of the effect of militancy on the origins of the open shop movement, see David Montgomery, "Machinists, the Civic Federation, and the Socialist Party," in his collection of essays, *Workers' Control in America* (Cambridge: Cambridge University Press, 1979), pp. 48–90. Also see Paul E. Sultan, "Historical Antecedents to the Right-to-Work," *Southern California Law Review* 31(April 1958):221–238.

6. Montgomery, *Workers' Control in America*, p. 63.

7. For a portrait of industrial struggles during these years, see Bruno Ramirez, *When Workers Fight: The Politics of Industrial Relations in the Progressive Era, 1898–1916* (Westport, Conn.: Greenwood Press, 1978).

8. David Brody, *Labor in Crisis: The Steel Strike of 1919* (Philadelphia: Lippincott, 1965), pp. 120–126; Haggai Hurvitz, "Ideology and Industrial Conflict: President Wilson's First Industrial Conference of October, 1919," *Labor History* 18(Fall 1977):515–524.

9. Allen M. Wakstein, "The Origins of the Open-Shop Movement, 1919–1920," *Journal of American History* 51(1964):460–475 and Allen M. Wakstein, "The Open Shop Movement, 1919–1933" (Ph.D. diss., University of Illinois, 1961). For a valuable essay charting the rise and demise of welfare capitalism and its impact on organized labor, see David Brody, "The Rise and Decline of Welfare Capitalism," in David Brody, *Workers in Industrial America: Essays on the 20th Century Struggle* (New York: Oxford University Press, 1980), pp. 48–81.

10. Address, George Meany to the National Industrial Conference Board, January 1956, Box 11, The Sligh Family Collection, Michigan Historical Collections, Bentley Historical Library, University of Michigan, Ann Arbor, Michigan (hereafter BHL).

11. In my discussion of the industrial relations impact of right-to-work legislation I have drawn extensively on William J. Moore and Robert J. Newman, "The Effects of Right-to-Work Laws: A Review of the Literature," *Industrial and Labor Relations Review* 38(July 1985):571–586. Unless otherwise noted, their article forms the basis of my comments.

12. Moore and Newman have an extensive bibliography of industrial relations research studies appended to their article, and complete citations are available there.

13. Charles M. Rehmus, Doris B. McLaughlin, and Frederick N. Nesbitt, eds., *Labor and American Politics* (Ann Arbor: University of Michigan Press, 1967, rev. ed. 1978), p. 188.

14. There are a number of full-length studies on this period of labor's political activities, or that include material on labor politics at the state level, but most do not go much beyond the 1950s. See, for example, Philip Taft, *Labor Politics American Style: The California State Federation of Labor* (Cambridge, Mass.: Harvard University Press, 1968); Gary M Fink, ed., *Organizing Dixie: Alabama Workers in the Industrial Era* (Westport, Conn.: Greenwood Press, 1981); Gary M Fink, *Labor's Search for Political Order: The Political Behavior of the Missouri Labor Movement, 1890–1940* (Columbia, Mo.: University of Missouri Press, 1973); George E. Bard-

well and Harry Seligson, *Organized Labor and Political Action in Colorado: 1900–1960* (Denver: College of Business Administration, University of Denver, 1969); Leo Troy, *Organized Labor in New Jersey* (Princeton, N.J.: D. Van Nostrand, 1965); George W. Lawson, *Organized Labor in Minnesota* (St. Paul: Minnesota Federation of Labor, 1955); Doris B. McLaughlin, *Michigan Labor: A Brief History from 1818 to the Present* (Ann Arbor: Institute of Labor and Industrial Relations, University of Michigan-Wayne State University, 1970); Evelyn L. Harris and Frank J. Krebs, *From Humble Beginnings: West Virginia State Federation of Labor, 1903–1957* (Charleston: West Virginia History Publishing Fund, 1960); George G. Kundahl, Jr., "Organized Labor in Alabama State Politics" (Ph.D. diss., University of Alabama, 1967); Grady Mullenix, "A History of the Texas State Federation of Labor" (Ph.D. diss., University of Texas, 1954); Murray Polakoff, "The Development of the Texas State CIO Council" (Ph.D. diss., Columbia University, 1955); and Donald C. Mosley, "A History of Labor Unions in Mississippi" (Ph.D. diss., University of Alabama, 1965). Some exceptions are Thomas Becnel, *Labor, Church, and the Sugar Establishment: Louisiana, 1887–1976* (Baton Rouge: Louisiana State University Press, 1980); Warren P. Sanders, Jr., "The Political Dimension of Labor-Management Relations: National Trends and State Level Developments in Massachusetts, 1946–1960" (Ph.D. diss., Massachusetts Institute of Technology, 1964); Melvin A. Kahn, *The Politics of American Labor: The Indiana Microcosm* (Carbondale, Ill: Southern Illinois University Labor Institute, 1970); and Jay S. Goodman, *The Democrats and Labor in Rhode Island, 1952–1962: Changes in the Old Alliance* (Providence: Brown University Press, 1967).

2

Labor Legislation and Right to Work

> No one has been hardy enough to contend that union men be compelled to work with non-union men, or that the former may, by law or judicial process, be prohibited from striking against the employment of the latter.
>
> —Samuel Gompers, *Open Shop Editorials*, 1904[1]

The story of the emergence of the right-to-work movement is also the story of the evolution of public attitudes toward labor relations since the 1930s. Between 1935 and 1949, the problem of union security bedeviled a renascent labor movement. Although the legislative innovations in labor law during the 1930s left the legal status of union security ambiguous, the subject emerged as a major point of controversy requiring legal definition during World War II. Favorable rulings granting union security by wartime agencies of the government drove home to the AFL and CIO its importance; at the same time, labor's ability to secure it by government fiat stimulated anti-labor forces and helped inaugurate a vigorous right-to-work movement. Then the strike wave of 1945–1946 and labor's initial organizing victories in the South immediately after the war intensified the effort to curtail union security, first on the state level and then through national legislation, culminating in the anti–union security features of the Taft-Hartley Act of June 1947.

The rival federations responded divergently to these unwelcome developments. The AFL stressed state and local lobbying and legal court challenges, while the CIO launched into electoral activism. Continuing rivalry, as well as the lack of foresight and structural inadequacies in both federations, inhibited organized labor from doing more than preventing the right-to-work tide from engulfing industrialized areas. By the end of 1947, fourteen states, most of them in the South and Plains, had passed right-to-work laws, and the conservative Eightieth Congress effectively protected the statutes from a court challenge by granting the states jurisdiction over the matter under section 14(b) of the Taft-Hartley Act. During these struggles, labor experienced in great detail the difficulties of attempting to wield special interest influence through its growing alliance with the fractionalized Democratic party. Even so, the defeats the labor movement suffered and the cooperation that its several branches began to develop in the right-to-work conflict helped pave the way for expanded political activity in the following decade.

UNION SECURITY IN THE 1930S

Of course, organized labor did not completely realize the ramifications of government regulation of labor relations when it gave its backing to the National Labor Relations Act (NLRA) in 1935.[2] Laborites regarded federal encouragement of union recognition and collective bargaining as an unmixed blessing. Even in the 1930s that evaluation was too optimistic, for there were many subjects still undergoing legal interpretation. The National Labor Relations Act, for instance, settled representation questions and penalized employers who discriminated against unionists, but was ambiguous on the topic of union security. The drafters of the law knew that most of the labor conflicts in the 1930s were over basic recognition, and they also knew that it would be hard enough to get business to accept collective bargaining, let alone union security. Therefore, in one of the many compromises necessary to win support for the bill, they included a provision that prevented union security from being held illegal under interpretation of the NLRA. That clause, however, left untouched any state legislation or common law doctrines making such provisions illegal.[3] For most unions this ambiguity mattered little, for their immediate objective was to win basic recognition of their right to bargain for their members. Union security always remained an important objective for most labor leaders, even to the level of rank-and-file activists, but an objective that would have to be won once the union gained a toehold in the workplace. The first job was to establish viable unions through organization. When those unions became strong enough, they could bargain for union security, if necessary, by threatening to strike.[4]

Though the conflict over union security appeared dormant for much of the 1930s, such was not the case. The contest had simply moved into the realm of legislative definition. From 1938 to 1941 business and political conservatives made a strong attempt to amend the Wagner Act, and at the center of their ideal revision was the desire to prevent the requiring of union membership as a condition of employment. Lobbyists of the National Association of Manufacturers and the U.S. Chamber of Commerce argued that Congress should change the law to prohibit "coercion from any source."

They obviously hoped that such a clause would function as a mandatory open shop provision under statutory interpretation, making it impossible for unions to obtain union security through bargaining. Union representatives, on the other hand, contended that under the evolving doctrine of majority representation it was only fair to allow labor organizations to negotiate a union security clause. In any given bargaining unit, unions would have to provide collective bargaining representation for all workers in the unit. Non-members of the union could receive the benefits of union membership without bearing any of the burden of supporting the union, financially and otherwise. In the interests of equitability, they believed, union security was a legitimate concern that could best be handled through collective bargaining. The NLRA's critics failed to amend the act before the war derailed their campaign. Nonetheless, their efforts signaled that the union security contest had moved into the legislative arena. Inherent in all their proposals for NLRA revision was the traditional employer position on the open shop—a fundamental insistence that union membership be a matter of individual choice.[5]

THE UNION SECURITY CRISIS IN WORLD WAR II

So stood the situation when Pearl Harbor brought the matter of union security not only to the forefront of labor-management relations, but into the realm of national security as well. In the months previous to the attack, the National Defense Mediation Board (NDMB), President Roosevelt's agency for expediting defense production, had exercised increasing control over labor relations. The board had public, business, and labor members, and previously the public and business representatives had combined to reject labor leaders' entreaties for agency grants of union security. In the eyes of the public and business members, union status, including security, should be frozen for the duration of the defense emergency. The board would grant a limited form of union security only in those extreme cases where local workers rebelled against a union leadership that cooperated with its policies. And even then the grant would not go beyond requiring workers to stay in a union they joined for the length of the contract. The NDMB called this compromise "maintenance of membership." Clearly, the board considered this rather limited form of union security as something of a necessary evil—and one it should not extend if at all possible.[6]

Unfortunately for the opponents of union security, keeping this form of organizational maintenance sequestered from the rest of unionized industry did not prove possible. The unique pressures of wartime production impelled unions, especially the new industrial unions, to seek security in exchange for cooperation on wages and strikes. Neither AFL nor CIO leaders liked the NDMB's policy on union security; for the AFL, however, it did not seem particularly threatening. Most union security clauses in existence were with AFL unions, and a freeze on the status quo did not threaten disaster. But the CIO was much more vulnerable. With increasing government control of wages, hours, and even strikes looming, many CIO leaders feared that rank-and-file support for their newly established unions would crumble. Unable to perform the functions of collective bargaining for workers inexperienced in unionism, CIO officials believed that their unions' organizational cohesion would atrophy. This would make CIO affiliates tempting targets for rival unions and hostile employers at the end of the war.[7]

Thus, in 1941 the leaders of the industrial union movement launched a campaign aimed at winning government support for union security in exchange for their cooperation. John L. Lewis vigorously pressed this cause within NDMB councils on behalf of the United Mine Workers. In order to establish the principle of a grant of union security as a quid pro quo for cooperation in the defense effort, Lewis insisted that the small number of miners in the steel-industry-owned "captive mines" be brought into the UMW. In this campaign he drew strong backing from other CIO leaders on the organization's executive board.[8]

Lewis did not accomplish his objective without a fight. Virtually the entire business community regarded any extension of union security, except in isolated cases, as setting a dangerous precedent. As U.S. Steel chairman Irving Olds told the NDMB, granting union security would presage "an aggressive closed shop drive in the steel industry and generally through that large segment of American industry which[,] like the steel industry[,] has always operated under the open shop principle."[9] The employer representatives generally agreed, but Lewis, through shrewd calculation and power brokering, finally forced the government to come to terms with his demand for protection. Leading the miners into two short work stoppages in the fall of 1941, Lewis hoped to pressure the NDMB into submission. When this failed and the board voted against the Mine Workers in November 1941, all CIO members resigned setting the agency on a course of disintegration. President Roosevelt, now knowing the issue could erupt into serious difficulties, appointed an arbitration tribunal, strictly limited to the Mine Workers case, which decided in favor of the UMW on the same day as the attack on Pearl Harbor. But even so, the government was left without a workable policy for wartime labor relations, and without an agency with which to effectuate it.[10]

On December 19, 1941, the president tried to mediate the union security crisis by calling a special labor-management conference to chart a course for peaceful industrial production. AFL and CIO functionaries met with business representatives and agreed to three things: there would be no strikes or lockouts during the course of the war; there should be a National War Labor Board (NWLB) to administer wartime labor relations; and the president should appoint that board.

On the subject that had led to the demise of the NDMB as a functioning agency they still could not agree, even at the height of a national emergency. "The big question," recalled George Meany, then secretary-treasurer of the AFL, "and really the only question, was union security." Conference moderators Senator Elbert Thomas (D-UT) and William Davis, a former official of the NDMB, could not get either side to budge. "We went around this ring-around-the-rosy for two and a half days," said Meany. The employers fought hard for their by now well-repeated position of a freeze on the status of union security. Meany suggested to Thomas that since they had not reached consensus, he should simply recommend to the president those questions on which they had agreed, leaving the rest for a case-by-case determination. "This meant the whole question of union security was left completely open and, of course, this was really a victory for the labor side," Meany later pointed out. "We didn't want affirmative action on the part of the government on this; we just wanted the government to say they wouldn't interfere." This turn of events "bitterly disappointed" industry member Roger Lapham, according to the secretary. Meany felt that the business members did not want to see labor make any progress during the war. "We said, 'The hell with that!' We don't see why we should stop organizing just because there is a war going on."[11]

While the AFL was content with that state of affairs, the CIO did not dare let the NDMB's successor, the NWLB, haphazardly develop policy on union security during the early war years. In 1941, hardly more than a year into the defense emergency, industrial unions in the basic industries had already begun to show the strains of war production. The Steelworkers, for instance, had many new recruits—mainly women and black workers—who saw, for one reason or another, little benefit in joining unions. Moreover, the CIO had only recently signed a contract with the vehemently open shop Little Steel industry. The union also had to deal with tremendous turnover and a sizeable number of unenrolled workers, making it necessary to devote considerable resources to organizing and staying organized. Even many regular members often failed to pay their dues on time, forcing union leaders, in late 1941 and early 1942, to place thousands of representatives on collection duties and to set up dues picket lines. This cost the union tens of thousands of dollars per month as well as a tremendous amount of staff time.[12]

Therefore, it became crucial for industrial unions to ensure that the heretofore limited NDMB grants of union security became commonplace under the new National War Labor Board. Working toward this end, CIO president Philip Murray and Lee Pressman, the federation's general counsel, privately lobbied the War Labor Board's public members for an extension of the concept. Through the first half of 1942, the NWLB struggled to find a workable compromise between the labor members and the business representatives, who stood their ground against government-mandated security provisions.

Finally, the labor and public members gradually moved closer and, in the *Little Steel* decision of July 1942, agreed to generalize the maintenance-of-membership form of union security—forcing workers to stay in the union they had joined for the length of the contract—in exchange for labor's acquiescence to the case's wage-restriction formula. Organized labor found that the policy solved most of the problems stemming from the peculiarities of wartime labor relations. Indeed, unions even prospered under its auspices. The Steelworkers, for example, had no further dues difficulties and soon had enough money to begin organizing plants in Texas and California.[13]

THE ORIGINS OF THE RIGHT-TO-WORK MOVEMENT

For the time being, the labor movement had won the fight over union security at the national level. It had fought off all attempts to amend the Wagner Act and, during the early war years, convinced reluctant government officials to extend union security to industries that had never experienced it before. However, that success was transitory, for the board's decisions set in motion forces determined to make all forms of union security as rare as possible.

The evolving response of industry NWLB members to the *Little Steel* decision clearly reflected this trend. In 1942, they had disliked the agency's solution but felt they had to live with it, and therefore made only token objections in their dissents. By 1944, the deep hostility of their constituency to the policy forced them to abandon their casual opposition, and they began to argue seriously against the extension of maintenance of membership. By the war's end, industry members' dissents in decisions extending union security reached a shrill pitch. In its 1946 termination report, the NWLB asserted that "no issue presented to the War Labor Board precipitated more furious debate than union security." By the close of the war it was clear that the "furious debate" would extend into peacetime.[14]

And it did, but not at the national level. Since the conservative resurgence of 1938, unions had been on the defensive in the state legislative arena, especially in South and agricultural Midwest. This was largely due to the fact that organized labor, particularly the CIO, regarded these areas as crucial to its future. The southern textile industry, for example, presented a tempting target to industrial unionists. As John L. Lewis told a 1939 executive board meeting, this industry held "one of the greatest opportunities to expand the numerical strength of the C.I.O." and consolidate the power of the new federation. Predictably, local business elites feared that increasing organization would threaten their position and prerogatives. As a southern manufacturer wrote his congressman, the "point we object to is a man coming in and telling our employees what they should do ... when we feel that we are in a better position ... to tell them how they can obtain better results as far as their employment is concerned."[15]

Thus, in the period from 1938 to 1944, numerous states passed harsh and sometimes punitive laws restricting union behavior, since it appeared that national labor policy would continue to favor the labor movement for the foreseeable future. Though some of the laws simply aimed to harass unions, they usually concentrated on two areas. They either restricted union security or imposed state regulation on strikes and picketing. Because of the doctrine of federal supremacy, however, much of this state anti-union legislation proved unconstitutional in those areas affecting interstate commerce. The Supreme Court had long held that congressional legislation in the field of interstate commerce preempted state legislation. Despite this, under the National Labor Relations Act there was one subject, which because of the vagaries of legislative decision making and its contentiousness, the drafters of the NLRA apparently intended to leave to the states—union security.[16]

THE AFL'S RESPONSE TO STATE UNION SECURITY RESTRICTIONS

Throughout the 1940s, the AFL responded to right-to-work activity at the state level in a highly legalistic, decentralized fashion. From 1944 to 1946 labor lost five states to right-to-work forces: Florida (1944), Arkansas (1944), South Dakota (1945 and 1946), Nebraska (1946), and Arizona (1946). In addition, unions faced strong challenges in California in 1944, in Texas in 1945, and in Louisiana in 1946, as well as less serious drives in other states. Where there was a strong and well-financed state federation, as in California, the national AFL's policy of remaining unobtrusive paid off. On occasion, as in the early stages of the Florida fight, a reliance on court challenges won victory. In general, though, the federation paid dearly for its reluctance to commit substantial resources to defeating right to work at the state level. Thus, in Arkansas's and Florida's 1944 referendums, narrow defeats for labor might well have ended in victory, as Florida local unionists declared, had AFL president William Green roused himself to action. By the time the issue came to a head in late 1945 and early 1946, Green and the national AFL were becoming deeply alarmed that lobbying action by state AFL officials would not be enough; the federation had barely defeated the issue in the Texas legislature in 1945 and lost South Dakota to right-to-work forces that same year through legislative enactment. Afterward, the AFL president began expanding the involvement of the national office on a limited basis in the Nebraska and Arizona electoral battles to bolster the efforts of the state federation officials. However, the assistance proved too little and too late.

While during the mid–1940s most of the CIO's concerns regarding union security lay in the realm of national labor policy, AFL leaders more properly feared this growing agitation for state-level restriction. Nothing that business proposed before the NDMB or NWLB promised devastation to the older federation, since an agreement to maintain the status quo presumably meant that AFL affiliates would keep their security. Much more important, from the AFL's point of view, would be state laws prohibiting the age-old efforts of craft unions to stabilize their trades against work-rule and wage-scale erosion. And, to make matters worse, many AFL unions were purely local in operation and escaped federal jurisdiction. Small-scale construction work, for example, was often not significant enough to affect interstate commerce. These statutes also bothered CIO functionaries, but for craft unionists they promised immediate difficulties.

The leaders of the AFL were well aware of, and concerned about, the broad-gauged state effort to hamper union effectiveness. And in most instances they combatted such legislation capably, either with preventative lobbying by state federation officials, or, when this failed, by legal challenges through the AFL general counsel's office. This reflected the time-honored division of responsibility within the federation: state politics was the province of the state federation, while complex legal suits affecting the whole trade union movement seemed better handled by the national organization.

State restrictions on union security, however, did not lend themselves well to traditional AFL strategy, mainly because they first gathered momentum as popular referendums. In the period from 1944 to 1946, the five states that passed union security laws—Florida, Arkansas, South Dakota, Nebraska, and Arizona—did so mainly by public vote, usually in the form of a state constitutional amendment which later required additional enabling legislation. Arkansas's 1944 constitutional change, for example, stated that no person shall be denied employment because of membership in or affiliation with or resignation from a labor union. And furthermore, no person shall against his will be compelled to pay dues to any labor organization as a prerequisite to or condition of employment. Nor could any corporation or organization enter into any agreement that would in effect accomplish any of the forbidden ends. The later campaigns in 1947 and 1948, in Texas, Virginia, Tennessee, Georgia, Iowa, North Dakota, and North Carolina, and in those states that passed supporting legislation to implement constitutional right-to-work amendments, relied almost totally on statutory enactment by the state legislatures. For the most part, the penalties for violation were either non-enforcement of the contract provision or a misdemeanor fine. Still, such laws could chill the desire to organize.

Though several archconservatives from Texas had been promoting the idea of constitutional amendments prohibiting union security in early 1941, the first serious attempt by mainstream business conservatives to destroy union security at the state level came in Florida later in that same year. Florida attorney general Tom Watson (D), at the urging of state business associations, undertook a suit attacking existing closed shop contracts in Florida as illegal and against public policy. Watson aimed to revoke the corporate charters of several shipbuilding companies that had entered into closed shop contracts, in the hope that this would discourage other businesses from signing union security agreements with their unions.[17]

In 1943, AFL general counsel Joseph Padway defeated Watson's suit on behalf of fourteen AFL unions of the metal and building trades departments interested in protecting their security. The AFL general counsel successfully argued before the Florida Supreme Court that closed shop contracts in war industries were under the jurisdiction of the federal government. The court agreed that, in the absence of any statutory prohibitions, members of organized labor were "free to work only with Union men" if they chose, Padway wrote to AFL president William Green.[18]

Despite the ruling, the Florida suit had important adverse consequences. For one thing, it prompted Watson to change the tactics of his attack on union security; afterward, he induced the Florida legislature to place a referendum on the state ballot for the 1944 elections. In a legislature composed entirely of Democrats, the measure proposing a constitutional amendment to the voters passed by 90 to 35. More importantly, the decision made AFL officials confident they could obtain court protection of union security and, in addition, the favorable ruling lent moral authority to labor's attempt to defeat the referendum. The case was "a great milestone in labor's struggle for recognition and protection of the union shop," Padway informed William Green in November 1943. And "it will prove of inestimable value in combatting the reactionary resolution for a Constitutional Amendment seeking to outlaw the closed shop."[19]

Despite Padway's comforting analysis, there were clouds on the horizon. By the early spring of 1944, other states had joined Florida. Anti–union security forces in both Arkansas and California succeeded in placing similar provisions on their ballots by initiative petition. Of the three state labor federations affiliated with the AFL, California's was the strongest and most experienced at fighting anti-labor legislation, and in fact had headed off a similar effort in 1938. Now it faced another attempt, sponsored by the open shop Los Angeles Merchant and Manufacturers Association. With effective leadership, sufficient funding, and a shrewd campaign strategy emphasizing that such a law would stimulate labor difficulties and harm the country's war effort, California's state federation defeated the proposal. As Table 2.6 indicates, out of nearly 3.2 million votes cast, approximately 1.9 million people voted against right to work, for a percentage ratio of 41 yes and 59 no. In addition, the issue garnered vote totals equal to 86 percent of the total vote for the highest elected office in that election—a high percentage for an issue referendum. With an estimated 769,893 union members in the state, representing a probable 29.2 percent of the work force organized, California's labor leaders had the resources and the voting base to build a solid victory over right-to-work forces in which labor won 37 of the state's 58 counties.[20]

In contrast to California, AFL affiliates in Florida and Arkansas faced much greater difficulties. The state labor leadership of these mostly rural areas lacked the resources to battle effectively on the electoral plane. Even though state and local labor officials at times resented upper-level interference in their affairs, the fear of their states outlawing union security convinced them they needed help.

Thus, early in the 1944 primaries, the Tampa (Florida) Central Trades and Labor Assembly warned AFL president Green that the proposed right-to-work amendment, as Florida papers now termed it, represented a national threat to the entire labor movement. In a remarkably prescient letter, W. E. Sullivan, a Teamster business agent and president of the assembly, criticized Green for his uninterest in the Florida situation. "Again we plead for attention to and action against this grave danger," he wrote. The amendment would pass unless someone could motivate the international unions, "who have as much at stake as anybody," he argued, into lending substantial financial assistance for an educational campaign. "The camouflaged nature of the amendment, misleading the public and even organized workers, makes it a national danger," Sullivan maintained.

While the passage of the amendment would be "a general setback of many years for the organized labor movement of the South," Sullivan wrote, there were additional reasons the national office should be concerned. The attempt presaged a national right-to-work drive. If "this scheme succeeds in Florida," the lobbyists of the National Association of Manufacturers "are ready to take it to legislators in other states," Sullivan argued, "and point out to them that here is an issue of proven popularity with the public." And legislators would find that promoting union security restrictions would earn them large business campaign contributions. "Then," he added, "the international unions would have on their hands a national fight costing many more times what it would take to head off or mitigate such a scheme in the first state in which this anti-labor trick will be submitted to a public vote." Sullivan closed by urging the AFL president's strong support for Tampa labor's educational efforts, as well as his help in arousing the internationals' interest.

Green responded peevishly by alleging that Florida labor had shown serious political deficiencies in the recent primaries. Sullivan then angrily reminded Green of his several requests for electoral aid from the national office and listed the political accomplishments of Tampa labor's education committee. He concluded, "we have done and are continuing to do everything that we know to urge state and international officials to help us with the statewide campaign." Unfortunately, as Table 2.1 shows, those educational efforts were not enough. The referendum passed by 25,090 votes; 147,860 yes to 122,770 no. While right-to-work supporters did win by a 55 to 45 percent margin, and took 57 out of 67 counties, it was not a deep victory as ten counties were marginal and labor either only narrowly won

2.1
Labor Defeats in Public Right-to-Work Elections, 1944–1948

STATE AND YEAR	YES RTW	NO RTW	TOTAL	%RATIO	COUNTY Y/N RATIO	# MARGINAL COUNTIES	% OF VOTE FOR HIGHEST OFFICE IN ELECTION	APPROXIMATE UNION MEMBERSHIP
South Dakota 1946	93035	39257	132292	70/30	68/0	0	81	11750(11.0%)
North Dakota 1948	105192	53515	158707	66/34	53/0	1	72	13943(14.1%)
Nebraska 1946	212465	142702	355167	60/40	89/4	8	93	47850(16.6%)
Arizona 1948	86866	60295	147161	59/41	12/2	4	83	41378(24.1%)
Arizona 1946	61875	49557	111432	56/44	14/0	5	95	35649(22.5%)
Arkansas 1944	105300	87652	192952	55/45	52/23	25	91	43386(17.1%)
Florida 1944	147860	122770	270630	55/45	57/10	10	56	83000(13.8%)

Source: Appendix B, Cox, and Troy. See explanation in Appendix B as to the derivation of percent of state vote and union membership.

or closely lost nine of the major urban or industrial-rural counties. In fact, a difference of a little over 6,000 votes in Florida's four major urban areas would have defeated the proposal. With a probable total of only 83,000 union members (an estimated 13.8 percent of the work force), Florida unionists had a difficult time convincing their fellow voters to support them on the issue, and indeed many of them did not even vote on the question. Only 56 percent of those casting ballots for president in 1944 also chose to express their opinion on right to work.[21]

Green had obviously disliked Sullivan's invitation to become more deeply involved in the Florida effort. The approach of the Arkansas State Federation of Labor in its right-to-work fight, however, was more akin to the AFL president's inclinations. In the legislative session of 1943, Arkansas labor lobbyists believed they had prevented a referendum from being submitted to the voters. Unfortunately, the well-financed radio campaign of right-to-work proponents convinced a sufficient number of Arkansas's voters to sign petitions authorizing an initiative vote. The state federation organized a publicity program against the right-to-work amendment, and although it received some funds from the national AFL, it generally did not press Green to involve the national organization in state politics in a major way, other than to ask Green to do some high-level lobbying involving the Arkansas congressional delegation, which he refused to do. Table 2.1 reveals that Arkansas's labor leaders also lost their fight by a narrow margin of 17,648 votes out of the 192,952 cast, a 55 to 45 percent spread, as in Florida. Having approximately 43,386 union members in the state (17.1 percent of the work force), Arkansas labor officials struggled in vain to carry their message beyond the labor movement, and eventually saw their opponents' initiative win 52 out of 75 counties. Twenty-five of those counties were marginal, however, with fourteen only barely passing right to work. As in California, the controversy aroused great interest, for 91 percent of voters voting for president also registered their opinions on the initiative.[22]

William Green's response to the Arkansas and Florida right-to-work fights revealed much. The structure of the AFL mandated that the area of state politics was the responsibility of the state and local organizations. Despite strong indications that state legislation restricting union security threatened to emerge as a national problem, organizational patterns of behavior inhibited the national officers from exercising effective leadership. Thus, Green felt comfortable rendering modest financial assistance, exhorting the state federations and affiliates to organize opposition, and occasionally assigning staff help, though even these contributions came late in the electoral campaigns.[23]

Unfortunately for the labor movement, Sullivan's prediction that the first right-to-work referendum would have a ripple effect turned out to be all too accurate. For example, Florida state representative Joseph C. Jenkins (D) actively promoted similar measures to the elected representatives of other states. In soliciting supporters, Jenkins recited a litany of labor's abuses of power, and then told how he believed a right-to-work law would be a panacea. "If you are interested in sponsoring a similar amendment to the Constitution of your State," Jenkins wrote to prospective allies, "I shall be delighted to furnish you further information on how we handled the matter in Florida." AFL representatives soon saw evidence of the Florida referendum's influence in a Georgia proposal. Indeed, by early 1945 similar promotional efforts placed South Dakota in the ranks of the right-to-work states. The legislature of this Republican-dominated state (which had only three Democrats in the House) voted 100 to 7 to pass statutory legislation prohibiting union security, and 96 to 11 to allow South Dakota's citizens to cast ballots regarding a parallel constitutional amendment in 1946. In addition, vigorous agitation for state union security restrictions surfaced in the Texas and Louisiana legislatures in 1945 and 1946, respectively, while right-to-work activists began initiative movements in Nebraska and Arizona in 1946.[24]

In these states too, the AFL's national officers followed their non-interventionist policy in state politics, particularly regarding state-level lobbying efforts. To some degree, though, AFL officials began to show greater concern for those states under the threat of a public vote. In the 1945 session of the Texas legislature, Texas union officials succeeded in fending off a strong drive in a totally Democratic legislature, losing 68 to 63 in the House, and narrowly avoiding a final vote in the Senate, having lost on a previous reading by 17 to 10. In Louisiana in 1946, in another totally Democratic legislature, organized labor actually lost the battle, 55 to 43 in the House and 23 to 15 in the Senate. The legislation failed, however, when the governor vetoed the measure. In these contests, the national office rendered marginal help. However, in the 1946 referendum engagements, national AFL officials stepped up their involvement somewhat. For example, in February 1946, AFL attorneys advised threatened Nebraska trade unionists on the necessity of developing good election strategy and suggested they correspond with California's AFL officials to find out how that state federation won its 1944 contest. Later, Padway's associate Herbert Thatcher participated in a special strategy session called by leaders of the Nebraska AFL. "In all states we found...the way...to defeat" such a referendum was through cooperation between the state federation and publicity committee overseeing the campaign, Thatcher told the conference delegates. Significantly, the AFL attorney had explicitly acknowledged the paramount importance of central leadership in such a battle, but neglected to discuss what role a national labor organization like the AFL could or should play. And in Arizona, Green sent national office personnel to speak at rallies in order to help generate and solidify labor activism in the upcoming vote.[25]

The AFL president's willingness to increase the involvement of national staff and regional AFL organizers showed an increasing awareness that such elections often required resources beyond those that some state federations could supply. It also protected him from being criticized for inactivity since right-to-work legislation had by now created some organizational turbulence within the AFL. Trade union officers began to ask the national hierarchy what the effects of union security restrictions would be on existing and future contracts and organizing campaigns. Thus it became more important, politically, for Green to be able to point to actions he had taken to prevent the adoption of right-to-work laws in the first place, in addition to challenging them once they were on the books.[26]

In contrast to Green's unwillingness to become an active leader in the field of state politics, he showed little reluctance to exert his considerable influence in marshalling a court challenge. Orchestrating a constitutional test of legislation was something the national hierarchy had done over and over again for decades. Padway's office moved quickly in 1945 to test the Florida law, and Green even considered instituting disciplinary action against Tampa's city central labor council when it pursued a test case separate from the AFL suit. In this area the national officers realized the need for coordination and leadership.[27]

Padway concentrated on testing the constitutionality of the Florida right-to-work amendment first, bringing it to the U.S. Supreme Court in late 1945. Unexpectedly, the Court sent the case back to Florida on a technicality. Somewhat concerned, the AFL general counsel wrote Green that perhaps a delay of a year or two would work to the AFL's advantage because the "present temper of the courts towards labor problems" was unfavorable. Sooner or later, though, AFL officials expected that the U.S. Supreme Court would rule the statutes in violation of the U.S. Constitution.[28]

Yet, even with some changes during 1946, the national AFL office continued to play a minor role in state right-to-work politics. Green had gone from giving pro forma assistance to contributing a minor amount of the national federation's resources and talent. Caught by surprise by the ability of right-to-work proponents to obtain ballot status with petitions, state federation officials in Arizona and Nebraska seemed taken aback and unsure of the best strategy. "We know that both yourself and your men in the AFL . . . have plenty of work to do," wrote an Arizona officer in a plaintive plea for help, "yet we are facing a battle here that is of the utmost importance to us in the labor movement in attempting to defeat this vicious attack on Labor at the polls." At least some state functionaries wanted the aid of the national office. When it came to state politics, though, the state federations and local centrals were basically on their own. Even when Green did send aid it had only marginal value, for AFL organizers could only contribute as much time as the press of their other duties would allow. And in Nebraska, Thatcher informed state people that if they wanted to find out how to defeat a right-to-work proposal, they should contact other state labor leaders for assistance. Overall, this did little to make for effective use of the labor movement's entire capabilities.[29]

Consequently, the right-to-work referendums in Arizona, Nebraska, and South Dakota in 1946 passed by wider margins than in Florida and Arkansas in 1944. As summarized in Table 2.1, Nebraska voters approved the initiative by 69,763 votes (212,465 yes to 142,702 no), with the proposal winning 89 out of 93 counties. In less populous Arizona, labor's foes won by 12,318 votes, 61,875 in favor and 49,557 against, with the measure carrying all fourteen Arizona counties. In both elections, right-to-work proponents won solid citizen approbation; 93 percent of Nebraska voters and 95 percent of Arizona voters who voted for the highest office in that election also expressed their desires on union security. In Nebraska, a state with an estimated 47,850 union members (16.6 percent of the work force), the percentage margin ended up at 60 to 40; in Arizona, with a somewhat higher percent organized (an estimated 22.5 percent or 35,649 members), the division was 56 to 44 percent.

To make matters even worse, South Dakota's voters registered appreciation of their legislature's 1945 action by running up the largest pro-right-to-work vote (in percentage terms) in 1946. The referendum on the constitutional amendment buttressing the state statute won by 70 to 30 percent, completely sweeping all 68 counties with not one in the marginal zone. Here too, the question attracted widespread public attention. Of those voting for the highest office on the ballot, 81 percent also voted on the union security question. With about 11 percent of the work force organized (approximately 11,750 members), South Dakota labor leaders could do little but watch forlornly as the proposal carried by vote of 93,035 to 39,257. All three 1946 elections substantiated the claims of the Tampa labor official who predicted in 1944 that the issue would be one that could gain in popularity with the public.

THE CIO'S RESPONSE TO RIGHT TO WORK

While prior to 1947 national AFL leaders had shown little desire to deeply involve themselves in fighting the expanding right-to-work movement at the state level, their CIO counterparts evidenced no such hesitation. In fact, industrial unionists correctly perceived that the attacks on union security presaged a broader attempt to weaken the revitalized labor movement. As early as 1942, CIO president Philip Murray saw great danger in the growing sophistication of conservatives' attempts to revise the complex of protective labor relations legislation that had done much to establish and consolidate the industrial union movement. And like him, Sidney Hillman envisioned a replay of the post–World War I destruction of nascent industrial unionism if the CIO did not turn to electoral politics—on every level—to defend itself.

They had been able to protect their union security through the National War Labor Board, but the war and the special labor relations policies it created would not last forever. To men like Murray and Hillman, then, organizing politically on the national, state, and local level was absolutely necessary to ensure the continued existence of the CIO and what it represented.

Unlike the AFL, which had an established organizational structure, the CIO found that its newness as an organization hampered effective political and legislative work. Until the middle of 1942, the national office did not even have a formally organized legislative department, and in late 1943 the CIO had state industrial union councils in only 35 states. Comparable in structure and function to the AFL's state federations, these councils sprang up first where the CIO's membership was greatest, and their political power paralleled the distribution of the CIO's economic power in the industrialized northeastern and midwestern states. AFL state federations had established records of participation in local politics and a more even impact from state to state. CIO industrial union councils were new and unsettled as political and legislative organs and influential in some areas while completely impotent in others.

For example, in 1939 the CIO had less than 1,000 members in New Mexico, Mississippi, and Arizona; between 1,000 and 2,000 in Florida and South Carolina; and between 3,000 and 6,000 in Georgia, North Carolina, Louisiana, and Arkansas. Following these were Texas with 8,500, Virginia with 17,800, Tennessee with 19,600, and finally Alabama with 28,600, the highest total of any state in the South. Indeed, the Alabama state IUC was typical of the difficult development of the CIO in this region. Formed in December 1937—with United Mine Worker locals predominating—it had no statewide convention until 1940 and had problems attracting local industrial union affiliation in its early years. Nevertheless, there were eleven industrial internationals or organizing committees active in the state, and nine local IUCs. By 1940, its officers claimed that they "have been more fortunate than any other state in the entire southern area" because not only was the ASIUC the largest CIO body, "but the largest organized labor group in any State in the deep South." Within two years, though, the disaffiliation of UMW members from the state organization left it with only 11,000 members and almost destroyed it.

There were other differences between the AFL and CIO as well. In the early 1940s, CIO leaders were still building up their organizational structures, developing policy for wielding political power, and trying to stimulate political and legislative consciousness in their new members. In contrast to the AFL's national leadership, CIO officers quickly realized that state-level agitation for restrictive labor legislation required a political response and direction from above in order to stimulate and guide grass roots activity. Unfortunately, the power realities made it difficult for the industrial federation to respond effectively. In the agricultural Midwest, as in the South, CIO membership was sparse in many areas. North and South Dakota registered no CIO presence in 1939, for example, while Nebraska had only 400 members. Kansas and Iowa fared somewhat better, with 4,000 and 15,000 respectively. More often than not, the industrial union movement had the fewest troops precisely where the threat was greatest.[30]

Thus, for the most part, the CIO's capabilities in the South and rural Plains states were unrealized in late 1942. John L. Lewis's autocratic rule left the national office and its new leaders ill-prepared to make a political impact, and the apathy of labor voters in the fall elections starkly revealed this unreadiness. "The unfortunate results of these campaigns," a 1942 post-election study of the CIO's political potential pointed out, "indicates the need for sustained political organization and for more fully developed systems of gathering political data." This report by national staffers Nathan Cowan, John Brophy, and J. Raymond Walsh informed CIO president Philip Murray that "the neglect of detailed political work which characterized the administration of the first president of the CIO made it necessary to begin building organizations and procedures anew from the ground up" after the end of Lewis's reign in 1940. Because of this inattention, the "councils have been carrying the main burden of our political and legislative work" without direction from Washington. Even when the national office participated actively in attempting to defeat noted anti-labor congressmen, as it did in two cases in the 1942 elections, it had little effect.[31]

Cowan, Brophy, and Walsh surveyed the CIO's field organization and found "the existence of considerable political machinery" within the IUCs. The CIO should follow a policy of being a catalytic agent, they advised, thus strengthening, supplementing, and solidifying, "these agencies, rather than supplanting or duplicating them." In some states these political organizations cooperated with AFL and Railroad Brotherhood legislative committees. This should be encouraged, they argued, for a "much broader coalition of labor than has ever been achieved in the past is desirable on the state level and can probably be accomplished in many places at the present time." Furthermore, they envisioned shared intra-organizational responsibility at the state level, in much the same way as the legislative, IUC, and research departments shared responsibilities in the national office. And by allowing political-electoral organizations to share in the legislative work between elections, they would be able to sustain interest in political activism.[32]

Significantly, in their blueprint for the construction of a new political apparatus for labor, Cowan, Brophy, and Walsh believed that the CIO should abandon the non-partisan approach of rewarding friends and punishing enemies. They recommended to Murray that the "work be carried on largely within the Democratic Party" and by building progressive coalitions. "We should not pretend that there is the slightest possibility of our achieving genuine influence in the Republican Party," they argued. In the Democratic party, however, labor's influence was considerable, "and can be increased greatly if the proper methods are followed." Even though Cowan, Brophy, and Walsh acknowledged problems with the Democratic party, they saw labor's voting strength as the solution. If only organized labor could marshall its resources effectively it could rid the Democratic party of conservatives. Though "it may prove true that the control of re-actionary interests over the Democratic Party is too strong to be broken," they wrote, the only way labor would ever find out was by making a prodigious commitment to electoral politics.[33]

More than anything else, the CIO leadership's interest in building a po-litical machine at the national, state, and local levels stemmed from a fear of legislative attacks. In early 1943, after receiving the Cowan/Brophy/Walsh report, Philip Murray broached the subject at a meeting of the CIO's ex-ecutive board. Intensely concerned about the federation's political ineffec-tiveness, and about the growing number of anti-labor bills in Congress and in state legislatures, he lectured the board members on the importance of politics. "I am going to say to you frankly and candidly—we fail at the top to do this job and do it the way it ought to be done."

For example, Murray went on, the leaders of the international unions gave the subject little attention, ignored the legislative meetings at the na-tional office, and neglected to circulate legislative and political information. This uninterest made it all too easy for the enemies of labor to succeed in their attacks. The results were obvious; as of February 1943 five southern states were considering labor legislation that "may very well destroy" unions, the CIO president said. "Senator [W. L.] O'Daniel [D-TX] is down in the State of Arkansas today, he is appearing before a session of the Arkansas legislature," the CIO president informed the board members, "and he is appealing to that body to pass legislation to stop closed shops, union shops, maintenance of membership...and so forth." Laws such as these presented a major challenge to labor. This "is a life and death struggle, and I want you to know that," Murray somewhat angrily pointed out. "Your union security is at stake, and with your union security at stake the very life of millions of workers is at stake also."[34]

The CIO president knew that this "all important" subject of "labor leg-islation" required him to assert vigorous leadership. After the executive board meeting in February 1943, he set Cowan and Brophy to work or-ganizing local legislative conferences, improving communications, and ar-ranging for the creation of national, local, and joint legislative committees in local and state industrial union councils. Such groups could also work with the proposed political agencies. Through these multiple layers of com-mittees CIO leaders hoped, as Murray put it, "to build some semblance of order out of this confused legislative situation." He also sought, at about the same time, to convince AFL president William Green to participate in "an organizational setup...composed of the Federation of Labor, [the] CIO, the Railroad Brotherhoods and the National Farmers Union," but Green's dislike of the idea ruined the plan.

Despite this rebuff, CIO leaders continued to seek inter-federation political cooperation and continued to reorganize their own structure. Cowan advised the executive board members that all CIO state and local legislative committees should initiate the organization of legislative coalitions at the local level. With the establishment of systematic legislative committees in the councils, led by the national office through "a never-ending flow of instructions and guidance from the national unions to their local unions," the CIO would be much more effective in warding off attacks.[35]

The growing threat of anti-labor legislation had provided a genuine incentive for CIO leaders to rationalize their legislative lobbying and increase their political activity on all levels. Murray reminded the executive board members at their May 1943 meeting in Cleveland that the "legislative straight-jacket" was "just around the corner," and asked affiliates' lobbyists to "exercise the greatest degree of vigilance in all of the States throughout the nation where anti-labor legislation was pending." Nonetheless, he and other CIO officials realized that there was a limit to what they could accomplish without parallel commitment at the state level. Little of lasting value could be accomplished unless it emanated from the grass roots level. "It is desirable that the legislative and political work of all CIO organizations be coordinated," wrote John Brophy to a state labor leader, but "the responsibility for such coordination falls in the last analysis on our state councils."[36]

And it was in the state councils that CIO officers had to exercise leadership through education. After touring state council conventions in the first half of 1943, John Brophy informed the executive board that "there is a great deal of dissatisfaction and some confusion...about what they shall do in order to bring together our political power more effectively." Many CIO members at the local level often lacked sophistication in political and legislative matters. Thus, to promote a better informed local membership, the national office organized a series of meetings with state industrial union leaders across the country, starting with the more industrialized states first. As Sidney Hillman admitted to his brethren in October 1943, in many areas CIO organizations were just "taking hold."[37] Nevertheless, there could be no substitute for political action in fighting state anti-labor legislation. CIO general counsel Lee Pressman told the 1943 convention delegates that of course his office would defend affiliates fighting union security restrictions. But, Pressman concluded, the courts often ruled on the basis of what people wanted, and the best way for CIO members to make those wants known was through electoral politics.[38]

By the end of 1943, then, CIO leaders saw electoral organization as a tool with which to struggle against their national and state legislative enemies. They felt no hesitancy in trying to generate activity at the state level, for more often than not they had been intimately involved in establishing industrial union councils. They had spent the last eight years building and consolidating the industrial union movement, and had seen how favorable legislation protected their gains. Any qualms CIO leaders had about becoming institutionally committed to politics through the liberal wing of the Democratic party vanished when officials remembered the near destruction of many industrial unions after World War I. They all recalled how quickly President Wilson's hope for industrial peace through collective bargaining had evaporated in the face of employer hostility to unionism, and how that hostility became the second open shop movement in the Republican 1920s.[39]

But no matter how badly they desired political influence, the difficulties of asserting political power where they had little economic power remained a thorny problem for CIO leaders. Through the efforts of Sidney Hillman, the Cowan/Brophy/Walsh blueprint had resulted in the establishment of the federation's Political Action Committee (PAC) in 1943. From 1944 through 1946, the industrial organization deepened its commitment to PAC, but, understandably, most of the federation's resources went into the areas where it had an economic power base. Although southern CIO people formed PACs—as early as 1944 in Alabama—they were mostly paper organizations and resulted in comparatively little electoral action in the South.[40]

This weakness vexed the leadership all the more because they saw the relationship between what was happening at the state level and what was now occurring in Congress. As Lee Pressman told the executive board in July 1945, many proposals for labor law revision at the national level contained provisions giving greater jurisdiction to the states. This was tantamount, Pressman said, to "suggesting to the states, 'you pass those laws,' and what's more, they will be all right because labor will not be able to argue that they interfere with the Wagner Act." Philip Murray pointed out that the new way to oppose unions was through legislation, and that this was becoming just as bad as the former use of labor injunctions. It was even a "more vicious way, in that it provides that whilst we want to be good to the unions, we will only be good to the unions under certain conditions and that is that you don't grow; that you become weak; and if you are a vacillating union, then you will be a good union." And, Murray continued, "this is just a beginning. If the Federal Congress dare enact legislation of this description, how far do you suppose the states may go?" Still, no matter how they would have liked to have been politically potent enough to defeat right to work in the South and Plains states, the CIO did not yet have the strength and organization. Where it had a presence, it fought hard with mixed success. Elsewhere, its weakness or disagreements with the AFL state leaders sapped its effectiveness.[41]

RESTRICTING UNION SECURITY AT THE NATIONAL LEVEL

The success of right-to-work advocates at restricting union security at the state level was soon duplicated in national labor policy. Obviously, both the AFL and CIO faced a difficult challenge from right-to-work forces, and the events of 1946 did nothing to make their job any easier. Leaders of organized labor had hoped that the anti–union security elections of 1944 and 1946, along with the legislative votes in several states, would be passing phenomena that could at least be limited if not reversed. But by 1946 the huge post-war strike wave and other problems of reconversion gave an added impetus to right-to-work proposals, as was evident in both the Nebraska and Arizona elections. Public opinion polls indicated that the critics of powerful unionism—anti–union security advocates foremost among them—had struck a popular chord. In this environment, right-to-work proponents could gain a much more sympathetic hearing.

And they did, especially in the southern states, where both federations planned massive organizing drives for after the war. In these conservative states a limited amount of craft unionism had existed for years, and it had rarely threatened to become a major force for social change. With the advent of the CIO, however, southern community leaders could not help but wonder what would happen if large-scale organization were to occur. In particular, the industrial federation's vocal support for social and racial equality received an even more unwelcome reception in the South than in other parts of the country.

Since 1937, in fact, conservative Democrats had warned the CIO of the South's inhospitability to industrial unionism. Often it took the form of red-baiting. In 1939, Georgia Congressman Eugene Cox (D) warned "John L. Lewis and his Communistic cohorts that no second 'carpetbag expedition' in the Southland, under the red banner of Soviet Russia..." would be tolerated. Even so, that did not stop the federation's organizers from organizing anyone they could, white or black. "The C.I.O. got a hold of our four colored janitors and two white boys and took us before the N.L.R.B.," complained a textile manufacturer to his congressman, Howard W. Smith (D-VA), in 1939. According to this Virginia businessman, labor now had "the upper hand and is going too far." Furthermore, when the CIO organized IUCs in southern states the national body insisted that all meetings be integrated and some of the organizations' first convention resolutions denounced the poll tax and employment discrimination. This disturbed southern officials so much that in 1942, for example, the mayor of Fairfield, Alabama, threatened to throw CIO leaders in jail if they allowed Negroes into their meeting.

If southern conservatives needed any further convincing of the danger to power relations posed by union growth, they had merely to look at the initial success of the AFL's and CIO's post-war organizing drives. From 1946 to 1948 the CIO raised approximately $770,000 for southern organizing and added 400,000 members. In essentially the same period, the AFL spent a little over $355,000 and gained approximately 500,000 new members. In addition, in many areas the two organizations competed for the allegiance of black workers. There was thus some evidence that unionization might indeed prove popular with the South's working class.[42]

The nexus of union growth, racial equality, and politics was quite apparent to southern conservatives interested in preserving the existing social order. However, given the control of national labor policy by liberal politicians, they had a limited sphere in which to operate. They might not be able to destroy unionism through state anti-labor legislation, but conservatives could make sure that unions never became secure enough to become a political force of consequence. At first, as in Texas in 1945 and Louisiana in 1946, conservative southern Democratic legislators supporting right to work found the going rough. Table 2.2 computes the index of cohesion for these states (a measure of how strongly the party supported or opposed the proposal, a positive value of 100 indicating total cohesion in favor of restricting union security, and − 100 signifying total cohesion against right to work). In both these states, the Democratic party's cohesion was relatively low in favor of restricting union security; an index of 8 in Texas and 15 in Louisiana, just barely over a total randomness measure of 0. This indicated at least some labor influence over legislators, even considering that cohesion in one-party states tends to be lower across the entire spectrum of issues. By 1947, however, Democratic opponents of labor in the South and Southwest found the going easier. In that year, Georgia legislators led the way by passing two bills with an 84 and 74 index, respectively. North Carolina followed with 71, Virginia with 60, Arkansas with 60, Tennessee with 51, Texas with 39, Arizona with 38, and finally New Mexico with 17. Clearly, conservative Democrats were acting on their belief that an effective way to hamstring organized labor was to pass a right-to-work law.

Consequently, the mass-organizing drives and rhetoric after the war, combined with huge strikes in the auto, railroad, electrical, and other industries, gave right-to-work advocates the public acceptance they had always sought. Moreover, the 1946 victories of conservative Republicans across the country strengthened the drive, pushing it northward and into the Mid-Atlantic region. Predictably, this put severe strains on union lobbyists' ability to block adverse union security legislation. In the strongly Republican states of South Dakota, North Dakota, New Hampshire, and Iowa, Republican legislators succeeded in passing several types of right-to-work legislation in 1947. Table 2.4 tabulates the index of cohesion of Republicans favoring right to work as 71 for South Dakota, 58 for New Hampshire (one chamber only), 57 for Iowa, and 21 for North Dakota. In one predominantly Republican legislature, Maine's, a proposal failed, although house Republicans

2.2

Rice Index of Cohesion of Democratic Party, in Southern and Southwestern State
Legislatures, on Right-to-Work Measures, 1943–1949

STATE/YEAR	TOTAL	INDEXES SENATE	HOUSE	BALLOTS CAST SENATE	HOUSE
Georgia 1947					
Bill 1	84	100	80	39	162
Bill 2	74	100	70	34	184
North Carolina 1947	71	39	83	46	118
Virginia 1947	60	66	58	35	91
Arkansas 1947	60	52	64	33	88
Tennessee 1947	51	71	43	28	74
Florida 1943	44	35	47	34	91
Texas 1947	39	70	32	27	124
Arizona 1947	38	47	35	19	49
New Mexico 1947	17	11	20	18	30
Louisiana 1946	15	21	12	38	98
Texas 1945					
Bill 1	8	26	4	27	131
Bill 2	-	NV	6	NA	113
Tennessee 1949	-	7	NV	28	NA

Source: Appendix A
Key: NV–No Vote, NA–Not Available
Index: +100(Totally Cohesive in Favor of Right to Work)
          -100(Totally Cohesive Against Right to Work)

in that state supported right to work with an index of 51. In two-party
Delaware, Republicans chalked up a perfect index of 100 while Democrats
opposed with a pro-labor − 65, as Tables 2.3 and 2.4 reveal in comparison.
New Mexico and Tennessee, the only other states with more than a handful
of Republicans, also yielded positive indexes for right to work for GOP
legislators, 67 in New Mexico and 24 in Tennessee. "Spreading from the
action taken in Florida," William Green wrote a labor sympathizer in the
spring of 1947, "legislation in opposition to closed shop agreements has
been passed in about a dozen other states. The movement seems to be on
all over the country," the distraught AFL president noted. "People seem to
be moved by... [hatred] toward labor. I do not know where it is all going
to end. It is arousing labor and creating widespread feeling everywhere."[43]

By early 1947, in fact, a pattern had emerged. Right-to-work groups
usually formed around a core of employer association activists—mainly
smaller manufacturers, retailers, and farmer-businessmen. Previously, right-

2.3

Rice Index of Cohesion of Democratic Party, Northern, Mid-Atlantic, and Plains State Legislatures, on Right-to-Work Measures, 1945–1949

STATE/YEAR	TOTAL	INDEXES SENATE	HOUSE	BALLOTS CAST SENATE	HOUSE
Massachusetts 1948	-100	-100	-100	14	80
Delaware 1949	-100	-100	-100	8	17
Maine 1947	-	DV	-100	NA	21
New Hampshire 1947	-	DV	-89	NA	112
Iowa 1947	-86	-50	-100	4	10
Delaware 1947	-65	-100	-54	4	13
South Dakota 1947	-50	ND	-50	ND	4
South Dakota 1945 Bill 1	-33	ND	-33	ND	3
Bill 2	-33	ND	-33	ND	3
North Dakota 1947	60	33	100	3	2
New Hampshire 1949	-	DV	VV	NA	NA
Nebraska 1947	NP	NP	NP	NP	NP

Source: Appendix A
Key: NA-Not Available, NV-No Vote, VV-Voice Vote, DV-Division,
           NP-Non-Partisan Legislature, ND-No Democrats
Index: +100(Totally Cohesive in Favor of Right to Work)
           -100(Totally Cohesive Against Right to Work)

to-work propagandists had substantial ties to extreme right-wing politics, but this component of the movement subsided somewhat by 1946. Now, mainstream political conservatives had clearly seen the usefulness of right to work in weakening unionism and had picked up the torch. The 1946 National Association of Manufacturers' (NAM) Declaration of Principles on Labor Law Reform, for example, affirmed as its first principle the right to refuse to join a union, and further stated that all union security provisions should be illegal. These manufacturing, retailing, and farming businessmen lobbied persistently for right-to-work statutes and were the main supporters—and sometimes the only supporters—in legislative hearings. They almost always denied any bias against collective bargaining and unions, simply stating that they wished to insure freedom of choice with regard to union membership. The backers often tried to capitalize on the anti-union feeling generated by local labor conflicts, as well as by the national labor situation, to finally push the legislation through.[44]

In the face of the legislative onslaught that these groups launched, the national offices of both labor federations continued their previous strategies.

2.4

Rice Index of Cohesion of Republican Party, All State Legislatures, on Right-to-Work Measures, 1943–1949

STATE/YEAR	TOTAL	INDEXES SENATE	HOUSE	BALLOTS CAST SENATE	HOUSE
Delaware 1947	100	100	100	9	20
Arkansas 1947	100	NR	100	NR	3
Arizona 1947	100	NR	100	NR	5
Georgia 1947 Bills 1&2	–	NA	100	NA	1
South Dakota 1945 Bill 1	90	100	86	33	71
Bill 2	83	88	80	33	71
Virginia 1947	78	100	67	3	6
South Dakota 1947	71	100	57	32	70
New Mexico 1947	67	67	67	6	18
New Hampshire 1947	–	DV	58	NA	238
Iowa 1947	57	59	56	44	95
Maine 1947	–	DV	51	NA	115
Tennessee 1949	–	50	NV	4	NA
Tennessee 1947	24	–20	38	5	16
North Dakota 1947	21	33	17	42	108
Delaware 1949	–20	71	–56	7	18
Massachusetts 1948	–93	–100	–92	22	128
North Carolina 1947	–	VV	VV	NA	NA
New Hampshire 1949	–	DV	VV	NA	NA
Florida 1943	NR	NR	NR	NR	NR
Louisiana 1946	NR	NR	NR	NR	NR
Texas 1945	NR	NR	NR	NR	NR
Texas 1947	NR	NR	NR	NR	NR
Nebraska 1947	NP	NP	NP	NP	NP

Source: Appendix A
Key: NA–Not Available, NV–No Vote, VV–Voice Vote, DV–Division, NP–Non-Partisan, NR–No Republicans
Index: +100(Totally Cohesive in Favor of Right to Work) –100(Totally Cohesive Against Right to Work)

The AFL pushed ahead with its legal challenge, and the CIO feverishly urged electoral activism. The Eightieth Congress, beginning in early 1947, promised to be a difficult one, for restrictive national labor legislation seemed a real possibility. With most of their resources committed to that fight, the national officers gave even less attention to state right-to-work initiatives. The CIO encouraged state-level cooperation; as late as the spring of 1947, however, the AFL remained confident that its court challenge would ultimately solve the problem.[45]

Working toward this end, AFL attorney Herbert Thatcher kept on the lookout for the most favorable cases to bring to the Supreme Court, and most state labor leaders readily accepted the national office's aid. "We are very anxious to bring this law to a test at the very earliest possible moment," wrote Tennessee state labor official Stanton Smith in March 1947, "as we are running into difficulties with the employers who are refusing to sign closed shop, union shop, or maintenance of membership contracts." By this point, however, Thatcher could do little more than advise trade unionists "to try to persuade employers to go along with you" on union security. Not only did quite a few states have a right-to-work law, but "a number of other states will probably pass such a law in the near future. All we can do is try to hang on to what we have pending the outcome of the litigation." It was because of the crucial importance of the issue that the AFL's national office had worked so hard to coordinate and direct the suits, without charge to the state federations. That way, Thatcher informed John Hand of the Tennessee state oganization, "we are assured that all our effort[s] are coordinated and that all our arguments are properly presented and all federal issues properly raised."[46]

On the other hand, CIO leaders believed the legislative situation in early 1947 further confirmed the correctness of their evaluation. If for no other reason than protection, labor had to become committed to systematic electoral organization and find a way to transform that commitment into legislative influence. The national leaders had called an IUC conference in late 1946 to aid state officers in dealing with the crisis in the state legislatures, thereby hoping to improve "methods of clearance and communication," according to John Brophy. In addition, southern CIO regional director Paul Christopher set the wheels in motion for a joint conference of southern CIO officials and international staff in May 1947. And Philip Murray once again tried to convince AFL officers that both federations should cooperate on the legislative and political front. All to little avail, however, for in the genteel words of the CIO diplomat who approached the older federation, the AFL's national officers, "expressed themselves rather vigorously that they had no use for PAC."[47]

Besides anger at the political affronts, a good deal of fear lay behind CIO officialdom's urgent entreaties. Unfortunately for the industrial federation, anti–union security measures no longer posed a vague, future threat—by

May 1947 they touched the heart of CIO power in the industrial northeast and Mid-Atlantic states. Right-to-work drives had edged up into states such as Maine, Massachusetts, New Hampshire, and Delaware, thus alerting the large mass-production affiliates that they too would soon experience the danger of the statutes firsthand. In fact, in May 1947 Lee Pressman thought the subject of sufficient importance to recommend specific executive board discussion.[48]

While right-to-work laws never found a formal place on the agenda, the executive board reviewed the problems created by anti–union security measures as part of its deliberations on the Taft-Hartley proposals in May 1947. More than anything else, this discussion revealed the difficulties of striking a proper balance between electoral and legislative work. It also highlighted the problems of functioning in a two-party system where labor's chosen ally, the Democratic party, often found itself badly divided on labor questions. Pressman informed the board that many state CIO officials initially felt that the Republicans elected in 1946 would not dare to pass anti-labor legislation, and that all they had to do was to wait for the 1948 elections. "As a result of that I am afraid that not too serious efforts were made in the various States to combat" adverse state legislation at the end of 1946 and into the first four months of 1947. That evaluation was disastrous, he insisted, for the "Republicans not only dared to do it, but they have done it with the able assistance of many of the Southern Democrats." The outcome was predictable. Right-to-work legislation had now become more than a phenomenon of the South and Plains states; it had moved into more industrialized areas.[49]

Pressman's indictment of the Republican-southern Democrat coalition was on the mark—although subject to interpretation as to who exactly was ably assisting whom. A comparison of available indexes of cohesion for Democratic legislators in the South and Southwest, and Republicans in the Plains states and Northeast, suggests a parallel conservative movement in early 1947. Table 2.2 shows that in 1947 southern Democrats' cohesion in favor of right-to-work legislation ranged from a high of 84 in Georgia to a low of 17 in New Mexico—a total of 9 indexes for an average index of 54.8. Comparing this to the Republican-dominated legislatures of South Dakota, Iowa, North Dakota, New Hampshire, and Maine, as charted in Table 2.4, we find a top index of 71 in South Dakota and a low score of 21 in North Dakota. These five 1947 votes yielded an average index of 51.6, taking into account that the Maine and New Hampshire indexes encompassed only one chamber. Thus, Democratic legislators in the South and Southwest and Republican state representatives in the Plains states and the Northeast voted remarkably alike on the right-to-work question in 1947, with southern Democrats averaging a slightly higher index in favor of restricting union security. Few of these states had much of a two-party pattern. The small number of Republicans in Virginia, New Mexico, and Tennessee chalked up positive indexes of 78, 67, and 24, respectively. The Democrats in a similar position in Maine, New Hampshire, and Iowa responded differently—they opposed right to work with negative indexes of −100 in Maine (one chamber), −89 in New Hampshire (one chamber), and −86 in Iowa. In 1947 Delaware was perhaps the only real two-party state that passed a right-to-work law. And there the two parties took directly opposite stances, which can be seen by comparing Tables 2.3 and 2.4. Delaware's Republicans had a perfect index of 100 while its Democrats compiled an index of −65. Thus, even in a notably anti-labor political climate, nonsouthern Democratic legislators stood by labor. Delaware, though, was an exception to the pattern. Because of the extensive Republican victories of 1946, it may have appeared to CIO general counsel Pressman that Republicans were leading the way. The legislative roll calls, however, indicated that each political grouping was a co-leader in the right-to-work movement.

Obviously, the CIO attorney continued, the fact that many of the statutes did not go into effect immediately had lulled CIO affiliates into dangerous complacency, as many thought that by the time their contracts came up for renegotiation, the courts would have declared the laws unconstitutional. Industrial unionists were just beginning to understand the laws' impact, "and their first impression is, you just can't do this to me. . . . why can't I get a renewal of . . . union security?" What was worse, many employers also interpreted the statutes liberally, arguing that right-to-work statutes made the checkoff illegal as well. And the laws had other ramifications, for they appeared to encourage employers to oppose collective bargaining. "Where . . . contracts are expiring," Pressman maintained, "the Unions are finding it more and more difficult to negotiate any kind of a contract. The issue is not confined to getting a renewal of union security."[50]

At the same executive board meeting in May 1947, Pressman also noted that as a complement to the state laws, the Taft-Hartley bill now proposed to restrict union security at the national level. First, it made unions go through extremely difficult and unfair NLRB ballots if they wanted to negotiate a union security provision. This, when combined with other features of the bill, made "a mockery of the union security clause." And second, if a state wanted more stringent restrictions on union security, the House bill intended to allow the states total jurisdiction over the subject, in direct contradiction to the doctrine of federal supremacy. Organized labor seemed to be in a state of shock, according to the CIO counsel, and consequently it had done little but repeat that politicians simply could not do that. "But unfortunately the answer is that they have done it. They have done it in the States, they have done it in the House of Representatives and they have done it in the Senate of the United States, and we are now merely on the last lap."[51]

Pressman's remarks produced a great deal of comment among executive board members. Some expressed uneasiness with the "missionary" fervor of recent years. Emil Rieve of the Textile Workers wondered, for example, "if our attempt to organize the South has not hastened this legislation." But most believed they were on the right track in emphasizing electoral work on behalf of liberal Democrats as a means of ultimately winning legislative power. George Baldanzi of the Textile Workers pointed out what organized labor could do if it only practiced the solidarity it preached. In South Carolina the CIO, AFL, and Railroad Brotherhoods combined to prevent a right-to-work law in a state dominated by conservative and business interests. With unobtrusive backing from the internationals, South Carolina unionists convinced the liberal legislators of the most organized districts to successfully filibuster right-to-work proposals. The episode was an excellent example, Baldanzi said, of using the strength of the national organizations behind the scenes to strengthen southern unionists. This allowed them to lead the campaign, for in the South, he noted, you could not speak with authority "unless you speak as a native of the state."[52]

But by mid–1947, the conservative tide reached such proportions that successful opposition to national anti-labor legislation was problematic. The Republican-dominated Eightieth Congress not only passed the Taft-Hartley bill, it passed it over President Truman's veto. In the original vote that sent the bill to the president, as well as in the veto override vote, there was a distinct difference between parties. Table 2.5 outlines the index of cohesion of both parties on this national labor legislation which, while encompassing union security, went far beyond that subject in imposing new restrictions on labor. Republicans in both chambers of Congress, as the table shows, united strongly in favor of the bill, compiling indexes of 81 in the House and 88 in the Senate on the initial vote, and 91 and 88, respectively, on the override. Democrats also tended to favor the legislation, but by a much smaller margin. The Democratic index of cohesion on the first vote was 5 in the House and 0 in the Senate; on the override the House index climbed to 20, but the Senate's tipped into the labor column with a −5 index. In such a legislative climate, even the most skilled labor lobbyist could accomplish little. Thus, the benefits of the CIO's calls for political activism, if realized, only held promise for the future. By this point, if organized labor had any chance at all of ridding itself of state union security restrictions, that chance lay with the Supreme Court's tendency to declare that national legislation preempted state labor laws.

The AFL, of course, had hoped for some time that the Court would render just such a ruling. Well aware of this, the drafters of the House's Hartley bill included a clause to protect state right-to-work laws from preemption. The Hartley committee recommended that Congress provide "expressly . . . that laws and constitutional provisions of any state that restrict the right of employers to require employees to become or remain members of labor organizations are valid, nothwithstanding any provision of the National Labor Relations Act." When this provision became section 14(b) of the

2.5

Rice Index of Cohesion of Congressional Parties, on National Labor Legislation
Involving Union Security Issues, 1947–1949

LEGISLATION/YEAR	AGAINST LABOR	FOR LABOR	TOTAL	PERCENT YES	PERCENT NO	RICE INDEX
Taft-Hartley Act 1947						
House Original						
D Vote	93	84	177	53	47	5
R	215	22	237	91	9	81
Senate						
D	21	21	42	50	50	0
R	47	3	50	94	6	88
Both Chambers						
D	114	105	219	52	48	4
R	262	25	287	91	9	83
Total	376	130	506	74	26	49
Veto						
Override						
House						
D	106	71	177	60	40	20
R	225	11	236	95	5	91
Senate						
D	20	22	42	48	52	-5
R	48	3	51	94	6	88
Both Chambers						
D	126	93	219	58	42	15
R	273	14	287	95	5	90
Total	399	107	506	79	21	58
Taft-Hartley Repeal 1949						
House						
D	62	193	255	24	76	-51
R	147	18	165	89	11	78
Senate						
D	23	29	52	44	56	-12
R	30	12	42	71	29	43
Both Chambers						
D	85	222	307	28	72	-45
R	177	30	207	86	14	71
Total	262	252	514	51	49	2

Source: Congressional Quarterly, Congress and the Nation, 1945-1964,
         (Washington, DC: Congressional Quarterly Service, 1965).
Index: +100(Totally Cohesive Against Labor)
         -100(Totally Cohesive in Favor of Labor)
         Rice Index Rounded to Nearest Integer

[joint] conference draft, Congress ceded its jurisdiction over union security
restrictions to the states. As a frustrated Virginia unionist complained at
the 1947 CIO convention, now "with the Taft-Hartley law in operation
our Virginia [right-to-work] law has the backing of the federal government."[53]

And so it did. The success of the right-to-work movement had led congressional conservatives to include specific protection for those state statutes in
the new national labor law. By inserting section 14(b), they significantly
weakened the AFL's legal challenge by narrowing the grounds on which
the federation could persuasively argue that the state statutes were uncon-

stitutional. After this, AFL attorneys would have to contend that state right-to-work laws violated some broad constitutional right protected by the amended National Labor Relations Act—a much more difficult task.

Until the Court decided, though, organized labor had to develop a workable response to the legislative events of 1947. Predictably, it denounced Taft-Hartley as a slave-labor law and resolved that nothing short of repeal would divert its wrath. And, of course, it strongly desired the same fate for state union security restrictions wherever possible, particularly after the NLRB stopped holding union shop elections in states with a right-to-work law. It was imperative, AFL officers told the 1948 convention, "that we fight for the repeal of the state anti-labor laws at the same time that we fight for the repeal of the Taft-Hartley Act."[54]

The key to this was to make sure that those legislators who had voted for Taft-Hartley and right to work did not return to Congress and the state legislatures in 1948. The Taft-Hartley experience had convinced even the most stodgy AFL leaders of the necessity of developing organizational structures with continuity that could oversee the federation's political agenda. Thus, in the wake of Taft-Hartley the AFL created Labor's League for Political Education (LLPE) to parallel the CIO's Political Action Committee. Both federations vowed an unending struggle to replace every representative who voted for the laws with someone committed to repeal.

And by 1948, an aroused organized labor had made some significant progress in reversing the unfavorable legislative outlook. This first became evident in early 1948 when the Massachusetts legislature overwhelmingly defeated a right-to-work proposal. A comparison of Tables 2.3 and 2.4 shows that both Democrats and Republicans in Massachusetts wanted nothing to do with the measure; Democratic legislators in both chambers compiled a perfect −100 index of cohesion in supporting labor, while Republicans in the House and Senate were only slightly less adamant with a −93 index.

On the heels of this lobbying victory came three electoral victories (Massachusetts, Maine, and New Mexico); one failed attempt to repeal through initiative (Arizona); and an electoral defeat (North Dakota). Tables 2.1 and 2.6 give the vital statistics on these elections in the fall of 1948. Nearly 1.8 million citizens of the Bay State, which had approximately 425,671 union members (35.3 percent of the work force), rejected the proposal to restrict union security by a 72 to 28 percent margin. While the initiative failed in ten of the state's twelve counties, the question attracted wide interest in Massachusetts—85 percent of those voting for president marked their ballots on right to work as well. Even in more conservative Maine and New Mexico, with far fewer workers who carried union cards—about 43,293 in Maine (16.8 percent organized) and 19,214 in New Mexico (13.4 percent organized)—voters chose not to add this legislation to their statute books. In Maine, 84 percent of those voting in the September 1948 primary election

2.6
Labor Victories in Public Right-to-Work Elections, 1944–1948

STATE AND YEAR	YES RTW	NO RTW	TOTAL	%RATIO	COUNTY Y/N RATIO	# MARGINAL COUNTIES	% OF VOTE FOR HIGHEST OFFICE IN ELECTION	APPROXIMATE UNION MEMBERSHIP
Massachusetts 1948	505575	1290310	1795890	28/72	2/12	2	85	425671(35.3%)
Maine 1948	60485	126285	186770	23/68	2/14	2	84	43293(16.8%)
California 1944	1304430	1893630	3198060	41/59	21/37	24	86	769893(29.2%)
New Mexico 1948	43229	60865	104094	42/58	14/17	4	56	19214(13.4%)

Source: Appendix B, Cox, and Troy. See explanation in Appendix B as to the derivation of percent of state vote and union membership.

expressed their views about union security. Maine labor leaders emerged from this election with a 68 to 23 percent victory (60,485 yes and 126,285 no), with only two out of sixteen counties falling into the opposition's column. New Mexico's election victory was narrower, however, and only 56 percent of those casting ballots for the highest office in the election cared enough to vote on the referendum. There labor won by a 58 to 42 percent margin overall (43,229 yes and 60,865 no), but the county yes/no ratio ended up at a slender 14 yes and 17 no division.

To some degree, the referendum losses in Arizona and North Dakota could be read as voter approval of previous action on right-to-work legislation. In Arizona, a labor-sponsored 1948 referendum attempt to undo the 1946 and 1947 measures failed with Arizona citizens, garnering 86,866 pros and 60,295 cons. This 59 to 41 percent difference was 3 percentage points more support than the proposal had in 1946, even though the unionization level was 24.1 percent of the work force in 1948 (41,378 union members). Similarly, North Dakotans ratified the 1947 action of their legislators by voting 105,192 to 53,515 to add a right-to-work amendment to their constitution. The state's 13,943 unionists (14.1 percent of the labor force) did not have the wherewithal to affect the 66 to 34 percent victory margin in this unindustrialized region. In both Arizona and North Dakota, as in most other states, citizens showed a relatively high level of interest in the controversy. About 83 percent of Arizona's presidential voters also voted on the question; in North Dakota, 72 percent of the balloters did the same. But despite the two defeats, 1948 still seemed to mark a reversal of political momentum at both the state and national levels. Both PAC and LLPE had thrown themselves into the 1948 elections with a vengeance, mostly working along parallel lines but collaborating on occasion. Their registration and get-out-the-vote drives produced a solid labor vote for the Democratic party in many districts. Not only did their efforts elect a more favorable Congress and save the presidency for Harry Truman, but their grass roots work left them in control of many local Democratic party structures.[55]

Moreover, labor's electoral gains in 1948 portended new legislative successes in 1949. In relatively short order, both Delaware and New Hampshire repealed their anti–union security statutes, yielding two offensive victories, although another repeal drive failed in Tennessee. Tables 2.2, 2.3, and 2.4 tell the story. Twenty-five Delaware Democrats scored − 100 on cohesion for the repeal effort (up from − 65 in 1947), topping the state's Republican lawmakers who also fell into the pro-labor column this time around with an index of cohesion of − 20. In New Hampshire repeal sentiment favored the pro-labor position, with labor lobbyists and their legislative friends winning a victory by voice vote and division. The Tennessee repeal campaign did not fare as well, coming to a vote in only one chamber where it met a narrow defeat. The 28 senate Democrats of the Volunteer State generally went in both directions with a low cohesion index of 7 (the small amount of Republican votes, a total of 4, added up to 3 in favor of right to work and 1 against). Furthermore, it looked as though a successful assault on Taft-Hartley was also possible in 1949. Here, however, despite yeoman work in the nation's wards and precincts on behalf of the Democratic party, organized labor found the Truman administration notably unsympathetic to its wishes regarding Taft-Hartley repeal. Further complications occurred when labor itself, knowing that outright repeal was an impossibility, failed to quickly agree on amendments acceptable to all segments of the movement. These tactical errors allowed a minority of Republicans and southern Democrats to organize an effective opposition; the final votes were close, but the compromise bill did not pass. In this 1949 repeal-revision drive, labor did get a somewhat better response from the Democratic congressional delegation, reflecting, at least, some acknowledgment of the potential electoral importance of organized labor to the party. Table 2.5 lists the respective party responses on Taft-Hartley repeal-revision. House Democrats tallied a −51 cohesion index and their Senate party brethren a −12. This was a definite (though insufficient from labor leaders' point of view) improvement on the index scores of 5 and 0 two years earlier. Overall, the Democrats scored −45 in support of revision and the Republicans 71 against—a clearcut difference no matter how one looked at it.[56]

Thus, in 1949 the odious law emerged unscathed from labor's assault, and the defeat greatly disheartened union activists. "We went into the fight knowing we had only an outside chance of accomplishing repeal on any sort of terms acceptable to all branches of labor," wrote labor lobbyist John Edelman to the Textile Workers' executive council. Now unions were either losing interest or looking toward the 1950 elections. "A defeatist policy of this sort seems utterly stupid from a political standpoint," said Edelman. Organized labor needed at least some minor legislative gains to keep up the political enthusiasm of the rank and file. "We will invite losses (which we cannot afford)," Edelman advised, "if we go to the voters with merely bitter denunciations of the perfidy of the [Republican-southern Democrat] coalition, and elaborate alibis for why we got nothing at all." The success of industry lobbies, he argued, is proof that Congress reacts "to carefully planned, sustained and well-organized pressures." Labor had to continue to produce those pressures.[57]

Nevertheless, it would be some time before the labor movement had another chance at significantly modifying the Taft-Hartley Act. The failure of the 1949 effort resulted in a secure underpinning for state right-to-work laws as well, for as long as section 14(b) remained a part of the law the statutes would be exempt from federal preemption. And befitting the intimate connection between the two levels of legislation, the decision on the AFL test suits came down shortly after the defeated repeal-revision attempt.

In *Lincoln Federal Labor Union v. Northwestern Iron and Metal Com-*

pany, the Supreme Court ruled that state right-to-work laws were constitutional exercises of state police powers. In a group of three cases, the Court rejected the AFL's argument that state union security restrictions violated the individual's constitutional right to join a union for self-protection. Historical experience had shown, the federation maintained in a brief prepared by researcher Boris Shishkin, that the right to free assembly was indispensable to human freedom. As it applied to unionism, this right of assembly would become useless if unions could not protect themselves with union security provisions. The union shop was a major element in forcing adherence to common rules, thereby guaranteeing the existence of unions and collective bargaining. The justices disagreed, pointing out that legislation now protected the right to join a union. In the tribunal's view, the existence of section 14(b) had forced AFL attorneys to base their arguments on broad issues which in context did not carry compelling weight. Right-to-work laws, the Court held, simply did not violate the right to organize collectively nor did they imply the destruction of unionism.[58]

Whether or not the Court was correct, organized labor's tradition of fighting the open shop prevented it from granting any validity to the justices' position. In any event, it was the Court's findings that determined the law— not the labor movement. And with the rendering of those findings, it become painfully obvious that both the AFL's and the CIO's strategy for combatting right to work had come up short. Padway's successor, J. Albert Woll, told the 1949 convention that the *Lincoln* decision "demonstrates clearly, I think, that we cannot channel into one line of attack our efforts to rid organized labor of restrictive legislation." The federation must use legislative lobbying, court challenges, and politics to oppose the attempts of its enemies to destroy its hard-won gains.[59]

Perhaps if that realization had existed in 1944 it may have made a difference in some right-to-work states. By 1949, however, if organized labor wanted to remove right-to-work laws in the South and in the Plains states, it did not have the strategic advantage of defending—it had to attack. And by that time the labor movement also began to realize that its apocalyptic rhetoric about the likely effects of open shop legislation had been overdone— or were at least premature. A 1949 report by Tennessee unionists, for example, indicated that the initial impact tended to quarantine labor rather than destroy it. But, the report argued, if state officials began to stringently enforce the law or if the state experienced hard times, devastation might well occur. Up until now, though, it seemed that only the weak and poorly organized industries had major difficulties. In addition, the right-to-work law formed the basis for more than a score of damage suits, costing Tennessee unions much time, energy, and money, "all of which could and should be directed toward more constructive purposes." "What the state law has done is to make it more difficult to establish an organization on a permanent basis," the report asserted. "The unfriendly employer hides behind the state law, which prohibits all forms of union security, [and uses it] as a vantage point from which to undermine the union's position."[60]

By this point, however, there was little that organized labor could do except fight off the extension of right to work to other states. Until political activism placed enough labor sympathizers in the state legislatures and in Congress, the labor movement would have to live with union security restrictions and the Taft-Hartley Act. Using the ambiguity on union security in national labor policy and the fear of growing labor power, right-to-work proponents had put together an impressive string of victories at the state level. Neither the AFL or the CIO had been effective in dealing with the first attempts of their opponents to establish the legitimacy of state union security restrictions through public votes. The national office of the AFL, following organizational traditions, put most of its energy into a legal challenge and neglected its political and educational functions. The CIO's leadership, on the other hand, saw political action and education as a tool with which to struggle against anti-labor legislation. It was difficult, however, to educate and stimulate a membership that was not there; more than anything else the CIO's 1946 organizing drive was an acknowledgment that economic organization must come before political influence.

The net effect of both approaches poorly equipped organized labor to respond to the 1944 to 1946 right-to-work thrusts, which were in the main referendums that required expertise in single-issue election campaigning. When the labor turmoil and organizing of 1946 spread right to work even further, anti-labor forces, composed of small-town Republicans and southern Democrats in about equal portions, had good reason to ensure that their revision of national labor policy took into account gains at the state level. With section 14(b) in the Taft-Hartley Act, Congress not only protected the statutes from the courts, it expanded the jurisdiction of the laws into the realm of interstate commerce. Then, despite a slight pro-labor reversal of the momentum on right to work in 1948 and 1949, the key legislative defeat on Taft-Hartley revision and the unexpected legal upset in the *Lincoln* decision put the final nail in the coffin. By the end of the decade, many labor leaders believed that trade unionism's great victories of the 1930s were in danger of being wiped out. Not by an economic fight between labor and management, the CIO's venerable Van Bittner maintained, "but by a government—our government, the government of the United States."[61]

Perhaps somewhere Samuel Gompers silently nodded in agreement. Government intervention in labor relations in the 1940s had in many ways affirmed voluntarism's observations about the state, observations that in the late 1930s and war years had seemed less valid than previously. After 1949, however, organized labor had a much more balanced appreciation of the role of the state and the depth of the difficulties inherent in its

relationship with the Democratic party. In 1944, AFL attorney Joseph Padway confidently told that year's convention delegates that we "might as
well, here and now, tell the State of Florida and the State of Arkansas" that
their right-to-work laws could never, ever force unionists to work with non-
union laborers. "It cannot and will not be done," he thundered angrily.
Five years later, no one in the AFL, the CIO, or any other part of organized
labor would have cared to repeat those words.[62]

NOTES

1. Quoted in Lamar T. Beman, comp., *Selected Articles on the Closed Shop*
(New York: H. W. Wilson Company, 1921), p. 83.
2. Several works on the development of the New Deal's labor policy in the
1930s and 1940s are Irving Bernstein, *The New Deal Collective Bargaining Policy*
(Berkeley: University of California Press, 1950) and *Turbulent Years: A History of
the American Worker 1933–1941* (Boston: Houghton Mifflin, 1970); James A.
Gross, *The Making of the National Labor Relations Board: A Study in Economics,
Politics, and the Law* (Albany: State University of New York Press, 1976) and *The
Reshaping of the National Labor Relations Board: National Labor Policy in Tran-
sition 1937–1947* (Albany: State University of New York Press, 1982); Harry Millis
and Emily Clark Brown, *From the Wagner Act to the Taft-Hartley Act* (Chicago:
University of Chicago Press, 1950).
3. Bernstein, *Turbulent Years*, pp. 327–328; Thomas R. Haggard, *Compulsory
Unionism, the NLRB, and the Courts* (Philadelphia: Wharton School, University of
Pennsylvania Press, 1977), pp. 145–171.
4. Robert H. Zieger, "The Limits of Militancy: Organizing Paperworkers, 1933–
1935," *Journal of American History* 63(December 1976):638–657.
5. The best study of the evolution of attempts to revise the NLRA in a more
conservative direction is Gross, *The Reshaping of the NLRB*.
6. I have drawn much of my discussion of the controversy surrounding the
union security question during World War II from Nelson Nauen Lichtenstein,
"Industrial Unionism Under the No-Strike Pledge: A Study of the CIO During the
Second World War" (Ph.D. diss., University of California, 1974). Also see Lichtenstein, "Ambiguous Legacy: The Union Security Problem During World War II,"
Labor History 18(Spring 1977):214–238, and his recent monograph, *Labor's War
at Home* (Cambridge: Cambridge University Press, 1982).
7. On this point see Joel Seidman, *American Labor From Defense to Reconversion* (Chicago: University of Chicago Press, 1953), chapter 6.
8. Lichtenstein, "Industrial Unionism," pp. 149–150.
9. Ibid., p. 151.
10. Ibid., pp. 154–162.
11. Archie Robinson, *George Meany and His Times: A Biography* (New York:
Simon and Schuster, 1981), pp. 110–111.
12. Lichtenstein, "Industrial Unionism," pp. 174–176, 217.
13. Confidential Memorandum, Conversation, William H. Davis with Philip
Murray and Lee Pressman, 14 April 1942, War Labor Board Headquarters, non-
case record, Series #3, Administration Policies and Processes, RG 202, National

Archives, cited in Lichtenstein, "Industrial Unionism," pp. 202–203, 197–201; Lichtenstein, "Ambiguous Legacy," pp. 232–233. For evidence of the importance that CIO unions, such as the UE, accorded the union security issue before the NWLB, see the Circular Letter #54, Organizing Department, 14 April 1942, Box 22, Local 932 Collection, WPRL. The UE instructed locals not to sign or renew any contract without a union security provision unless so authorized by the international.

14. See Howell John Harris, *The Right to Manage: Industrial Relations Policies of American Business in the 1940s* (Madison: University of Wisconsin Press, 1982), pp. 48–50, 107–111, for business's continuing antipathy to union security. The Termination Report of the NWLB is quoted in Seidman, p. 108.

15. CIO, *Executive Board*, 14 October 1939, WPRL; David Donati to Congressman Howard W. Smith, Virginia, 19 January 1939, Box 219, Howard W. Smith Papers, Alderman Library, University of Virginia, Charlottesville, Virginia.

16. For a good overview of the extent of the spread of state statutes restricting union behavior in this period, see Millis and Brown, *From the Wagner Act*, pp. 316–326. The AFL believed much of this state anti-labor legislation to be the work of right-wing fringe elements which, to some extent, it was. The mainstream conservative establishment did not take long to inject its participation, however. With regard to some of the earliest agitation see George N. Green, *The Establishment in Texas Politics, 1938–1957* (Westport, Conn.: Greenwood Press, 1979), pp. 61–66, 104–107, and Press Release, "Statement by the Executive Council of the American Federation of Labor," 21 May 1943, American Federation of Labor, State Legislation Files (hereafter AFL State Files), State Historical Society of Wisconsin, Madison, Wisconsin (hereafter SHSW).

17. Joseph Padway to the Members of the Executive Council, AFL, 19 May 1943, and Padway to William Green, 19 November 1943, both Box 1, AFL State Files, SHSW; Arkansas Constitutional Amendment 34 (1944). For an annotated compilation of state right-to-work statutes see "State Right-to-Work Laws," annotated, National Right to Work Committee Publication, April, 1977.

18. Padway to Green, 19 November 1943, Box 1, AFL State Files, SHSW.

19. Ibid. In this study, all citations to legislative votes on right-to-work measures at the state level are taken from Appendix A. This appendix also contains the Rice Index of Cohesion (RIC), a statistical measure of group solidarity, for the respective political parties in each vote. See the explanation in Appendix A for information on the RIC's significance and the methodology used for its derivation.

20. Philip Taft, *Labor Politics American Style: The California State Federation of Labor* (Cambridge, Mass.: Harvard University Press, 1968), pp. 232–233. All statistics on state right-to-work elections, arranged within each chapter in tables, come from official state tabulations. Appendix B contains a listing of each state that has had such an issue put before its citizens from 1944 to 1978. With regard to state union membership, I have derived my estimates from two sources: Leo Troy, *Distribution of Union Membership among the States, 1939 and 1953* (Washington, D.C.: National Bureau Of Economic Research), 1957, table 1, and Leo Troy and Neil Sheflin, *U.S. Union Sourcebook: Membership, Finances, Structure, Directory* (West Orange, N.J.: Industrial Relations Data and Information Services, 1985), tables 7.1 and 7.2. See explanation in Appendix B for the method used to estimate absolute and percent organized membership figures as well as the method used to determine the percent of vote for highest office.

21. For the Sullivan-Green exchange, see W. E. Sullivan to William Green, 28 June 1944; William Green to W. E. Sullivan, 6 July 1944; Sullivan to Green, 18 July 1944; all Box 1, AFL State Files, SHSW. For an examination of the Florida campaign, see John G. Shott, *How Right-to-Work Laws Are Passed: Florida Sets the Pattern* (Washington, D.C.: Public Affairs Institute, 1956), pp. 60–61.

22. W. C. Mullins to W. H. Winchester, 11 February 1943, Brotherhood of Locomotive Engineers Files, 38–4–8, Texas Labor Archives (hereafter TLA), University of Texas at Arlington, Arlington, Texas (hereafter UTA), cited in George Green, *Texas Politics*, p. 63; E.H. Williams, Director, Arkansas State Federation of Labor, to William Green, 19 October 1944, Box 1, AFL State Files, SHSW. Also see James E. Youngdahl, "Thirteen Years of the 'Right to Work' in Arkansas," *Arkansas Law Review and Bar Journal* (Fall 1960):222.

23. At the same time that Green was asking Sullivan what the national AFL could do to stimulate the internationals, he was writing to Charles MacGowan of the Boilermakers that the national AFL had "called upon" the Florida state federation to oppose the amendment, implying that the national officers were leading the charge. See MacGowan to Green, 2 July 1944; Green to MacGowan, 20 July 1944; William Green to T. L. Carlton, Carlton to Green, both 27 September 1944; all Box 1, AFL State Files, SHSW. In his study of the passage of the Florida right-to-work law Shott concluded that Florida labor's main failure was its inability to sustain an educational program and public relations campaign over eighteen months. See Shott, pp. 60–61.

24. Max Wedekind to William Green, with attachments, 7 February 1945, Box 1; Memo, George Googe, AFL Southern Representative, n.d. [February 1945?], Box 2; Francis McDonald, Executive Secretary, South Dakota Federation of Labor, to William Green, 18 February 1945, Box 5; J. J. Guenther, President, Nebraska State Federation of Labor, to William Green, 4 January 1945, Box 3; Harry W. Acreman, Executive Secretary, Texas State Federation of Labor, to William Green, 6 February 1945, Box 5; Wade Church, Secretary-Treasurer, Arizona State Federation of Labor, Circular Letter to the Presidents of All Internationals with Locals in Arizona, 2 May 1946, Box 1; all AFL State Files, SHSW. Millis and Brown found that eleven state legislatures had nearly identical right-to-work proposals submitted in the 1945 legislative sessions, see pp. 326–332. For an in-depth examination of the Arizona right-to-work battle see Michael S. Wade, *The Bitter Issue: The Right to Work in Arizona* (Tucson: Arizona Historical Society, 1976).

25. Herbert S. Thatcher to Kenneth P. Lewis, 26 February 1945; "Transcript of the Address of Herbert S. Thatcher, Anti–Closed Shop Conference," 2 June 1946; both Box 3, AFL State Files, SHSW. For the background of the Louisiana right-to-work campaigns, see Thomas Becnel, *Labor, Church, and the Sugar Establishment: Louisiana, 1887–1976* (Baton Rouge: Louisiana State University Press, 1980), pp. 179–183.

26. James A. Suffridge, President, Retail Clerks International Association, to William Green, 2 March 1946; and Florida State Legislation folder, generally, both Box 1, AFL State Files, SHSW. For the national office's participation in the Nebraska and Arizona elections, see J. J. Guenther and Patrick McCartney to William Green, 21 May 1946; Green to Guenther, 23 July 1946; Guenther to Green, 9 November 1946; all Box 3; John J. Durkin, Secretary, Tucson Central Trades Council, to William Green, 16 July 1946; Durkin to Nelson Cruikshank, 22 August 1946; Green

to Durkin, 12 September 1946 and 4 October 1946; all Box 1, AFL State Files, SHSW.

27. Padway to William Green, 21 February 1945; George Googe to William Green, 11 May 1945; William Green to Padway, 12 April 1945; all Box 1, AFL State Files, SHSW.

28. Joseph Padway to William Green, 20 November 1945, Box 1; Francis MacDonald to William Green, 18 February 1945; Green to MacDonald, 1 March 1945; Padway to William Green, "Re: Report on South Dakota Anti–Closed Shop Test Suit," 16 April 1946; all Box 5, AFL State Files, SHSW; American Federation of Labor, *Report of Proceedings of the Annual Convention*, 1946, 136–137 (hereafter AFL, *Proceedings*).

29. John J. Durkin to William Green, 25 September 1946; J.J. Guenther to William Green, 7 November 1946; both Box 1, AFL State Files, SHSW. Also see Wade, p. 82, for the background to the Arizona agitation. For the 1945–1947 struggle over right to work in Texas see George Green, *Texas Politics*, pp. 65–66, and Thomas B. Brewer, "State Anti-Labor Legislation: Texas—A Case Study," *Labor History* 11(Winter 1970):58–76.

30. Florida's IUC, for example, had not been organized until 1943. See Congress of Industrial Organizations, *Report of Proceedings of the Constitutional Convention*, 1943, pp. 51–52 (hereafter CIO, *Proceedings*). The official's quote is in Philip Taft, *Organizing Dixie: Alabama Workers in the Industrial Era* (Westport, Conn.: Greenwood Press, 1981), pp. 121–123. Also see Murray Polakoff, "The Development of the Texas State CIO Council" (Ph.D. diss., Columbia University, 1955). CIO membership figures are taken from Troy, table 1.

31. Report, Nathan Cowan, CIO Legislative Representative, John Brophy, Director of Industrial Union Councils, and J. Raymond Walsh, Director of Education and Research, to Philip Murray, 30 December 1942; copy in Metropolitan Detroit AFL-CIO Collection (Wayne County), Series II, Box 25, WPRL.

32. Ibid.

33. Ibid.

34. CIO, *Transcript of Proceedings of the Meeting of the Executive Board, CIO* (hereafter CIO, *Executive Board*), 5 February 1943, pp. 77, 88–89, 92, WPRL.

35. Ibid., pp. 9–14, 63–70, 74–77, 95.

36. CIO, *Executive Board*, 14–15 May 1943, pp. 27, 33, WPRL; John Brophy to Ernest Bennett, 29 March 1943, Box 25; Metropolitan Detroit AFL-CIO Collection, WPRL.

37. CIO, *Executive Board*, 7–8 July 1943 and 29 October 1943, pp. 229–232 and 147–159 respectively, WPRL.

38. CIO, *Proceedings*, 1943, pp. 51–53, 320–323.

39. Ibid., p. 245.

40. CIO, *Executive Board*, 13–14 July 1945, pp. 318–321.

41. Ibid., pp. 132, 154–157. The record of AFL/CIO legislative cooperation at the state level was generally good, but there were instances in which craft-industrial or personal rivalries harmed joint efforts. William Green, for example, urged the Nebraska AFL to make plans separate from the "rebel, rival movement" in its right-to-work campaign. To some degree, this also occurred in Arkansas. See William Green to J. J. Guenther, 15 January 1945, Box 3, AFL State Files, SHSW, and Walter

H. Harris to James B. Carey, 17 January 1947, Box 84, CIO Secretary-Treasurer's Collection, Pt. I, WPRL.

42. Cox quoted in "Cox, Edward Eugene," *Current Biography*, 1943; B. O. Cone, President, Crawford Manufacturing Company, to Congressman Howard W. Smith, 10 January 1939, Box 219, Howard W. Smith Collection, Alderman Library, University of Virginia, Charlottesville, Virginia. For a discussion of labor's 1946 militancy, see Seidman, pp. 213–269. For details on the AFL's and CIO's southern organizing campaigns, see F. Ray Marshall, *Labor in the South* (Cambridge, Mass.: Harvard University Press, 1967), pp. 252–265.

43. William Green to Woodrow Wilson Davis, Sr., 21 March 1947, Box 1, AFL State Files, SHSW. A further explanation of the Rice Index of Cohesion is found in Appendix A. For a discussion of the sources of local right-to-work support, see Joseph R. Dempsey, *The Operation of Right-to-Work Laws: a comparison between what the state legislatures say about the meaning of the laws and how state court judges have applied these laws* (Milwaukee: Marquette University Press, 1961), pp. 24–26, and Paul E. Sultan, *Right-to-Work Laws: A Study in Conflict* (Los Angeles: University of California, Institute of Industrial Relations, 1958).

44. Dempsey, *The Operation of Right-to-Work Laws*, p. 15. The pattern, of course, often had local variations. In Arizona, early supporters of right to work were a group of veterans supposedly shut out from employment because of union security. In Texas larger corporate interests were instrumental in passing the law. See Wade, pp. 2–10, 28–82, Brewer, p. 76, and Green, pp. 104–107. Typical models for the passage of right-to-work legislation were Florida and Virginia. See Shott for Florida and John M. Kuhlman, "Right to Work Laws: The Virginia Experience," *Labor Law Journal* 6 (July 1955):453–462, for Virginia. The pattern should not suggest that big business liked union security, just that small business leaders usually took the most active role. George Romney, head of the Automotive Council on War Production, for example, had been conspicuous in supporting right-to-work principles in 1945–1946. Also see *Fortune*'s big-business poll, "They Judge The Closed Shop Coldly," *Fortune*, November 1941, pp. 203–204.

45. William Green to the Executive Council, AFL, AFL Executive Council Minutes, 21–25 April 1945, pp. 34–36, quoted in Marshall, pp. 252–253.

46. Stanton E. Smith to Herbert Thatcher, 10 March 1947, Thatcher to Smith, 12 March 1947, Box 1095, Chattanooga Area Labor Council, Southern Labor Archives, Georgia State University, Atlanta, Georgia (hereafter SLA); Thatcher to Patrick E. Gorman, 3 March 1947; Thatcher to John L. Hand, 4 March 1947; both Box 5, AFL State Files, SHSW.

47. Paul R. Christopher to Lee Pressman, "Re: Tennessee Anti–Closed Shop Law," and Christopher to Van Bittner, "Re: Anti–Closed Shop Law in Tennessee"; both 28 February 1947, Box 128; "Van Bittner, 1946–1947," CIO Organizing Campaign Papers, Tennessee, Duke University, Durham, North Carolina. CIO, *Executive Board*, 16–17 May 1947, pp. 12–18, 44, WPRL; "Report of President Philip Murray to the 9th Constitutional Convention of the C.I.O.," 13–17 October 1947, copy in UAW President's Office: Walter P. Reuther Files, Box 103; WPRL.

48. Lee Pressman to Philip Murray and James B. Carey, 9 May 1947, Box 73, CIO Secretary-Treasurer's Office, Pt. I (hereafter James Carey Files), WPRL; Maurice Sugar, UAW General Counsel, to Walter P. Reuther, 25 April 1947 and 5 May 1947, "Re: Delaware Anti-Labor Law"; Reuther to Sugar, 24 June 1947, Box 157;

UAW President's Office: Walter P. Reuther Files, WPRL; Textile Workers Union of America, "A Program of TWUA Activity Against State Anti-Labor Legislation," n.d. [1947?], Box 10, John W. Edelman Collection, WPRL. The TWUA advised its locals to spend money to send representatives to lobby against right-to-work legislation because "a union without a treasury is preferable to a treasury without a union."

49. CIO, *Executive Board*, 16–17 May 1947, pp. 271–272, WPRL.

50. CIO, *Executive Board*, 16–17 May 1947, pp. 271–272, WPRL. There are a number of good studies that provide a picture of the political milieu at the state level. For the South in the 1940s, V. O. Key, Jr.'s classic, *Southern Politics in State and Nation* (New York: Alfred A. Knopf, 1949), is the best source. For the West, see Frank Jonas, ed., *Western Politics* (Salt Lake City: University of Utah Press, 1961). A similar study for New England is Duane Lockard, *New England State Politics* (Princeton, N.J.: Princeton University Press, 1959). Unfortunately, none of these studies focus exclusively on labor politics within these states and mention labor as an organized political force only in passing.

51. CIO, *Executive Board*, 16–17 May 1947, pp. 273–278, WPRL.

52. CIO, *Executive Board*, 16–17 May 1947, pp. 328, 356, WPRL.

53. See the comments of Delegate Charles Weber of the Virginia IUC in CIO, *Proceedings*, 1947, p. 216; U.S. Congress, House, Committee on Education and Labor, 80th Cong., 1st sess., 1947, H. Rept. 245 on H.R. 3020, p. 44.

54. AFL, *Proceedings*, 1948, pp. 171–172.

55. James C. Foster, *The Union Politic: The CIO Political Action Committee* (Columbia, Mo.: University of Missouri Press, 1975), pp. 108–132.

56. Benjamin Aaron, "Amending the Taft-Hartley Act: A Decade of Frustration," *Industrial and Labor Relations Review* 11(April 1958):330; Gerald Pomper, "Labor and Congress: The Repeal of the Taft-Hartley Act," *Labor History* 2(Fall 1961):323–343; and Gerald Pomper, "Organized Labor in Politics: The Campaign to Revise the Taft-Hartley Act" (Ph.D. diss., Princeton University, 1959).

57. John W. Edelman to Textile Workers of America, Executive Council, 14 May 1949 and 3 October 1949, both Box 95, John W. Edelman Collection, WPRL.

58. 335 U.S. 522 (1949). Consistent with the CIO's somewhat passive role in legally contesting right to work, the industrial federation filed as an amicus curiae in the case. For the original complaint, see Document 65 in Box 3, AFL State Files, SHSW. A good discussion of the *Lincoln* decision is in Dempsey, *The Operation of Right-to-Work Laws*, pp. 29–40.

59. AFL, *Proceedings*, 1949, p. 402.

60. Memo, "Answers to Certain Questions Concerning the Tennessee So-Called Right to Work Law," 1949, Box 1095/174, Chattanooga Area Labor Council, SLA.

61. CIO, *Executive Board*, 16–17 May 1947, p. 316, WPRL.

62. AFL, *Proceedings*, 1944, p. 353.

3

Principles and Politics

The gulf between organized labor and management can not be bridged by amicable gestures or attitudes of goodwill. It is the result of a fundamental difference on a matter of principle—the right of an individual employee to get and hold a job without being compelled to join a union.
—Staff Report, National Association of Manufacturers, 1956[1]

Between 1950 and 1956, the labor movement stepped up its attempts to respond effectively to the right-to-work problem within the context of its ambivalent relationship with the Democratic party. During these years, organized labor tried four distinct strategies aimed at securing reform or preventing further enactment of union security restrictions. Through 1952, most of the activity focused on individual union lobbying, largely reflecting the disarray that followed the failed Taft-Hartley amendment drive of 1949. Then, in 1953 and 1954, faced with the unwelcome accession of the Eisenhower Republicans to power, both federations launched Taft-Hartley revision campaigns—each of which included key amendments to the act's union security provisions—only to find that labor's highly visible Democratic partisanship undermined the effort. Disappointed by the meagre results of these initiatives, George Meany, now president of the newly merged AFL-CIO, sought to deflect the increasing right-to-work agitation in late 1955 by engaging in unsuccessful high-level negotiations with representatives of employers associations.

During this time, labor lobbyists saved five states from right-to-work forces while losing six others. In those battles, the Democratic party's performance at the state level improved. The anti-labor vote of southern Democrats was less cohesive than in the 1940s, and in two-party areas Democrats supported the labor position on right to work. Coinciding with the failure of the preferred national-level approach to labor law reform, this

relative improvement in state-level performance forced the labor movement's political strategists to scrutinize both their methodology and their
relationship with the Democrats.

It became increasingly clear to union officers that at the national level,
when labor issues involved divisive "principles" like right to work, the party
leadership was uninterested in enforcing conformity. Organized labor's answer to this problem—in effect its fourth strategy—was to tighten and
expand the mechanics of its political operations and to focus once again on
the state political arenas, where events in 1955 and 1956 foreshadowed
future success. Key victories over right-to-work proposals—in Kentucky,
Kansas, and Maryland in 1955, and especially in Louisiana and Washington
in 1956—left labor's legislative leaders feeling upbeat, for the victories indicated the potential effectiveness of a reinvigorated grass roots labor politics
which had the dual aim of halting right-to-work encroachments and puri-
fying the Democratic party.

INDIVIDUAL UNION LOBBYING AND THE NATIONAL DEMOCRATIC ALLIANCE

Though most of the right-to-work battles of the decade occurred between
1954 and 1958, the outlines of organized labor's problematic and vexing
relationship with the Democratic party on the question of union security
appeared early in the decade. After the 1940s right-to-work struggles in the
South, labor officials acknowledged that their influence in most southern
state Democratic parties was weak. On the national level, though, AFL and
CIO leaders expected their voices to carry enough weight within the party
to be able to set a minimum agenda on labor-related issues. But here they
discovered over and over again that the conservative elements of the party
held enough power to impose positions independent of the more numerous
representatives of the ideological center. As United Auto Workers (UAW)
Washington lobbyist Paul Sifton wrote to Walter Reuther in June 1950, the
interaction of the one-party system in the South and the seniority system
in Congress left liberals out of power even when the Democrats were in the
majority. The unwanted intervention of southern Democrats in the 1949
Taft-Hartley amendment attempt was only the most recent example. "At
some point in our political life," Sifton observed in 1950, "this question of
re-alignment of power within the Democratic Party must be faced up to by
both labor supporters . . . and the Fair Deal segments within the Democratic
Party." Labor could just not "keep on getting out the vote for 2 and 4 more
years of defeat by persons . . . who, while technically Democratic," work
with Republicans to defeat reforms "our members support through PAC,
registration, and voting."[2]

The conservatives' dominance of the national congressional party was
also only one aspect of the problem. All too often, noted some analysts

close to the scene, even liberal legislators would have preferred that labor's legislative representatives not pressure them. For example, in 1950 when Textile Workers of America (TWUA) lobbyist John Edelman pressed usually sympathetic lawmakers into holding hearings on the adverse effects of the Taft-Hartley Act on the textile industry, he got a decidedly lukewarm reception. As he informed his union's executive council, "with so many diversions absorbing the time and energies of the Senators—all of which seemed to offer better opportunities for publicity and fewer headaches—our job was constantly postponed."[3]

Thus, when labor leaders sought to shape Democratic Party policy on national labor law reform, they found themselves confronted by a party with a powerful and hostile conservative wing and an at times diffident liberal element. This did not mean that congressional Democrats did not listen to labor viewpoints—they did. It did mean, however, that it usually required an atypical situation for labor to be effective in an administrative or legislative offensive. When dependent upon normal, work-a-day channels of legislative influence, labor lobbyists' plans often ran aground on the sympathetic nods of politicians intending to take no action. When special circumstances combined to increase labor's political leverage, however, union chiefs could successfully pursue their objectives.

In 1951 and 1952, for instance, segments of organized labor won from a Democratic administration and Congress several important changes in union security at the national level. No doubt the Korean War had much to do with this, as President Truman's need for uninterrupted industrial production overrode other considerations. For example, in 1951 the politically astute railroad brotherhoods capitalized on both their critical economic position and lack of effective employer opposition to push through an amendment repealing the Railway Labor Act's decades-old prohibition on union security clauses. Then, through the threat of a strike, the rail unions collapsed the last-ditch efforts of disorganized employers to prevent institution of the practice. As Table 3.1 shows, the long history of government regulation of the industry, the lack of unified corporate opposition, and the critical timing led both Democrats and Republicans in Congress to support railroad labor. In fact, Republicans outdid the Democrats by compiling a pro-labor −76 index of cohesion (−84 in the House and −50 in the Senate). Irreconcilable southern Democrats, however, brought down their party's cohesion score to −58 (−61 in the House and −38 in the Senate). Thus, within two years the railroad brotherhoods had effectively established union security in an industry that had operated for many years under a law prohibiting it.[4]

Similarly, during the 1952 steel crisis, the Wage Stabilization Board (WSB), like the NWLB before it, granted the United Steelworkers a union shop in basic steel in exchange for wage moderation—even over strenuous corporate objections. Though U.S. Steel chairman Benjamin Fairless warned

3.1
Rice Index of Cohesion of Congressional Parties, on National Labor Legislation Involving Union Security Issues, 1951–1954

LEGISLATION/YEAR	AGAINST LABOR	FOR LABOR	TOTAL	PERCENT YES	PERCENT NO	RICE INDEX
Railway Labor Act 1951						
House						
D	42	176	218	19	81	-61
R	10	115	125	8	92	-84
Senate VV						
D But RC On	13	29	42	31	69	-38
R Amendment	10	30	40	25	75	-50
Both Chambers						
D	55	205	260	21	79	-58
R	20	145	165	12	88	-76
Total	75	350	425	18	82	-65
Taft-Hartley Amendment 1951						
House						
D	13	154	167	8	92	-84
R	5	152	157	3	97	-94
Senate						
D	VV	VV	VV	VV	VV	VV
R	VV	VV	VV	VV	VV	VV
Both Chambers						
D	13	154	167	8	92	-84
R	5	152	157	3	97	-94
Total	18	306	324	6	94	-89
Taft-Hartley Revision Drive 1954						
House						
D	NV	NV	NV	NV	NV	NV
R	NV	NV	NV	NV	NV	NV
Senate Vote						
D to	0	46	46	0	100	-100
R Recommit	42	3	45	93	7	87
Both Chambers						
D	0	46	46	0	100	-100
R	42	3	45	93	7	87
Total	42	49	91	46	54	-8

Source: Congressional Quarterly, <u>Congress and the Nation</u>, 1945-1964,
         (Washington, DC: Congressional Quarterly Service, 1965).
Key: VV-Voice Vote, NV-No Vote, RC-Roll-Call
Index: +100(Totally Cohesive Against Labor)
         -100(Totally Cohesive in Favor of Labor)
         Rice Index Rounded to Nearest Integer

that a government directive ordering the union shop could lead the country toward becoming "a strange socialistic Utopia where freedom is unknown," it was clear that the president's wartime anti-inflation objectives took precedence. As another steel executive said unhappily of Truman's speech backing the WSB, the president "dealt with money, but omitted principle."[5]

In addition to these two legislative changes grounded in the special conditions of wartime, in 1951 organized labor won the removal of the union shop authorization election from the Taft-Hartley Act. This victory was largely due to the lack of an organized opposition. From 1947 to 1951, corporations jousted with unions in these union shop contests. Faced with the fact that labor won 97 percent of over 46,000 polls, business leaders as well as conservative politicians such as Senator Robert Taft (R-OH) saw little need to spend more tax dollars on the elections. Taft and Senator Hubert Humphrey (D-MN), an ardent liberal and warm friend of labor, co-sponsored a repeal bill which passed in the fall of 1951. Reflecting the unity of both parties on the issue, Table 3.1 lists the indexes of cohesion as being a pro-labor − 94 percent for the Republicans and a − 84 percent for the Democrats. Thereafter, in non-right-to-work states, labor and management could negotiate a union security clause without a special election.[6]

These events all had one thing in common. It apparently took more than just having a Democratic president and Congress for organized labor to gain legislative reform of labor relations laws. The failure of the building trades unions' attempt to repeal section 14(b), as well as the uneven regional response of state Democratic organizations to right to work, highlighted this fact. If labor's political leaders wanted more than just perfunctory nods from Democratic officials at the national level, they had to somehow increase the amount of power they could wield in setting the legislative agenda on the thorny issue of national labor relations policy.

Indeed, the prominence of union security questions at the national level through 1952 meant that labor leaders still regarded it as immensely important to the future of their organizations. A closer examination of the union shop election statistics reveals why. Though undeniably reflecting a victory for unionism and union security, the round numbers hid unsettling facts. It was true that unions won 97 percent of the elections. However, it was also true that a significant number of workers eligible to vote in the elections either voted against the union shop or did not vote at all. In the 1950 General Motors union shop elections, for example, 75 percent voted for the UAW position, while 9.5 percent voted against the union and 13.5 percent did not cast ballots. The Steelworkers leaders also found that after big union shop election campaigns in 162 plants (where the union won 153 and lost 9), only 66 percent of the employees voted for union security in 1950. Thus, a third of the workers in both the UAW and USWA elections wanted either no union shop or failed to vote (14 percent and 20 percent respectively). Likewise, the International Association of Machinists' (IAM) 1951 Boeing elections revealed that while 64 percent supported the IAM, 12 percent were dead set against union security and 25 percent did not bother to vote. Overall union shop election statistics implied that between 5 and 12 percent of bargaining-unit members in these large industrial unions definitely opposed the union shop, and between 12 and 19 percent did not care enough to vote.[7]

When confronted with such numbers, an astute union leader might well conclude that a union security clause could be extremely useful in bolstering organizational cohesion. With such a device, labor officials could work to educate the uncommitted to support the union. If right-to-work laws became widespread, however, trade union officers could not count on union security to aid them. With constant turnover, unions might experience a rising proportion of non-members at the workplace and, the election statistics seemed to suggest, some unions could lose up to 15 percent of their membership while still having to represent those workers in collective bargaining and grievance handling. Even worse, the subsequent dues decline would drain resources from other valued programs.[8]

These were grim considerations. If union security restrictions continued to spread to new areas, and if public officials enforced the statutes religiously, many international unions would lose at least some power and influence. This was a real possibility, for as the AFL general counsel reported to the 1951 convention, the forces of organized labor battled against more right-to-work agitation during the preceding state legislative sessions than at any time since 1947. Of all those states considering proposals in 1951, the sole defeat for labor came in Nevada. Representatives of both parties combined to pass a right-to-work statute as well as a subsequent referendum for the 1952 election. Republicans led the way with a 60 percent Rice Index of Cohesion and even the Democrats voted aye by a 20 percent margin, as shown in Tables 3.3 and 3.4. The breadth of the agitation caused labor's legislative strategists to turn once again to the national political arena for succor. And it seemed to many of them that the most cost-effective approach would be to make repeal of section 14(b) a part of a general Taft-Hartley amendment drive after the coming 1952 elections.[9]

There were several reasons why this was the most attractive course. While frustrating, the less-than-ideal relationship with the national Democratic party had indeed produced near-victory in the Taft-Hartley campaign of 1949. By changing the liberal-conservative Democratic mix and winning the White House for the Democratic party, labor functionaries hoped that grateful politicians would repay labor's electoral aid by voting for labor law reform. This top-level strategy proved doubly attractive as piecemeal repeal of state right-to-work laws continued to be difficult to achieve. Under the doctrine of federal preemption, removal of 14(b) would invalidate existing state laws and decapitate further state agitation in one fell swoop. In addition, a national drive would be more focused and hopefully gain the resource commitment of many internationals. And perhaps above all, labor's top leaders could not resist making 14(b) repeal a part of a general Taft-Hartley amendment package because they wanted other changes in the act. Most trade union officers at this level had still not accepted the hated "slave-labor" law as a permanent part of the industrial scene.

SPECIAL INTEREST INFLUENCE AND THE REPUBLICANS

It was in this context, then, that organized labor entered into the 1952 elections determined to make Taft-Hartley amendment *the* campaign issue for both parties. This tactic seemed plausible because powerful AFL union leaders believed, not without some justification, that a possibility existed of influencing the Republicans on the issue; moreover, even stridently anti-Republican CIO strategists realized the importance of hedging their bets before the election. Thus, both federations withheld presidential endorsement until the nominee for each party promised action on Taft-Hartley. The strategy worked, for both presidential rivals agreed that change of some sort was necessary, though neither rushed to proclaim a reform position. The Democrats' Adlai Stevenson belatedly promised repeal and won labor's united backing, but even the Republicans' Dwight Eisenhower, the eventual winner, made a campaign promise to work for ameliorating amendments.[10]

By insisting on making Taft-Hartley an issue in 1952, labor's political strategists had succeeded in laying the basis for another legislative assault. Unfortunately, the election results left labor in a poor position for such an attack, because after November 1952 the labor movement faced a Republican president and Congress. Though Eisenhower had promised modest revision in the interests of fairness, his party's position on labor-backed amendments was lukewarm, to say the least. Both the AFL and CIO now reaped the harvest of their electoral commitment to the Democrats. Federation functionaries had to devise a way to influence the Republican party, which they had opposed, while keeping all Democrats committed to amendment. And, in a situation made for confusion and miscalculation, matters only became worse when the AFL refused to cooperate with the CIO and pursued an independent amendment strategy.

The older federation opted for this alternative because the election outcome necessitated working with the Republicans and, of the two national labor centers, the AFL was the more serious about gaining relief from the law. Many of its craft affiliates in the building trades had experienced major problems with the boycott, injunction, and right-to-work provisions of the statute. These same unions were among the most powerful within the federation and generally constituted the core of Republican support in organized labor. Therefore, officials of the craft unions believed that conditions made it mandatory that they work with the administration, and they saw no reason why the president would summarily reject their entreaties. Moreover, Eisenhower's nomination of plumbers' union president Martin Durkin as secretary of labor seemed to imply a desire to cooperate on a program of change.[11]

While CIO leaders likewise felt compelled by their past rhetoric to propose and lobby for changes, the industrial federation's strong attachment to liberal Democratic ideology tended to make its leaders less hopeful about revising labor legislation. They did not seriously expect the Republicans to rectify the unjust provisions of the law. Any changes the party supported, they believed, would at best be window dressing to fulfill the campaign promises of the president. Furthermore, CIO executives suspected that the

Republicans would try to split the AFL and CIO by offering amendments limited to the building trades, perhaps to the detriment of competing industrial unions. Still, even though the Republican margin was slim, 48 to 47 in the Senate and 221 to 212 in the House, there were great hazards in allowing the Republicans to shape the form and substance of any Taft-Hartley amendments—which the party in power would normally do. All of this did not mean that the industrial federation should not seek revision on behalf of its affiliates. As UAW lobbyist Paul Sifton wrote to the newly elected CIO president, Walter Reuther, in November 1952, "the fact that the election of Eisenhower was not a Republican landslide—and that the members of Congress know it—will tend to . . . [prevent] a lynching bee against unions." In all likelihood, the relative balance between the parties would enable the CIO to head off any conservative efforts to make the act worse. And it was just possible that the industrial federation might secure some improvement if it proceeded on its own.[12]

Therefore, by early 1953 both federations had resolved to seek amendment through essentially divergent strategies. After soliciting suggested revisions from affiliates, the AFL's Taft-Hartley steering committee constructed a campaign of pure special-interest lobbying. The craft federation's leadership entered into negotiations with the Eisenhower administration by tacitly allowing Secretary of Labor Durkin to represent their interests. AFL attorneys even began independently exploring areas of possible agreement with prominent and influential management lawyers in the hope of reaching an understanding with business that would defuse opposition to changes.[13] In contrast, after garnering proposals from CIO general counsels and legislative representatives, the industrial federation worked through the Democratic party to fashion an acceptable bill.[14]

The AFL's and CIO's different approaches reflected not only the internal tendencies within each federation, but also the leaders' assessments of political possibilities. And in some ways the craft unionists' reading of the Taft-Hartley amendment situation was the more accurate. During his presidential campaign, Eisenhower had expressed concern about alienating labor and the working-class vote by appearing too pro-business. For instance, as a candidate and as president-elect, the former NATO general thought it useful when advisers Henry Cabot Lodge, Jr. and Harold Stassen solicited support for Eisenhower from prominent Republican union leaders such as Maurice Hutcheson, president of the Carpenters and Richard Gray, director of the AFL's building trades department. In fact, it was through Stassen's influence that Eisenhower agreed to choose Durkin for secretary of labor. Behind the efforts of people such as Lodge and Stassen was the belief that if the Republican party wanted more from the future than minority-party status, it dare not continue to leave itself too open to the criticism that it was the captive of business interests. The appointment of Durkin, a Stevenson Democrat and labor leader, was one step in the right direction.

Furthermore, there were many other things that the Republican party could do to wean certain segments of the labor movement away from the Democrats.[15]

Indeed, John Lannin, a coordinator of the Republican party's labor division, made just such a recommendation in a policy paper prepared for the Republican National Committee before the 1952 campaign. Noting that the party had all but ignored the labor vote, he pointed out that Republicans "will have serious difficulties in 1952 if the Democrats succeed in establishing themselves as the 'Labor Party.' " Realistically, he argued, not much could be done to win the allegiance of most of the officers of the international unions and national federations. But younger officials at the local level, he believed, felt shut out by the dominance of the older unionists. "Experience during the last election," Lannin argued, "proved that the younger labor leaders are anxiously awaiting the Republican invitation." He suggested bringing these local union presidents and business agents into the party structure and creating an office of director of labor for the RNC. "To accomplish the alienation of labor from the Democrat[ic] Party will take much effort," he wrote, "and we will have to prove our sincerity by action."[16]

Such an evaluation dovetailed nicely with the president's own concern for the future of the Republican party. Eisenhower's oft-repeated support for moderation and consensus decision making were tactical responses to a larger strategy. The party, in his view, had to be pragmatic enough to win the allegiance of enough elements of the body politic so that it could serve as an effective counterweight to the social-welfare drift of the New Deal Democrats. If, in fact, his administration could strengthen and build its labor backing, the party's long-term prospects would brighten considerably. By attracting a sizeable portion of organized labor away from the social-democratic segment that had attached itself to New Deal politicians, the Republicans could fracture part of the coalition that had held power for the last twenty years and thereby help maintain a balance against creeping socialism. Finding a workable compromise with conservative unionists on Taft-Hartley amendment would go a long way toward undermining charges that the party was anti-labor.[17]

Therefore, the president knew that an administration-sponsored, generally pro-labor Taft-Hartley amendment package could turn out to be much more than a simple fulfillment of his campaign pledge. It was in this spirit that his administration entered into negotiations with all interested parties. After a series of labor-management conferences under Durkin's direction came to naught, Eisenhower's chief of staff Sherman Adams ordered intra-administration meetings between the Labor and Commerce departments. Considering Durkin's labor background and Commerce Secretary Sinclair Weeks' management ties, these talks in effect represented the contending forces involved in Taft-Hartley amendment. When it became apparent that

neither side would budge, White House aides Bernard Shanley and Gerald
Morgan took over by initiating a series of separate conferences with each
department beginning in the spring of 1953.[18]

Shanley and Morgan found soon after they began that the most hotly
contested issues between Labor and Commerce were the secondary boycott
restrictions and section 14(b). Try as they might, they could not bring either
side around to a compromise on these two subjects. Sherman Adams had
instructed Shanley that the right-to-work section of Taft-Hartley was off
limits for negotiation because the president had publicly expressed support
for individual choice regarding union membership. Nevertheless, the two
White House aides knew that they would make little progress unless they
could find a way of dealing with these most controversial items.[19]

In order to get around the impasse, in mid–1953 Shanley called in Senator
Robert Taft and Labor Committee chairmen Congressman Sam McConnell
(R-PA) and Senator H. Alexander Smith (R-NJ). Shanley later wrote that
he expanded the group "for the purpose of seeing if this issue [of federal-
state jurisdiction] could not be resolved by a larger group." This informal
committee met five times, once with the president, and by late July the
participants had again reached agreement on other amendments, but not
on 14(b). Surprisingly, while Senator Taft supported state control over union
security, he was troubled by 14(b) because it allowed control in only one
direction—against labor—and this bothered his sense of fairness. During
the time he was considering the problem, however, he fell ill and could no
longer attend the conferences.[20]

At this point, the committee began negotiations about accepting a series
of informal agreements reached by the AFL-management lawyers group.
This series of private negotiations had developed at the same time as the
Labor and Commerce departments conferences during the spring of 1953,
and had reached compromises on mandatory injunctions, voting rights for
economic strikers, pre-hire agreements for casual employment, and a number of other matters. After Morgan and Shanley's informal committee incorporated some of these suggestions, however, the AFL's Taft-Hartley
steering committee rejected the work of its own attorneys, forcing Durkin
to backtrack on his previous agreements. Once again, Morgan and Shanley
began individual meetings between Labor and Commerce in the summer of
1953, and this time they seriously explored the possibility of repealing or
modifying 14(b) since it was apparently a major obstacle separating the
parties. They even approached the president on the subject in early June,
hoping to get his backing in order to sell the doubtful Labor Committee
chairman on the feasibility of including significant changes to attract the
AFL.

By July 31, 1953, Shanley had drafted a proposed presidential message
on an administration amendment bill, which he sent along to all those
involved with an attached draft of the new, pro-labor Durkin proposals

which included 14(b) repeal. Among other changes were the elimination of mandatory injunction in secondary boycott cases, the authorization of pre-hire agreements for industries with casual employment, the authorization of voting rights for economic strikers, the exemption of struck work from secondary boycott provisions, and various administration reforms in NLRB procedure. Republicans on good terms with labor found much import in the document. "I trust that the significant and tremendous conclusion that has been reached," Department of Labor Solicitor Stuart Rothman wrote to Shanley, "is fully appreciated in terms of what it can mean to the Administration." The White House had been correct to reject the advice of anti-labor people in the Commerce Department. "Here is the opportunity to gainsay once, and I believe, for all time, that this is solely a businessman's administration."

Within three days, however, an unknown source leaked the message and Durkin's pro-labor proposals to the *Wall Street Journal*—in all likelihood to arouse the business community against the changes. In addition, Senator Taft's untimely death set the informal committee adrift. With the glare of publicity focused on the administration, and with the loss of the prestige that Taft would have lent had he given his assent to White House proposals, Morgan and Shanley suffered their most serious setback yet.[21]

The leak, in fact, did a better job than its instigator could have hoped, for in short order anguished cries of betrayal emanated from conservative Republicans and the business community. Arizona senator Barry Goldwater (R) told the president that the reforms would grant "monopolistic powers to labor leaders beyond the fondest dreams of the Roosevelt and Truman Administrations. I cannot believe...that the reports of your intentions are correct." "Of particular and immediate concern to me," the senator continued, is the "recommendation which would nullify...'right to work' laws.... Never, even in the days of the Wagner Act, was the Congress inclined to pre-empt the rights of the states to enact and enforce laws on the subject of compulsory unionism." Clearly, he wrote in disappointment, the president was repudiating his own opposition to extending federal control over the economy, as well as the 1952 platform position of the Republican party. He could only hope, he closed, "that I have been misinformed on the subject."[22]

The business community reacted just as heatedly. "Now, I am not an expert in labor legislation," wrote the president's brother, Milton Eisenhower, in early September. "But I live in an industrial State and there is now almost hysterical interest in the suggestions for Taft-Hartley Act changes." "I am being besieged with material, all of it extremely critical," he informed Sherman Adams. For a while the president deflected criticism of the leaked draft by pointing out that Senator Taft had been a part of the committee considering changes, and that he had agreed to all of them except the secondary boycott revisions and 14(b) repeal. "He thought that something had to be changed in the law in both instances," the president wrote one important critic, "but was not exactly sure what was the right thing to do." This tactic, however, could not last forever, for Taft's posthumous prestige among conservatives was bound to lessen in time.[23]

Faced with such an uproar, administration chief Adams decided to hold off on any presidential submission to Congress. This led to even more embarrassment for Secretary of Labor Durkin, who, believing that he had had Morgan and Shanley's agreement to the majority of his proposals, resigned when the administration began to backpedal on the issue. The two White House aides, Durkin told the president, had "broken faith" in bargaining with him. By now the situation had become a public embarrassment, and Eisenhower asked for a step-by-step outline of the whole affair. In response, Shanley and Morgan chronicled the difficult negotiations and informed the chief executive that they were "still trying to get people together on what should be done about the Taft-Hartley Act."[24]

Despite all these problems, throughout the fall of 1953 the administration still tried to piece together a workable bill. By this time two things had changed. James Mitchell, Durkin's replacement and a former personnel manager, could not accurately reflect AFL thinking on amendment. And the publicity flap surrounding possible 14(b) repeal had convinced the president to avoid the subject in any future administration bill. In a meeting on Taft-Hartley reform in early November 1953, Eisenhower told his advisers that although "every labor leader who comes into his office froths at the mouth about Section 14(b) [and] says that it will destroy unions," he felt it should stay in the act because Senator Taft had not seen fit to support repeal. Therefore, the president believed, any recommendations they made should not "'go below' those standards for which Taft worked before his death." The best they would probably be able to do, according to former Taft aide Michael Bernstein, would be to modify the section so that states could permit stronger forms of union security than authorized by Taft-Hartley—the closed shop, for instance—if they so desired. This "would go part of the way toward meeting union criticisms" of 14(b) and help put across the bill to organized labor. AFL representatives had assured Bernstein that this change, in combination with a few other equitable reforms, "would be satisfactory" to the federation, and "particularly [to] the building trades unions."[25]

Nevertheless, the continuing disappointment voiced by prominent business supporters of the administration gave notice that the issue could be politically hazardous to the president. Throughout December Eisenhower found he had to explain continually to corporate officers that he had never supported the closed shop. General Electric chairman Philip D. Reed, for example, cautioned the president against weakening the law, especially its crucial union security restrictions. Certainly there could be no political benefit in it, advised conservative supporter Lew Douglas. The public was definitely on the side of protecting the right to work, he argued. "It is, I believe, of doubtful wisdom to make concessions which are hostile to the American tradition," Douglas maintained, "in the hope of attracting trade union leaders to the Republican party. They are irrevocably bound and united to the Democratic organization."[26]

Ultimately, these entreaties had their effect and the president opted for prudence. The Republican Labor Committee chairman shaped the substance of the administration bill submitted in January, and in particular, the president made no moves to reform Taft-Hartley's union security sections. As one adviser counseled, the president could steer clear of right-to-work controversy by standing for the status quo. That way, he could say he was against the closed shop—but for unions—and that he accepted both the union shop and right-to-work clauses of the current law. The president should simply state that "in a very complex and controversial situation... [this] was about as accurate a representation of fairness to both sides as can be devised."[27]

Thus, by early 1954 the AFL's strategy for revising the Taft-Hartley Act, and at the same time destroying state right-to-work laws through 14(b) repeal, had floundered. The CIO's approach, however, proved even less effective. During the time the AFL had been attempting to arrange a deal with the Eisenhower administration, the CIO had proceeded with its plan of working through its Democratic friends in Congress. With its affiliates it presented testimony before the Labor committees and lobbied representatives—all to no avail for clearly most legislators were waiting to see the outcome of the administration's negotiations. By the middle of September 1953, the federation's legislative representatives knew that they had not only failed to generate interest in reform, they had not even convinced the representatives that there was a political need to amend the law. A poll of 221 members of Congress, for instance, revealed that only a minority of the legislators thought Taft-Hartley reform would be an issue of note in the 1954 elections. Only 25 percent of the Republicans thought it might be important and 38 percent of the Democrats. When adjusted for the inclusion of predictably anti-labor southern Democrats, the percentage rose nine points—still a minority of the Democratic respondents.[28]

With such a non-unified attitude on the part of friendly congressional Democrats, for the rest of 1953 CIO legislative operatives could do little to advance changes and watched the AFL developments from the sidelines. By early 1954, though, the president's backpedaling on amendment had paved the way for an assault by conservative lawmakers. Textile Workers' lobbyist John Edelman reported that a confidential draft of the House Labor Committee's bill, as it emerged from the administration's original proposals in January, "would forbid any and every sort of union security, including the union shop or maintenance of membership." It even included a broad grant of jurisdiction to the states, he informed his union's chief officials, "giving almost dictatorial power over unions to the state legislatures—a power which, of course, most legislatures in the South and elsewhere will use." This was a crisis, he pleaded. "We must somehow get over to these legislators that we are aware of the dangers in the proposed legislation and are fighting mad about it." Eventually they did, for unified labor opposition to changes of this type prevented the bill from reaching a floor vote.[29]

Senator Goldwater led the move by Senate conservatives to bring to the floor a companion bill that had as its key feature a broad grant of jurisdiction over labor relations matters to the states, as well as other changes unfavorable to labor. Here, however, the CIO's congressional work yielded results. While labor lobbyists could not convince Democratic party leaders to push pro-labor amendments vigorously, they did find them willing to lead a movement designed to protect the Taft-Hartley Act from amendments damaging to labor. In a frenetic effort to prevent disaster, CIO representatives insisted that labor's liberal supporters force the party's leadership to come to its aid. Consequently, Senate Minority Leader Lyndon Johnson (D-TX) persuaded a sufficient number of southern Democrats to vote for recommittal. Table 3.1 indicates that both political parties had high indexes of cohesion on anti-labor Taft-Hartley revision—but on opposite sides of the issue. The Republicans tallied a solid 87 percent against labor's position while Democratic senators compiled a perfect, pro-labor −100 in support of a motion to recommit. Thus, the conservative counteroffensive stalled in the spring of 1954. Overall, though, the CIO's lobbying effort was hardly impressive. According to CIO president Walter Reuther, the industrial federation's representatives too often preferred to associate with kindred spirits. When they lobbied Congress, he claimed, they did not try hard enough to convert neutrals and the opposition. "We would come back with a very tightly knit little minority," he told the executive board. "We were righteous as hell, but we didn't get anyplace."[30]

By mid-1954, then, both the AFL's and the CIO's offensive strategies had failed to change the Taft-Hartley Act. The AFL had tried to act as a typical pressure group, but the building trades unionists most concerned about the law had no real way of convincing the Eisenhower administration that they could bring the rest of the federation into the "modern Republican" fold. The president initially intended to back whatever the members of the administration's informal committee recommended. By late 1953, however, he realized that the unionists who supported him could not deliver a massive labor vote. Most labor leaders, he agreed in one meeting, would never embrace his goals. Therefore, by the beginning of 1954 he abandoned any hope of garnering political benefits by amending the Taft-Hartley Act to organized labor's satisfaction.[31]

Nor was the CIO's approach any better. Its denunciations of the Republican party made it difficult for the voice of moderate and liberal lawmakers and advisers to carry persuasive weight—a prerequisite when so many Democrats were either anti-labor or uninterested. This approach would not work while the Democratic party remained ideologically fractured and relatively immune to labor's influence. In order to be effective it had to instill a genuinely pro-labor liberalism into the party's dominant philosophy and find some way to discipline wayward legislators.

MEANY-NAM NEGOTIATIONS

With the failure of the attempts to amend Taft-Hartley, organized labor found that its goal of decapitating the right-to-work movement had failed as well. This was particularly unfortunate for in 1954 and 1955 it was clearly evident that the movement had revived at the state level. Within a span of a little over a year and a half, five states passed statutes restricting union security and three had elections.

Four of the five state legislatures assenting to right-to-work proposals were in the deep South: Alabama added the law in 1953; and Louisiana, South Carolina, and Mississippi followed in 1954. These states had no Republican representatives and thus the Democrats again held responsiblity. In the early 1950s, however, southern Democrats at the state level were somewhat less cohesive in voting the anti-labor position than they had generally been during the 1940s. Table 3.3 lists the indexes of cohesion as 48 for South Carolina (one chamber), 46 for Alabama, 41 for Mississippi, and 19 for Louisiana—an average of 38.5 (as compared to 54.8 in the 1940s). In two-party Nevada in 1951, Democrats also favored restricting union security with an index of 20. Here, though, the dominant Republican party led the way with a 60 percent cohesion score, as shown in Tables 3.3 and 3.4. With the inclusion of Nevada, the total average Rice Index of Cohesion for state Democratic lawmakers dropped to 34.8.

Two states also had right-to-work elections (one of them twice) between 1952 and 1954 and Table 3.2 outlines the statistics. In 1952, 93 percent of Nevada's citizens who voted for the highest office in the general election narrowly approved the 1951 action of their legislators. The ratification carried by a 51 to 49 percent margin, 38,823 yes to 37,789 no. Nevada's 21,377 union members (30.4 percent of the work force) made the battle close. In Arizona in the same year, labor did not fare as well, though it had a similar percent of the labor force organized (approximately 27 percent or 54,482 unionists). State labor leaders attempted to repeal their right-to-work law by initiative and lost by 48,353 votes, a 63 to 37 percent split with 70 percent of those casting ballots for president also voting on the question. And finally, in 1954 Nevada labor leaders also tried repeal with just about the same results they had achieved in 1952—a close election but no victory.

In addition to these losses, there were many other states in which labor officials barely stopped adverse legislation. The agitation affected organized

3.2
Public Right-to-Work Elections, 1952–1956

STATE AND YEAR	YES RTW	NO RTW	TOTAL	%RATIO	COUNTY Y/N RATIO	# MARGINAL COUNTIES	% OF VOTE FOR HIGHEST OFFICE IN ELECTION	APPROXIMATE UNION MEMBERSHIP
Arizona 1952	115389	67036	182425	63/37	13/1	3	70	54482(27.0%)
Nevada 1956	49585	42337	91922	54/46	14/3	3	95	29442(33.9%)
Nevada 1952	38823	37789	76612	51/49	13/4	2	93	21377(30.4%)
Nevada 1954	38480	36434	74914	51/49	14/3	4	97	24418(32.1%)
Washington 1956	329653	704903	1034560	32/68	3/36	6	90	390558(50.3%)

Source: Appendix B, Cox, and Troy. See explanation in Appendix B as to the derivation of percent of state vote and union membership.

3.3

Rice Index of Cohesion of Democratic Party, in All State Legislatures, on Right-to-Work Measures, 1951–1956

| | | INDEXES | | BALLOTS CAST | |
STATE/YEAR	TOTAL	SENATE	HOUSE	SENATE	HOUSE
South Carolina 1955	50	NV	50	NV	113
South Carolina 1954	-	VV	48	VV	108
Alabama 1953	46	44	47	32	91
Mississippi 1954	41	51	37	45	134
Nevada 1951	20	33	17	6	24
Louisiana 1954	19	22	17	36	99
Alabama 1955	-	NV	11	NV	85
Tennessee 1955	-	4	NV	25	NV
Louisiana 1956	-11	-8	-13	39	101
Maryland 1955	-	VV	-31	VV	90
Kentucky 1956	-	NV	-54	NV	39
Idaho 1955	-	NV	-57	NV	23
Kansas 1955	-69	-50	-71	4	35
South Dakota 1955	-70	-33	-86	6	14
Utah 1955	-100	-100	-100	6	27

Source: Appendix A
Key: NV–No Vote, VV–Voice Vote
Index: +100(Totally Cohesive in Favor of Right to Work)
         -100(Totally Cohesive Against Right to Work)

labor in two ways. It led both federations—at first separately, and after the merger, together—to refocus as well as re-energize their political efforts. The state right-to-work drives also prompted one top labor leader to undertake a private initiative in the hopes of quieting the agitation.

To most observers it seemed that organized labor had done all that could be done until its renewed commitment to electoral activity started paying returns. AFL-CIO president George Meany, however, was unwilling to have the united federation undertake the extensive and expensive activities necessary for self-defense if he could arrange another means of protection. Therefore, he resolved to try one last alternative before leading the AFL-CIO headlong into electoral politics.

Experience had shown that the most active proponents of right-to-work laws continued to be employers associations of one type or another; this was as true in 1954 and 1955 as it had been in 1947. In addition, in early

3.4
Rice Index of Cohesion of Republican Party, in All State Legislatures, on Right-to-Work Measures, 1951–1956

STATE/YEAR	TOTAL	INDEXES SENATE	HOUSE	BALLOTS CAST SENATE	HOUSE
Utah 1955	100	100	100	13	33
South Dakota 1955	71	66	75	29	55
Kansas 1955	64	77	58	35	77
Nevada 1951	60	60	60	10	20
Idaho 1955	-	NV	28	NV	36
Kentucky 1956	-	NV	25	NV	8
Tennessee 1955	-	20	NV	5	NV
Maryland 1955	-	VV	-5	VV	21
Alabama 1953	NR	NR	NR	NR	NR
Alabama 1955	NR	NR	NR	NR	NR
Louisiana 1954	NR	NR	NR	NR	NR
Louisiana 1956	NR	NR	NR	NR	NR
Mississippi 1954	NR	NR	NR	NR	NR
South Carolina 1954	NR	NR	NR	NR	NR
South Carolina 1955	NR	NR	NR	NR	NR

Source: Appendix A
Key: NV-No Vote, VV-Voice Vote, NR-No Republicans
Index: +100(Totally Cohesive in Favor of Right to Work)
          -100(Totally Cohesive Against Right to Work)

1955 a group of conservative employers backed the formation of the National Right to Work Committee, founded mainly by small businesspeople who recruited disgruntled unionists to their cause, agitating for union security restrictions as a single-issue pressure group. Heretofore, organized labor had for the most part faced isolated state by state campaigns. Meany feared the results of an organized assault by a coalition of the National Association of Manufacturers, the U.S. Chamber of Commerce, and the new NRTWC—a distinct possibility considering the swelling controversy surrounding the issue. So rather than immediately confronting employers with political action, he confronted them with rhetoric while exploring the possibility of negotiating a peace agreement.[32]

Meany's concern about the incipient combativeness of national business activists was well founded. In a mid–1954 meeting of the National Association of Manufacturers executive committee, for example, one businessman complained that the association was "going downhill." Since "it had been a long time since we had had any criticism from labor leaders...[we are apparently] becoming a 'do-gooder' organization...which puts up no aggressive fight about anything." One thing that many NAM members agreed needed "aggressive" attention was the labor movement; the merger, in the eyes of these free enterprise activists, had created a tremendously powerful labor monopoly that had the potential for undermining the American way of life. "Ever since last November I have been tremendously concerned over the political plans of the labor bosses," wrote NAM promoter and steel company official Charles Hook to association president, Charles R. Sligh, Jr. in the fall of 1955. The militant Labor Day speeches of Walter Reuther and George Meany only confirmed the fact that business must organize for solidarity or face a powerful attack on the free enterprise system. All NAM members must do everything they can to counter labor propaganda, he wrote. "From all that I have said, you will realize how scared I am and how serious I think this situation is."[33]

It was in this context, then, that Meany agreed to speak at the sixtieth annual congress of the NAM following the AFL-CIO merger convention in 1955. Both he and NAM president Charles R. Sligh, Jr. traded thoughts on the topics of "What Labor Expects From Management" and "What Industry Expects From Organized Labor" and Meany, speaking first, designed his speech to appeal to his audience. "I stand for the profit system...I believe it's a wonderful incentive. I believe in the free enterprise system completely," he told his business audience. And furthermore, "I believe in return on capital investment..." and "in management's right to manage." So in "believing in all these things, as a representative of free labor, what is left for us to disagree about?...We have so much in common that it seems rather silly to be fighting about the things we do not have in common," Meany concluded. If management would recognize that only organizations of workers could represent workers and accept unions as valuable institutions there could be cooperation. Labor could not cooperate, on the other hand, "if those on the other side of the table are actively engaged in a campaign to destroy our very existence as trade unions" through right-to-work laws.[34]

Despite Meany's conciliatory words, NAM president Sligh, according to an association staff report, "told Mr. Meany and the audience a few truths which had to be told about abuses of power by union leadership." Industry wanted economic responsibility and bargaining integrity from unions, he said, but first and foremost it wanted labor to respect American tradition and "refrain from efforts to coerce people into unions against their will." Moreover, it also expected unionists to "cease their unremitting efforts to remove or circumvent legal protections of this right which are contained in federal and state laws." Only then would management and labor be able to work together toward common goals.[35] With both speeches emphasizing right to work, it was not surprising that after the luncheon Meany and Sligh heatedly debated union security further—much to the delight of the assembled reporters and the few association members left in the room. "It seems to me you really had him in a corner on your union shop question," one right-to-work partisan smugly wrote to Sligh. And, like most NAM members, he dismissed Meany's pro-business speech as self-serving propaganda. As one business leader wrote, "I don't suppose any sane man believes that his utterances were sincere."[36]

One NAM leader who did discern some sincerity, however, was Sligh. Within three days he cabled the labor leader and thanked him for his "friendly and statesmanlike speech." "I agree with you that labor and management should seek mutual understanding and a basis for amicable relations," Sligh wrote. "I suggest that you and I meet privately and alone and see what can be developed in frank discussion." Meany accepted his offer. "I think it would be best if we could get together without any preconditions except a definite understanding that we should try to resolve our differences with the best interests of the country...as the prime target," the labor chieftan telegraphed in response.[37]

Meany's willingness to speak before the NAM had obviously piqued Sligh's interest. According to NAM staffer Edward Maher, the coming meeting could possibly be "an event of historic importance" in labor relations. Apparently, Maher advised Sligh in late December 1955, the AFL-CIO president was "anxious for some kind of understanding with management" because of the lack of recent progress in organizing and politics. Despite organized labor's best efforts, the leadership had "not succeeded in getting any right-to-work laws repealed and are fighting rear-guard actions in many states to prevent more of these laws from being adopted." Perhaps Meany was searching for a different approach, although it was doubtful that union leaders' ultimate aims had changed. "Their objective still remains the same— to unionize the whole country—but...they want to see what can be done by diplomacy rather than aggression."[38]

By working out a peace agreement with business, Maher wrote, labor could then "negotiate" people into unions through union security clauses. This, of course, was something the NAM would never support. Most of the problems in labor relations "stems from this belief on the part of union leaders that compulsion is necessary." Union leaders felt the need for "compulsion in order to maintain their own power; to make the rank-and-file do what they want done; to conduct successful strikes; to give substance to their political activities; and to do nearly everything else unions want to do." According to the NAM staff member, if only Sligh could convince Meany that it was in his self-interest to back voluntary unionism, the NAM and the AFL-CIO could perhaps find other areas of agreement. Still, it would be difficult, for Meany's "opposition to right-to-work laws is conditioned by what he believes to be the exigencies of running a labor union." Nevertheless, Maher counseled later, "Mr. Meany evidently is anxious to lead a

respectable and responsible labor movement which will become a constructive force in our society" and thus might be amenable to the business leader's
arguments.[39]

With both sides so committed to their respective positions, any high-level
meeting between Sligh and Meany would first have to resolve the fundamental disagreement over right to work if there was to be any hope of
further progress. This proved even harder than Maher anticipated, for as
rumors about the impending peace conference circulated, hard-line anti-
unionists within the NAM criticized the idea. "All in all, I am extremely
pessimistic that any good purpose could be served by maintaining a public
channel of connection open with Mr. Meany or any other labor leader of
his stature," wrote a member of the NAM's industrial relations committee
to Sligh. The association should abandon the executive approach, advised
another member. "I have seen so many so-called executives" only wanting
to toss "an occasional creampuff from behind the cloistered protection of
the private club." How much better it would be, he believed, to "slug it
out" with labor in the style of "high-class individualists like Herbert H.
Kohler."[40]

Faced with sentiment such as this, it was apparent that the only person
who could give on the union security issue would be Meany. He, however,
was no more willing to revise his position than was the NAM president.
When the two met in February 1956, their negotiations immediately ran
aground on the question of union membership. In the words of a NAM
staff report on the conference, "Mr. Sligh could not come to any compromise
without throwing overboard the basic principle . . . of free choice; Mr.
Meany felt the very existence of unions depended on what organized labor
calls 'union security provisions' in contracts." The meeting ended inconclu-
sively, and although Meany later suggested one more attempt, Sligh informed him that it was futile since the core of their disagreement was
unresolvable. As Sligh finally put it, "I can say unequivocally" that the
NAM executive board will never abrogate the principle of voluntary unionism.[41]

REINTENSIFICATION OF POLITICAL ACTION

With Sligh's unequivocal rejection, organized labor's last national-level
attempt at countering the expanding right-to-work movement had failed.
The unsuccessful Taft-Hartley drive, the continuing anti–union security agitation, and Meany's failed rapprochement with NAM provided all the proof
that most labor leaders needed that a sizeable portion of American management remained enamored of the open shop. Still in its infancy, the AFL-
CIO could not afford to face such a challenge without a well-oiled electoral/
political machine that could generate action at all levels of government. For
this reason, the new federation's leaders gave high priority to the activities

of the AFL-CIO's new political arm, the Committee on Political Education (COPE). Various levels of COPE would educate unionists all across the country on national, state, and local political issues, register them to vote, take labor voters to the polls on election day, and raise funds for pro-labor candidates. And the right-to-work movement provided most of the impetus, for what better reason could there be for extensive electoral activity than defense of trade union rights?

Indeed, this process had begun in both federations well before the merger. "Not since the black Taft-Hartley era of 1947," wrote John Edelman to a friend in April 1954, "have the reactionary forces been so successful in lobbying anti-union legislation through the state legislatures." No wonder the Taft-Hartley amendment campaign had involved such a determined drive to expand state jurisdiction in addition to other restrictions desired by conservatives. Declared Edelman, employers "are concentrating their efforts on the state legislatures and want more and more leverage from the Federal Congress to assist in this project."[42]

Without a doubt, both federations could expect little aid at the national level. Certainly, President Eisenhower saw nothing in the 1954 elections to make him change his mind. There "appears to be no doubt that the dominant influence in the Democratic Party has come to be the CIO, or at least the CIO and the AF of L in combination," he wrote a good friend and confidant. "I am told that labor unions were by far the greatest contributors to the Democrats in the recent campaigns." And, judging by the liberal-oriented candidates they backed, the most organized force for "paternalistic government."[43]

Understandably, the Republicans might not want to aid labor, considering the movement's lopsided Democratic candidate endorsements in the elections. But less understandably, neither did the congressional leadership of the Democrats. Both House Speaker Sam Rayburn (D-TX) and Senate Majority Leader Lyndon Johnson (D-TX) disliked wasting legislative credits by confronting their adamantly anti-labor southern Democratic kin.

For example, labor officials found the party's leaders unsympathetic to their request for the removal of especially vociferous anti-labor southern Democrats from the House Labor Committee after the 1954 elections. When AFL building trades department president Richard Gray and LLPE chair James McDevitt tried to pressure Lyndon Johnson into informally interceding with Speaker Sam Rayburn on the matter, Johnson glibly told them he himself had appointed "some of the strongest liberals" in the Senate to that body's labor committee and that the Texas AFL supported his record. Relatedly, a high-level CIO political analysis of labor's problems with the Democratic party zeroed in on conservative southern Democrats' domination of the congressional party as the source of the difficulty. "They select the issues on which a fight will be made and the issues for which only a token battle will be made," outlined the industrial federation's 1955 policy review. Labor rarely reaped any rewards for its electoral footwork, it seemed. Basically, the analyst concluded, if "any change . . . is to take place it will take place only at the initiative and insistence of the CIO. The majority of Democrats are well satisfied with the present status."[44]

Even so, labor officials of both federations could never quite bring themselves to return to pure-and-simple non-partisan voluntarism. Whatever the problem regarding divisive issues such as labor legislation, what continued to attract the CIO, and increasingly the AFL, to the national Democrats was the party's overall record. In comparative analysis, the two parties' voting patterns showed marked differences. On the broad range of legislation in which organized labor had an interest, CIO researcher Hyman Bookbinder wrote to Legislative Director Robert Oliver in September 1953, the Democrats proved much better than the Republicans. Even including the conservative southern Democrats, labor was better off with the Democratic party because labor had more potential friends in it, and when the Democrats were in the majority, most congressional committees would be in better hands. There were some places, Bookbinder did acknowledge, where a Democratic majority did little to aid the movement. For the most part, labor's trouble lay in conservative obstructionism in the powerful House Rules Committee and both chamber's labor committees. But even here, he noted, the percentages showed that the Democrats voted "right" many more times than the Republicans. Oliver informed him that they should circulate these facts widely. More than anything else, he wrote, it proves that under Eisenhower the Republican party "lives up to its reputation for being more interested in the welfare of big business, while the Democratic Party lives up to its reputation of being a friend to the little man."[45]

An analysis of state legislative roll call on right-to-work proposals from 1951 to 1956 generally confirmed that observation. Table 3.3, which lists the Rice Index of Cohesion of state-level Democrats, indicates that even southern members of the party were not as overwhelmingly cohesive in supporting restrictions in the 1950s as they had been in the 1940s. South Carolina had the highest anti-labor cohesion index with 50 (one chamber, in a 1955 repeal attempt), followed by 48 for the same state in 1954. Alabama Democrats came next with 46 in 1953. Five other states tallied positive, anti-labor indexes for the Democrats: Mississippi with 41, Nevada with 20, Louisiana with 19 (1954), Alabama with 11 (1955 repeal attempt), and Tennessee with 4 (one chamber, 1955 repeal attempt). In the border, midwestern, and western states, and even one southern state, Democrats ran up negative pro-labor indexes of cohesion. Utah Democrats were totally unified with a −100; South Dakota's party representatives were somewhat less cohesive with a −70 (on a 1955 anti-labor amendment). Following South Dakota came Kansas with −69, Idaho with −57 (one chamber), Kentucky with −54 (one chamber), Maryland with −31 (one chamber),

and Louisiana with − 11 (1956 repeal). The average index score for the
South was 26 (eight votes), indicating a good deal less cohesion on restricting
union security among southern Democrats than had been the case in the
1940s. For the non-southern states the average index ended up at a pro-
labor − 51.6 (7 votes). Overall, the Democratic state-level average index
score for 15 votes was a marginally pro-labor − 10.2.

In comparison, Table 3.4 tabulates the Rice Index scores of Republicans
(except for Alabama, Louisiana, Mississippi, and South Carolina, which
had no Republicans). Republican state legislators in the border, midwestern,
and western states almost duplicated the Democratic response in range and
magnitude but mirrored it in an anti-labor direction. Utah Republicans had
the highest index with 100. Next came South Dakota's GOP members with
71, Kansas's with 64, Nevada's with 60, Idaho's with 28 (one chamber),
Kentucky's with 25 (one chamber), and Tennessee's with 20. Maryland
Republicans were the only state party representatives to vote in the pro-
labor column, with a − 5 index of cohesion (one chamber). The average
Rice Index scores for the 8 votes in states that had Republican legislators
was 45.4, significantly higher than even the southern Democrats' 26.

Thus, the attractiveness of the social-welfare facets of Democratic policy—
as well as the party's acceptable support against right to work in two-party
states—kept labor leaders from casting off familiar moorings. According to
CIO president Walter Reuther, labor law reform would eventually come
when the public realized and began to appreciate the role labor had played
in pressing for progressive legislation. To hasten this process, labor needed
to rid the Democratic party of its reactionary and obstructionist elements.
Therefore, labor's political activists would have to place increasing emphasis
on electoral activity in a long-term effort to restructure all levels of the
Democratic organization.

Each federation, however, would have to make adjustments in order to
do this. For CIO leaders this meant a reevaluation of their preference for
focusing on national politics. According to a staff report proposing a state
legislative department for the national office, liberal-labor forces at the local
level needed reorganization to make them politically potent. Even within
the CIO itself, national officers had paid too little attention to the importance
of their counterparts at the state level. Ever since the beginning of its southern organizing drive, Operation Dixie, CIO national staff members "were
pretty much divorced from our Industrial Union Councils, both state and
local," wrote Southern Regional Director Paul Christopher in August 1953.
Consequently, the councils had to work with the talent they had on hand,
and "they became weaned away from competent CIO leadership."[46]

Such a division within the ranks could have great impact on the fight
against right-to-work legislation. In an effort to deal with this problem, in
1954 the new Industrial Union Council (IUC) director, John Riffe, began
a series of regional IUC conferences aimed at assisting state unionists with

developing professional political action programs. And in short order they made an impact. As a confidential Republican memorandum informed Eisenhower administration officials, there was "steadily mounting evidence that political action with respect to state delegates is becoming a standard, systematic activity of State CIO Councils. There is little evidence," the report warned, "that conservative elements are interested or prepared to counter such activity with a comparable, systematic, and organized approach."[47]

Concurrently, the CIO's research department began examining the possible effects of right-to-work statutes on industrial unionism. In the fall of 1954, the department devoted an entire issue of its official organ, *The Economic Outlook*, to the problem. The publication cautioned that recent NLRB decisions limiting federal intervention in labor relations made "state legislation more important than at any time in the past 20 years." Without the ability to negotiate a union security clause, industrial unions might find themselves subject to unending jurisdictional wrangles with other unions seeking to raid their membership.[48]

Of course, the three 1954 state right-to-work legislative victories (in Mississippi, South Carolina, and Louisiana) affected the AFL as well. At the federation's convention in November, no fewer than eight resolutions from affiliates denounced the laws and called for action, one of them urging that the national office establish a steering committee to monitor the agitation and a campaign fund from which state federations fighting to prevent or repeal right-to-work laws could draw aid. The resolutions committee combined all the requests into a weak directive ordering officers to "study" the problem and "consider" calling special conferences, but the large amount of attention generated by the recent losses suggested that the issue would gain increasing prominence in AFL councils.[49]

Organized labor's growing determination to increase its grass roots political activity—and the probability that Democrats would benefit from it—did not escape the notice of Republicans sympathetic to unionism. In a surprising address to the 1954 CIO convention, for example, Secretary of Labor James Mitchell denounced right-to-work statutes and their promoters. Concerned about the political fallout from the administration's stance on labor law reform, Mitchell sought to balance the anti-labor proclivities of other presidential advisers and bolster the administration's moderate image. While the president quickly informed the press that the secretary had spoken only for himself, the flap caused by Mitchell's speech heightened the controversy.[50]

Throughout the first half of 1955, the national offices of both federations stepped up involvement with their respective state organizations. The AFL's *American Federationist* published a spate of anti-right-to-work articles outlining the techniques of opposition, both in the lobbying and electoral spheres, and closely monitored state agitation nationwide. The national legislative committee also started a limited program of bill analysis and began collecting reference materials on the subject. The CIO's legislative department encouraged IUC people to seek out repeal possibilities and offered help—although somewhat late, in the opinion of some state leaders. "You spoke directly in your letter of the interest of the National CIO in right to work legislation," wrote a Nevada activist to CIO assistant regional director Irwin DeShetler. "This interest is not now unexpected to me, although a lot of us in affected states think it none too soon." Overall, however, Tables 3.3 and 3.4 show that both the AFL and CIO's activity yielded ambiguous results: labor blocked proposals in Maryland, Kansas, and Idaho; failed to repeal laws in Nevada, Tennessee, Alabama, and South Carolina; and lost battles in Utah and South Dakota (on an anti-labor amendment).[51]

Nevertheless, the events of the last two years had had desirable side effects. The two segments of the labor movement had clearly moved closer together. In combination, the failure of Taft-Hartley reform, the 1954 right-to-work losses, and the 1955 legislative jockeying had produced an environment conducive to inter-federation collaboration. CIO leaders began directing more of their energy toward local politics and strictly trade union issues. Relatedly, AFL officials' appreciation of the need for systematic electoral commitment grew in direct proportion to their continuing disappointment over labor law revision and their anger at union security restrictions. More and more, both federation's officers felt the need to work together toward common objectives, not the least of which was the need to elect lawmakers at all levels of government opposed to restricting union security—a factor in the decision to merge in 1955.[52]

By early 1956, it was clear to labor's political strategists that the alternate pathways of fighting right to work had narrowed, for the time being, to state political action to prevent passage and effect repeal of union security restrictions. Such a job would be difficult, for the newly merged federation had not completed the process of unification at the state level. Furthermore, it meant developing even more effective coordination and communication between national and state political organizations so that trade unions would become the most cohesive political force in any given area. And finally, it meant that organized labor would have to commit sufficient resources to building the kind of political influence the movement desired. This commitment would not only aid in fighting the right-to-work movement but, if pursued with diligence, would most likely have the added benefit of gradually increasing the number of liberal Democrats in Congress as well.

Nor did labor politicians have to wait long for anti–union security activists to press them into action. In 1956 the labor movements in Kentucky, Louisiana, Nevada, and Washington state engaged in the first right-to-work struggles since the merger. In the Kentucky legislature, a right-to-work proposal floundered after losing on the house floor. In Nevada, Table 3.2 reveals that labor's 1956 attempt to repeal the state law lost by a 54 to 46 percent margin (49,585 yes to 42, 337 no), a somewhat wider spread than in the 1952 and 1954 elections. In two of the states, however, top AFL-CIO leaders believed labor had made significant strides in developing procedures to fight the opposition. The success of Louisiana and Washington unionists in repealing and repelling union security restrictions caused the national leadership to view the campaigns as models for future action.

Louisiana labor started off 1956 right for both itself and the newly merged federation with its successful fight to have the state's anti—union security statute repealed. More than anything else, the 1954 law had been the result of agitation on the part of agricultural interests trying to prevent unionization of their farmworkers. The imposition of the law prompted the Louisiana State Federation of Labor and the Louisiana State Industrial Union Council to pool their resources in a joint effort to ensure that the legislators responsible for the outrage did not return for the next session. CIO PACs, AFL Leagues for Political Education, and Machinists' Non-Partisan Leagues set up facilities for voter registration in the urban areas and parishes where there were high concentrations of union members. In addition, they formed political clinics all across Louisiana to teach the art of practical politics, and did not foucus simply on union security. "We wanted to show that we were not just against something, like right-to-work," said state federation president E. H. Williams, "but that we were also for things that the public would accept." After activists had finished utilizing all the clinics, sound trucks, and door-to-door canvassing they could find strength for, they had registered approximately 70 percent of Louisiana's estimated 142,000 union members (about 19.1 percent of the work force). The hard work paid off. By targeting their efforts on marginal districts and supporting or opposing candidates depending on how they stood on right to work, labor leaders defeated six of the seven sponsors of the law and two key house legislators who had backed it in 1954. Otherwise, the legislature did not look much different. But, as E. H. Williams commented, "It's not how many you beat, it's who you beat."[53]

According to the national AFL-CIO's Committee on Political Education (COPE), Louisiana's grass roots campaign could serve as an "object lesson" in lobbying effectiveness generated by electoral activism. There was no need for the AFL-CIO education department's growing complement of anti-right-to-work literature; the repeal effort was not a campaign of mass communication, as in an election. Instead, the newly merged Louisiana State Labor Council (LSLC), one of the by-products of the cooperation, turned to lobbying a repeal bill through the legislature. Under the direction of Victor Bussie, the new president of the council, the LSLC's legislative committee had the tacit support of Governor Earl Long (D). Bussie's strategy in this all-Democratic state was simple. After talking with lawmakers, he knew there would be no repeal unless the non-agricultural segment of Louisiana labor agreed to allow the law to remain in effect for agricultural workers.

Reluctantly, the council acceded to this condition. With that concession, Bussie and the legislative committee split the opposition and won exemption from union security restrictions for non-agricultural unions. The vote to repeal was 57 to 44 in the house and a much closer 21 to 18 in the senate.[54]

In 1956 Nevada citizens voted on a labor-sponsored repeal initiative, but in Washington organized labor faced an initiative petition attempting to establish a right-to-work law. For the first time Washington state labor leaders found themselves arrayed against the operatives of a local right-to-work committee—an offshoot of the National Right to Work Committee formed in late 1955. While the original founders of the NRTWC stated that their group was to be an informational and educational network, their state associates clearly intended to do more. The Washington Right to Work Committee, in fact, sponsored, printed, and paid for 800,000 petitions, indicating that agitation was a major part of its function.[55]

However, in contrast to most other state labor movements that had fought anti–union security referendums, Washington labor was strong and well organized with an estimated 390,558 members totalling 50.3 percent of the organizable labor force (Table 3.2). It also proved well prepared to defend itself. To prevent their antagonists from associating their petition with ringing phrases about "freedom," Washington labor leaders convinced election officials to name the proposal neutrally as Initiative 198. Then, when their opposition mailed the petitions out, the Washington State Machinists' Council made sure that union members knew what they might be signing by taking out paid ads in the press. Both tactics certainly helped, for by early July 1956 the right-to-work committee filed 58,000 signatures—enough to put the question on the ballot but far below the 300,000 supporters had predicted.

By now Washington labor officials had grown increasingly confident. The public's response to the right-to-work proposal had been anemic at best, and unionists all over the state came together to fight Initiative 198. Under the leadership of E.M. Weston, president of the state federation, and Harold Slater, secretary-treasurer of the Washington CIO Council, the Machinists, Longshoremen, Carpenters, Railroad Brotherhoods, and Woodworkers joined the United Labor Advisory Committee Against 198. This steering committee then employed advertising and public relations professionals to design radio and television ads, posters, and billboards. Through this media, and through adjunct citizens committees, Washington labor aimed to persuade the citizenry that a right-to-work law would be harmful to everyone in the community and hence Initiative 198 was not simply a "labor" issue. To buttress this effort the Seattle Central Labor Council held public-speaking seminars and unions tried to make their community service activities more visible.

Perhaps even more importantly, a survey by the advisory committee revealed through cross-referencing that many union members and their families had not registered to vote. The major internationals and central organizations therefore undertook to make sure that their members would be able to cast their votes against 198 on election day. Through an intense registration drive over 200,000 new names entered the voting rolls for the 1956 election.

The media campaign and the political activism had their effect. The candidates for both parties for senator and governor came out against the proposal, as did many civic and fraternal organizations. The final splash of advertising and televised labor rallies topped off the well-thought-out and organized defense of union security. Initiative 198 went down to defeat by a 68 to 32 percent margin. Table 3.2 indicates that 90 percent of the presidential voters also cast ballots on 198, which lost in 36 of Washington's 39 counties. The final tabulation came out at 704,903 no to 329,653 yes, definitely a resounding victory. Washington labor's campaign, wrote labor editor William Holloman, "may well be the blueprint" for other states searching for methods and procedures to defeat right to work.[56]

National AFL-CIO leaders looked upon the Louisiana and Washington state campaigns warmly, especially since the 1956 elections changed neither the occupant of the White House nor the composition of Congress to any appreciable degree. Secretary of Labor Mitchell caused a flurry when he occasionally voiced his opposition to right-to-work laws, but for the most part the president and his aides simply desired to avoid further trouble. For example, when an assistant secretary of commerce suggested that the administration should clarify its support for 14(b), Sherman Adams bluntly told him he doubted "whether it is wise to stir this matter up" at the present time.[57]

Labor's relationship with the congressional Democratic leadership continued along its rocky course. Labor leaders had little trouble influencing party platform planks, but they had a great deal of trouble influencing action in support of them—increasingly even on social-welfare legislation. The preference of Lyndon Johnson and Sam Rayburn for consensus politics and pragmatism often overrode the party's ideological commitments—much to labor leaders' dismay. As UAW citizenship director Roy Reuther complained to the chairman of the Democratic National Committee, "It seems to me that the Southern leadership of the Party has completely dominated and paralyzed the National Party from acting as a party in the interests of the people." Autoworkers lobbyist Donald Montgomery put the problem in harsher terms to Walter Reuther in mid–1956: the Democrats should be told that they could not have labor and their southern brethren too; and until they decided the party had no moral unity.[58]

Thus, with the successful defense in Kentucky, the offensive in Nevada, and the Louisiana and Washington victories, it seemed to labor officials that the momemtum on right to work had shifted in their favor. While the successful ingredients for a ballot repeal may not as yet have been found, the Louisiana campaign could serve as a model for the repeal of laws passed by a state legislature (even in an all-Democratic southern state), and the Washington offensive was an example of how labor's interests could be defended in single-issue elections. Louisiana labor's strategic analysis that legislators' sensitivity to lobbying varied in proportion to the amount of electoral aid or opposition they received from labor became, in effect, the operating philosophy of the COPE structure within organized labor and a prime practical example of what could be done—even in hostile territory. The campaigns highlighted the importance of activism, professionalism, and unity. Labor needed activism in order to register voters and monitor public issues; it needed professionalism in order to plan, organize, and market campaigns; and above all else, it needed unity to make everything work to its utmost potential. As a COPE analysis of the 1956 national election concluded, in "local instances in which there were sharp labor issues," as in some of the right-to-work contests, "effective political mobilization of labor forces was achieved." While the 1956 right-to-work struggles were the immediate cause of the communication of these lessons, labor's political activists could use these insights on any issue. As the U.S. Chamber of Commerce organ *Nation's Business* editorialized uneasily, the Louisiana repeal effort symbolized the AFL-CIO's "growing power and sharpening shrewdness in practical politics."[59]

Organized labor's education, however, had not come without great frustration. From 1950 to 1956 most union leaders interested in politics had operated under the assumption—or hope—that they could easily transform the Democratic party of the 1950s into the party of the 1930s and early 1940s. Moreover, they believed that their network of personal ties with the party's waning liberal wing could produce the kind of influence needed to make labor into an offensive political force. The constant skirmishing over right to work revealed the shakiness of these assumptions. When the national Democratic party leadership had an overriding concern for which it needed labor's cooperation—during the Korean War, for instance—it would exert the kind of arm twisting necessary on divisive subjects like labor legislation. At the state level, the party operated much the same way. Except for Louisiana in 1956, most of the pro-labor votes received from Democrats were defensive in nature. Although the situation had improved somewhat from the 1940s, the party simply did not contain many dependable advocates of labor's cause regarding the inequities of labor relations legislation. Most of the party's leaders, it seemed, were willing to do little more than maintain the status quo. That way they could point to their votes to protect labor as justification for continued support while distancing themselves from charges that they were tools of the "labor bosses."

Perhaps it was predictable, then, that one of the prime purposes of the newly merged federation would be to develop a finely tuned electoral/political machine. It was unfortunate but understandable that organized labor's relationship with the Democratic party had undermined its ability to influence the Republicans. Less understandable was the Democratic party's general indifference to the problems the labor movement faced with labor legislation. As the failed Taft-Hartley drive and the state legislative situation taught, labor needed to expand its capability to force the Democrats to revive, at the grass roots level of the political system, the type of liberalism that viewed the promotion of the labor movement as social progress. Top-level influence could only be effective insofar as labor activists grounded it in local electoral action. Not to do so promised disaster. As AFL-CIO assistant regional director Irwin DeShetler wrote Director of Organizing John Livingston in December 1956, even municipalities had begun passing right-to-work ordinances. "When cities start doing these things," he noted uneasily, "you can well imagine what the States will do."[60]

NOTES

1. National Association of Manufacturers, Staff Report, "The Meany-Sligh Discussions Concerning Labor-Management Peace" [March, 1956], Box 11, The Sligh Family Collection, Michigan Historical Collections, Bentley Historical Library, University of Michigan, Ann Arbor, Michigan (hereafter BHL).

2. Memo, Paul Sifton to Walter P. Reuther, 5 June 1950, "Who Actually Run(s) the U.S. Government, How and Why," Box 66, UAW Washington Office: Donald Montgomery Files, WPRL.

3. Memo, John W. Edelman to the Textile Workers Union of America, Executive Board, 24 May 1951, Box 96, John W. Edelman Collection, WPRL.

4. U.S. Congress, House Committee on Interstate and Foreign Commerce, *Railway Labor Act Amendments: Hearings on H.R. 7789*, 81st Cong., 2d sess., 1950; U.S. Congress, Senate Committee on Labor and Public Welfare, *Hearings on S.R. 3295, To Amend the Railway Labor Act*, 81st Cong., 2d sess., 1950; U.S. Emergency Board, *Transcript of Proceedings, Emergency Board No. 98*, Washington, D.C., 1951–1952. For a critical appraisal of the railroad brotherhoods' actions, see James R. Morris, "Repeal of the Railway Right-to-Work Law: An Appraisal," *Labor Law Journal* (February 1956):69–72, 103–111.

5. Quoted in Jerome L. Toner, "Union Shop in the Steel Crisis," *Labor Law Journal* (September 1952):589–594.

6. On General Motors' attempts to use the union shop election to weaken the UAW, see John W. Livingston, Vice-President UAW, to Don Montgomery, 1 June 1948, Box 58, UAW Washington Office: Donald Montgomery Files, WPRL. The union shop election figures are cited in James W. Kuhn, "Right-to-Work Laws—Symbols or Substance?," *Industrial and Labor Relations Review* 14(July 1961):587–594. The CIO leadership was especially concerned about amending the union shop election provision because of a technical ruling by the Supreme Court that threatened thousands of union shop contracts in industrial union agreements. See Philip Murray to Congressman Augustine Kelley, 20 September 1951, Box 103, UAW President's Office: Walter P. Reuther Files, WPRL. Significantly, without the intervention of special factors, building trades unions found it impossible to win beneficial changes

on union security restrictions in the construction industry. See U.S. Congress, Senate Committee on Labor and Public Welfare, *Hearings on S. 1973: A Bill to Amend the National Labor Relations Act, with reference to the Building and Construction Industry*, 82nd Cong., 1st sess., 1951.

7. I have drawn extensively on the analysis of James W. Kuhn for these observations. See Kuhn, "Right-to-Work Laws—Symbols or Substance?," pp. 589–591.

8. Ibid., pp. 591–592.

9. AFL, *Proceedings*, 1951, p. 144.

10. Memo, George L-P Weaver to James B. Carey, 9 August 1952, Box 71, CIO Secretary-Treasurers' Collection: James B. Carey Files, WPRL.

11. Gerald Pomper, "Labor Legislation: The Revision of Taft-Hartley in 1953–1954," *Labor History* 6(Spring 1965):144.

12. Memo, Paul Sifton to Walter P. Reuther, 6 November 1952, "Taft Plan to Toughen Taft-Hartley Act," Box 208, UAW President's Office: Walter P. Reuther Files, WPRL; Memo, Robert Oliver, CIO Legislative Director, to Walter P. Reuther, 23 December 1952, "Taft-Hartley"; Memo, Thomas E. Harris, CIO Legislative Representative, to Walter P. Reuther, "Re: Taft-Hartley," 22 December 1952; both Box 81, CIO President's Office: Walter P. Reuther Files, WPRL.

13. Pomper, "Labor Legislation," p. 144.

14. CIO, *Executive Board*, 6 February 1953, pp. 78–98, WPRL.

15. Sherman Adams Oral History, p. 48, Dwight D. Eisenhower Library, Abilene, Kansas (hereafter DDEL); Memo, Henry Cabot Lodge, Jr., to Governor Sherman Adams, 21 August 1952, Box 943, Dwight D. Eisenhower, Records as President, 1953–1961, White House Central Files (hereafter WHCF), General File, 126-C, "AFL," DDEL.

16. Memo, John Lannin, Coordinator, Labor Division, to the Republican National Committee Labor Division, "Analysis of Present Political Labor Situation," Box 938, WHCF, General Files, 126, "Labor 1952–1953 (1)," n.d., DDEL.

17. For an examination of Eisenhower's long-range hopes for the Republican party see Michael Foley, *The New Senate: Liberal Influence on a Conservative Institution, 1959–1972* (New Haven, Conn.: Yale University Press, 1980), pp. 18–20.

18. Bernard Shanley and Jerry Morgan, Memorandum for the President, "Various Efforts to Secure Agreement on Taft-Hartley Act Amendments," 30 September 1953, Box 41, Dwight D. Eisenhower, Papers as President of the United States, 1953–1961, Ann Whitman Files (hereafter Whitman Files), Administration Series, DDEL.

19. Secretary of Commerce Sinclair Weeks' representative, Stephen Dunn, lobbied for a strengthening of states' rights in response to the expanding Court-defined doctrine of federal preemption regarding labor law. Durkin, on the other hand, pushed for a repeal of section 14(b), opposed increasing state jurisdiction, and wanted secondary boycott restrictions narrowed. Of course, there were also many other points under discusssion. See Ibid. For Adams' instructions to Shanley see Memorandum for Mr. Shanley, 28 May 1953, "Taft-Hartley Amendments," Box 83, WHCF, Confidential File, "Taft-Hartley Working Papers (7)," DDEL.

20. Shanley and Morgan, Memorandum for the President, "Various Efforts to Secure Agreement on Taft-Hartley Act Amendments," 30 September 1953, Box 41, Whitman Files, Administration Series, DDEL; Bernard Shanley Diaries, vol. 4: White House Days, pp. 873–1100, DDEL; Michael Bernstein, Senate Labor Committee

Aide, to I. Jack Martin, White House Administrative Assistant, "Senator Taft's Last Views on Revision of the Taft-Hartley Act," 3 November 1953, Box 82, WHCF, Confidential File, "Taft-Hartley (5)," DDEL.

21. The evidence on exactly how far Eisenhower administration officials were willing to go on section 14(b) repeal is suggestive rather than definitive. Shanley's diary reveals that the subject of 14(b) repeal received extensive discussion and was in again and out again during the course of composing possible amendments. By July 30 and 31, 1953, Morgan had apparently developed a strategy for getting around the political difficulties that had developed over Taft-Hartley's right-to-work provision. Most likely, what Morgan and Shanley considered was placing the entire subject of repeal in a study commission along with the Commerce Department's proposals for strengthening states' rights. That way, they could segregate the divisive issues from the rest of the amendment bill. Shanley, in his oral history, insists that the draft of proposals favored by Durkin did not have his or Morgan's approval and was merely a working paper. However, his diary indicates that on the day after circulating the presidential message and draft, which was also the day after Senator Taft's death, Commerce Secretary Weeks and his assistant Stephen Dunn were extremely disenchanted with the draft they had received. However, he also states that Durkin "was quite elated about it." This implies that the interested parties were treating the draft and suggested amendments as the probable administration position. See Shanley Diary, vol. 4, White House Days, pp. 873–1188, especially 1108–1120; Memo, Tom Shroyer to Senator Alexander Smith, 31 July 1953; Memo, Senator Smith to Bernard M. Shanley, 1 August 1953; Stuart Rothman to Bernard Shanley, 31 July 1953; all Box 83, WHCF, Confidential File, "Taft-Hartley (5)," DDEL.

22. White House aides convinced the senator that it was not in the interests of party unity to publicly release his critical letter. See Barry Goldwater to the President, 1 September 1953; Bryce Harlow to Bernard Shanley, 2 September 1953; both Box 83, WHCF, Confidential File, "Taft-Hartley (5)," DDEL.

23. Milton Eisenhower to Sherman Adams, 8 September 1953, Box 641, WHCF, Official File, 124-G, "Taft-Hartley Act 1953 (4)"; the President to Arthur Eisenhower, 11 September 1953; the President to Charles R. Hook, Armco Corporation, 23 September 1953; both Whitman Files, Box 3, "DDE Diary Aug.-Sept. 1953 (1)," DDE Diaries Series, DDEL.

24. The President, Memo, Re: Secretary of Labor Affair, 8 October 1953, Whitman Files, Box 4, "DDE Diary Oct.-Dec. 1953," DDE Diaries Series, DDEL; Memo, the President to Mr. Shanley, 26 September 1953, Whitman Files, Box 3, "DDE Diary Aug.-Sept. 1953," DDE Diaries Series, DDEL; Bernard Shanley and Jerry Morgan to the President, 30 September 1953, "Various Efforts to Secure Agreement on Taft-Hartley Act Amendments"; Bernard M. Shanley to the President, 30 September 1953; both Box 41, "Taft-Hartley," Whitman Files, Administration Series, DDEL.

25. Michael Bernstein to I. Jack Martin, 12 November 1953; Bernstein to Martin, 9 November 1953, "Suggestions for Amending the Taft-Hartley Act"; both Box 82, WHCF, Confidential File, DDEL; Memo, Legislative Meetings, 7 November 1953, Box 42, "Sinclair Weeks 1952–1955 (2)," Whitman Files, Administration Series, DDEL.

26. Philip D. Reed to the President, 23 December 1953, Box 41, "Taft-Hartley," Whitman Files, Administration Series, DDEL; the President to Clarence Francis,

General Foods Corporation, 19 December 1953; Memo, Lew Douglas to the President, 16 December 1953, both Box 4, "DDE Diary Dec. 1953 (1)," Whitman Files, DDE Diaries Series, DDEL.

27. The President, Memorandum of Conversation with Roy Roberts, 11 December 1953, Box 4, "DDE Diary Oct.-Dec. 1953," Whitman Files, DDE Diaries Series, DDEL.

28. For the CIO's objections to the Taft-Hartley Act in general and section 14(b) in particular, see "Statement, Walter P. Reuther, President of the Congress of Industrial Organizations, Before the House Committee on Education and Labor," 12 March 1953, copy in Box 82, CIO President's Office: Walter P. Reuther Files, WPRL; Arthur J. Goldberg to the CIO Executive Board, 19 August 1953, "Memorandum on Proposed Message by President Eisenhower on Taft-Hartley," Box 46, CIO Secretary-Treasurer's Office: James B. Carey Files, WPRL; Memo, Hyman H. Bookbinder to Robert Oliver, CIO Legislative Director, 9 September 1953, "Taft-Hartley Revision as an Issue in 1954," Box 81, CIO President's Office: Walter P. Reuther Files, WPRL.

29. Minutes of CIO Legislative Committee Meeting, 15 February, 22 February, 1954, 15 March 1954, "Special Legislative Meeting on Taft-Hartley," 5 April, 23 April, 29 April, 1954, 6 May 1954, all Box 76, CIO President's Office: Walter P. Reuther Files, WPRL; Memo, John Edelman to TWUA Officers, Joint Board Managers, PAC and Education Staff, "Proposed Taft-Hartley Amendments Now Being Considered by House Labor Committee," 26 February 1954; Edelman to TWUA Officers, "Fight Opens in House on Worsening Taft-Hartley," 2 April 1954; both Box 7, John W. Edelman Collection, WPRL.

30. By late July of 1954 the AFL adopted the CIO position of opposing *any* amendments, although the building trades unions continued to pursue negotiations with the Eisenhower administration on revisions limited to their industry. Fearing that such changes would be detrimental to industrial unions involved in jurisdictional battles with craft unions, CIO leaders refused to support any modifications that would grant building trades special Taft-Hartley exemptions. See Minutes of the CIO Legislative Committee Meeting, 19 July 1954, Box 76, CIO President's Office: Walter P. Reuther Files, WPRL; Thomas Harris to James B. Carey, 11 June 1954, "Construction Trades Amendments to Taft-Hartley," Box 74, CIO Secretary-Treasurer's Office: James B. Carey Files, WPRL; Arthur J. Goldberg to Robert Oliver, 18 June 1954, Box 25, CIO President's Office: Walter P. Reuther Files, WPRL; CIO, *Executive Board*, 29 June 1954, pp. 54–69.

31. Memo, Legislative Meetings, 7 November 1953, Box 42, "Sinclair Weeks 1952–1955 (2)," Whitman Files, Administration Series, DDEL; Memorandum by the President, 8 October 1953, Box 4, "DDE Diary Oct.-Dec. 1953," Whitman Files, DDE Diaries Series, DDEL; Jack Martin, Memorandum for Mrs. Ann C. Whitman, n.d., Box 1, "Nov.-Dec. 1953," Whitman Files, Ann C. Whitman Diaries Series, DDEL.

32. For an example of the involvement of state business associations in the right-to-work movement, see W.R. Brown, Research Director of the Missouri State Chamber of Commerce, "State Experience in Defending the Right to Work," *Commercial and Financial Chronicle*, 13 May 1954, pp. 18–19. For some recent labor comments regarding the foundations of the National Right to Work Committee, see Karen Chenoweth, "Disguising Bosses as Workers," *AFL-CIO News*, 14 June 1986, p. 2.

33. Memo, "Informal Minutes of Executive Session of NAM Executive Committee, Chicago, June 15, 1954," Box 23; Charles R. Hook to Charles R. Sligh, Jr., 15 September 1955, Box 24; both The Sligh Family Collection, BHL.

34. Address, George Meany, "What Labor Expects From Management," 9 December 1955, Box 11, The Sligh Family Collection, BHL.

35. Address, Charles R. Sligh, Jr., "What Industry Expects From Organized Labor," 9 December 1955, NAM Staff Report, n.d., "The Meany-Sligh Discussions Concerning Labor-Management Peace," [March 1956], both Box 11, The Sligh Family Collection, BHL.

36. E. T. Hamilton to Charles R. Sligh, Jr., 12 December 1955; Gus Ottenheimer to Sligh, 31 January 1956; both Box 11, The Sligh Family Collection, BHL. Sligh and Meany engaged in a "tense exchange" after the luncheon, according to a *New York Times* reporter, involving both right to work and labor's political ambitions. At one point Meany threatened the creation of a labor party if the two mainstream parties continued to ignore labor. See Homer Bigart, "Meany Says N.A.M. Attempts to Curb Union Labor Vote," *New York Times*, 10 December 1955, p. 1.

37. Charles R. Sligh, Jr., to George Meany, 12 December 1955; Meany to Sligh, 14 December 1955; both Box 11, The Sligh Family Collection, BHL.

38. Edward Maher to Charles R. Sligh, Jr., 27 December 1955, Box 11, The Sligh Family Collection, BHL.

39. Maher to Sligh, ibid.; Memo, Ed Maher to Charles R. Sligh, Jr., March 1956, Box 12, The Sligh Family Collection, BHL.

40. Address, George Meany before the National Industrial Conference Board, "Basic Concepts for Peaceful Labor-Management Relations," 19 January 1956, Box 11; Memo, Sybil Patterson to Coordinating Committee, "Suggested Draft of NAM's 1956 Campaign on Labor's Abuse of Its Monopoly Power," 5 January 1956, Box 13; Robert C. Landon to Charles R. Sligh, Jr., 14 February 1956, Box 11; J. H. Friedman to Sligh, 27 January 1956, Box 11; all in The Sligh Family Collection, BHL. The remark about Kohler referred to the then current and bitter struggle between the UAW and the Kohler Company in Wisconsin.

41. Though Meany believed that the meeting would be totally private, the NAM staff had arranged a press conference following the get-together—much to Meany's dismay. NAM public relations people took great pleasure in Meany's discomfort and lack of preparation. "I was really happy over the way you looked on the [television] screen, over the way you gave your story and *know* that it made IMPACT," gushed a PR staffer to Sligh. See NAM Staff Report, "The Meany-Sligh Discussions Concerning Labor-Management Peace," n.d. [March, 1956]; Memo, Johnny to Chuck [Sligh], n.d. [24 February 1956], George Meany to Charles R. Sligh, Jr., 21 March 1956; Sligh to Meany, 4 April 1956; all Box 11, The Sligh Family Collection, BHL.

42. John W. Edelman to George Fecteau, 27 April 1954, Box 23, John W. Edelman Collection, WPRL.

43. The President to E. E. Hazlett, 8 December 1954, Box 8, "DDE Diary Dec. 1954 (2)," Whitman Files, DDE Diaries Series, DDEL.

44. For some labor perceptions of the problematic relationship with the Democratic party, see George L-P Weaver to James B. Carey, 18 September 1953, Box 71, and Memorandum, 4 November 1955, Box 174, both CIO Secretary-Treasurer's Office: James B. Carey Files, WPRL; CIO, *Executive Board*, 29 June 1954, pp. 60–

65; Richard Gray to William C. Hushing, 14 July 1954, Box 84, AFL, AFL-CIO Department of Legislation, George Meany Memorial Archives, George Meany Center for Labor Studies, Silver Spring, Maryland (hereafter GMMA).

45. Memo, Hyman H. Bookbinder to Robert Oliver, 3 September 1953; Oliver to Bookbinder, 23 October 1953; both Box 76, CIO President's Office: Walter P. Reuther Files, WPRL.

46. Memo, "Proposal for Establishing a State Legislation Department in the National CIO Headquarters, Washington, D.C.," n.d. [1952], Box 76, CIO President's Office: Walter P. Reuther Files, WPRL; Paul R. Christopher to Carl McPeak, 26 August 1953, AFL-CIO Region 8 Collection, SLA.

47. Memo, Confidential, "Labor Political Action: The State Level," 15 April 1954, Box 34, "Labor," WHCF, Confidential File, DDEL.

48. CIO, Proceedings, 1954, p. 138; Jack Barbash, "Outline: The Right to Work Problem," February, 1954, Box 81, CIO President's Office: Walter P. Reuther Files, WPRL; CIO Department of Education and Research, Economic Outlook 15(September 1954):65–66.

49. AFL, Proceedings, 1954, vol. 2, pp. 191–192, 380–419, 520.

50. CIO, Proceedings, 1954, p. 394; Memo, George Lodge and John Leslie, to the Secretary [of Labor], "Subject: Meet the Press (for) Right to Work Laws," n.d. [15 April 1955], Box 36, James P. Mitchell Papers, DDEL; Jim [Mitchell] to Walter P. Reuther, 28 October 1954, Box 304; Matt Weinberg to Walter P. Reuther, 10 February 1955, Box 394, both UAW President's Office: Walter P. Reuther Files, WPRL.

51. AFL, Proceedings, 1955, pp. 161–171; Harry Cohn and J.C. Turner, "We Beat 'Right to Work [Maryland, 1955],' " American Federationist, May 1955, pp. 17–19; Gene Derrickson, "Right to Work Laws Can Be REPEALED [Delaware, 1949]," American Federationist, February 1955, p. 15. For the AFL's monitoring see memos by A.J. Biemiller to George Meany, 8, 9, 11, 14, 18 February 1955, 10 March 1955, 15 July 1955, AFL-CIO Office of the President, George Meany, Box 33, GMMA; David S. Turner, Secretary-Treasurer of the Utah Federation of Labor, to Saul Miller, 2 February 1955, Box 84, AFL, AFL-CIO Department of Legislation, GMMA. For the CIO's response, see Irwin L. DeShetler to William Friel and N. C. Dragon, 26 January 1955; William Friel to DeShetler, 1 February 1955; both Box 22, Irwin DeShetler Collection, WPRL; Jack Barbash to Robert Oliver, 16 February 1955, "Status of Right to Work Bills in State Legislatures," Box 81, CIO President's Office: Walter P. Reuther Files, WPRL.

52. In fact, the importance of united political action was evident in George Meany's use of right to work to sell the idea of the merger to skeptical AFL unionists at an executive council meeting in Chicago in October 1954. See Archie Robinson, George Meany, pp. 176–177.

53. "Labor's Political Punch Scores a Knockout," Nation's Business, August 1956, pp. 23–25, 57–59; Victor Bussie, "Louisiana Progress," American Federationist, September 1956, pp. 24–25, and Bussie, "This Is How We Repealed 'Wreck' Law," American Federationist, October 1956, pp. 26–27.

54. "Labor's Political Punch"; Memo, John W. Livingston to all AFL-CIO Regional Directors, 5 June 1956, Bulletin No. 17, Box 54, Irwin L. DeShetler Collection, WPRL. See also Thomas Becnel, Labor, Church, and the Sugar Establishment: Louisiana, 1887–1976 (Baton Rouge: Louisiana State University Press, 1980), pp.

179–197, and Memo, Fred C. Pieper, Regional Director, Region 19, AFL-CIO, to Walter P. Reuther, 17 August 1956, "Louisiana Repeal—'Right-to-Work' Bill," Box 325, UAW President's Office: Walter P. Reuther Files, WPRL.

55. William T. Holloman, "This Is How We Licked 198," *American Federationist*, January 1957, pp. 4–7, 29. Unless otherwise noted, all the information about the Washington right-to-work election is drawn from Holloman's article.

56. Ibid., p. 4.

57. The President to Henry Cabot Lodge, Jr., 21 February 1955, Box 9, "DDE Diary Feb. 1955 (1)," Whitman Files, DDE Diaries Series, DDEL; Frederick Mueller, Assistant Secretary of Commerce, to Sherman Adams, 18 October 1956; Adams to Mueller, 19 October 1956; both Box 641, "124-I, OF," Official File, WHCF, DDEL.

58. Roy L. Reuther to Paul Butler, Chairman of the Democratic National Committee, 23 January 1956, Box 63, UAW Washington Office: Donald Montgomery Files; Donald Montgomery to Walter P. Reuther, 19 July 1956, "Hell's Canyon, A Lesson in Politics," Box 208, UAW President's Office: Walter P. Reuther Files, both WPRL.

59. COPE Research Department, "Analysis of Returns from Selected States," 18 December 1956, Box 27, AFL-CIO President's Office: George Meany Files, GMMA. The U.S. Chamber of Commerce considered the Louisiana campaign of such importance that it sent an editor from *Nation's Business* to personally investigate the right-to-work repeal effort. See "Labor's Political Punch Scores a Knockout," *Nation's Business* August 1956, p. 23.

60. Irwin L. DeShetler to John W. Livingston, CIO Director of Organization, December 1956, Box 50, Irwin DeShetler Collection, WPRL.

4

"COPE"ing with Right to Work

Involvement in partisan politics makes the job of passing Right To Work more difficult, but not impossible. The simple principle of freedom of choice, when it stands alone, will receive the support of a majority of both Democrats and Republicans....[and] it will triumph eventually. The question of outlawing compulsory unionism is not one of if *it* will be done, but how *soon* will it be done.
— Reed Larson, then Executive Vice-President of Kansans for The Right to Work[1]

In 1958 the National Right to Work Committee and its allies tested organized labor's political mettle to the utmost. Capitalizing on the adverse publicity generated by the McClellan labor racketeering investigation, in the 1957 state legislative sessions right-to-workers lost in Louisiana but only narrowly failed in Idaho, won a referendum ballot in Kansas for the following year, and passed a statute in Indiana. By mid–1958 they had succeeded in getting public votes in California, Ohio, Idaho, Colorado, and Washington, as well as Kansas. The threatened penetration of right to work into heavily industrialized areas and centers of union power caused craft and industrial labor leaders to put aside their differences and come together for a prodigious electoral defense of union security. Organized labor's victory in every state except Kansas also contributed toward an impressive national victory for labor-endorsed candidates, most of them Democrats. The 1958 elections seemed to mark the emergence of COPE, the AFL-CIO's political subdivision, as a liberalizing electoral force to be reckoned with.

Interpreting the 1957 Indiana law and subsequent agitation as not only a threat to union organizations but also an attempt to destroy labor's growing political representation of the less affluent, AFL-CIO vice-president Walter Reuther took a leading role in the federation's fight against right-to-work state legislation in 1958. Although labor's Democratic friends in the six state legislatures under right-to-work peril in 1957–1958 normally would vote against restricting union security, when right-to-work evangelists turned to the ballot route in 1958, unionists could not count on their political allies participating to the utmost in these sure-to-be highly controversial campaigns. Therefore, Reuther joined wholeheartedly with craft unionists battling the restrictions. The UAW president prodded the national office into rationalizing its organizational structure for fighting right to work by establishing an executive council monitoring committee. He used his influence in the liberal community to stimulate the formation of pro-labor citizens coalitions and also subsidized campaign funding through the Industrial Union Department as a means of activating international union involvement. With top leaders putting aside organizational and personal difficulties arising from the merger, COPE committees carefully screened candidates and registered labor voters as they had seldom done before. Moreover, the steering committees responsible for directing the single-issue referendum battles reached new levels of sophistication and professionalism in political communication.

The broad and energetic political response of trade unionists yielded five victories for labor and a significant increase in the number of Democrats in the state legislatures and Congress. Unexpectedly, the struggles over right to work had blended the diverse political traditions of business and social unionism and channeled them toward a common goal. COPE's "baptism by fire" in 1958 gave labor's political chiefs reason to believe that the future pointed toward an ideological purification of the Democratic party along pro-labor liberal lines, and thus an end to their vexing inability to achieve labor law reform.

THE IMPACT OF THE INDIANA RIGHT-TO-WORK VICTORY

To a large degree, these developments originated in the 1957 challenges in Louisiana, Kansas, Idaho, and especially Indiana. The lawmakers of Kansas, in a mood to restrict unions, outflanked a threatened gubernatorial veto by passing—84 to 36 in the house and 30 to 9 in the senate—a referendum for the 1958 elections. In Idaho, a statute narrowly failed, carrying in the house 33 to 26 but losing in the senate 19 to 25. It was in Indiana, though, where right-to-work forces humbled one of the most powerful state labor movements in the country. Taking advantage of adverse public opinion, the Indiana Right to Work Committee (INRTWC) resoundingly beat Indiana labor lobbyists in the state legislature. By patiently molding public opinion, winning the active support of several influential Republican leaders in a Republican state, and outclassing the opposition in effectiveness, the INRTWC won passage of a state union security restriction and set the stage for the electoral battles of 1958. Indeed, so heartened were conservatives that they began to contemplate similar federal legislation.[2]

This was no mean accomplishment, for in 1955 the Indiana labor movement consisted of over 400,000 members: 220,000 in the CIO (in 25 internationals and 420 locals); 141,000 in AFL unions (in 100 internationals and 1,000 locals); and the balance in unaffiliated unions. And besides having 36 percent of the state's work force organized, Indiana union leaders had achieved some form of union security in 78 percent of their contracts. Obviously, the NRTWC and its offspring had come a long way in a short time. Originally formed from a core of anti–union shop railroad unionists and a group of small businessmen, including former congressman Fred Hartley, Jr., this single-issue pressure group devoted its entire attention to agitation against union security. The NRTWC established or assisted in the formation of state-level counterparts like the INRTWC and coordinated the efforts aimed at pushing anti–union security legislation through the state legislatures by lobbying or public votes. From late 1956 on, in fact, National Association of Manufacturers staff members readily directed any employer inquiries about political action on behalf of right to work to the NRTWC. As NAM's assistant industrial relations director Sybyl Patterson wrote to a concerned businessman, the NRTWC was only too "glad to explain the modus operandi of the campaign and the techniques which proved most effective" in lobbying.[3]

And, in fact, the modus operandi that proved most effective for Indiana employers consisted of the same factors that had worked to labor's advantage the year before: activism, professionalism, and unity. At the instigation of the Indiana Chamber of Commerce, a coalition of state and local chambers, as well as the Associated Employers of Indiana and the Indiana Manufacturers Association, formed the Indiana Right to Work Committee to lobby, ostensibly as a concerned citizens group. Headed by chamber officials Jack Reich and William Book, the INRTWC's "Working Together" program sought to stimulate business's political activism. The right-to-work group's efforts were well rewarded for the committee received excellent cooperation on legislative action from 156 local chamber affiliates and 72 state trade associations. To further promote its program, according to the U.S. Chamber of Commerce's journal, *Nation's Business*, the INRTWC met frequently for coordination and "used every technique of communication available" to create a favorable climate for the passage of a right-to-work statute. Operating out of the Indianapolis office of the state chamber, the INRTWC hired public relations specialists to capitalize on public hostility toward strike violence associated with a UAW strike against the Perfect Circle Corporation in 1955. Throughout 1956 the committee published pamphlets, took out newspaper and radio ads, and ran a speakers bureau— all to generate interest in its arguments that restricting union security would make unions behave "responsibly." Then, in 1956, when another violent strike incident, involving the wounding of an infant, further fanned the flames of public indignation, the INRTWC found that the climate of opinion had turned in its favor.[4]

Thus, after the 1956 elections the committee's lobbyists continued to cultivate legislators at breakfast meetings, and found many representatives receptive to their entreaties. Furthermore, right-to-work proponents also gained the influential support of Republican leaders Lieutenant Governor Crawford Parker and House Speaker George Denier by playing on their future political ambitions. By the beginning of March 1957, a right-to-work bill had passed the house by 54 to 44 and the senate by 27 to 23. Republican governor Harold Handley refused to veto the bill and allowed it to become law without his signature—"the easiest way to keep himself off the spot," wrote an AFL-CIO operative following the situation.[5] It was truly an ignominious defeat for Indiana's labor lobby. "We don't know what hit us," a bewildered Stanley Elliot, vice-president of the Indiana State Federation, told a reporter.[6]

Several factors besides the impressive business lobbying had hurt the Indiana labor movement. Foremost among them was disunity stemming from personal animosities and political preferences. In fact, in 1957 organized labor in Indiana was anything but unified. In the midst of state-level negotiations for an AFL-CIO merger, state labor leaders were divided by antagonisms over who should lead the united state organization as well as conflicting attitudes toward party preferences. Suspecting that Indiana's industrial union leaders coveted the merged organization's prized leadership positions, AFL unionists thought CIO leaders arrogant and uncompromising.[7] But even more importantly, AFL and CIO officials butted heads on the best strategy for influencing Indiana's political establishment. The craft unionists favored a decentralized, non-partisan, business/unionist approach. On the other hand, according to state federation officer Hobert Autterson, CIO people respected hierarchy and were devoted to the Democratic party. He wrote to state federation president Carl Mullen that CIO leaders followed "advice and counsel from their National office regardless of conflict with their own ideas or programs."[8]

Even worse, in the eyes of several AFL officers, their industrial union counterparts had unwisely bound themselves to one party. The "C.I.O. in Indiana is owned body and soul by the Democratic Party," wrote an AFL man to Mullen, "which I believe makes them more of a political organization than a labor union." In the opinion of a state federation executive council member, CIO unionists could "see no good in the Republican party, nor do they believe that anything good will ever come from them." As a case in point, he noted that the industrial union leaders refused to participate in the AFL's pre-passage demonstration rally against the right-to-work bill. Had "the bill been stopped in the legislature, or by a veto, it would have had to be done by and through the Republicans," he informed Mullen. And "it seems to me that what happened was just what they wanted to happen, to strengthen their position with the Democrats."[9]

In view of the closeness of the vote, such divisiveness had obviously contributed greatly to the law's passage. The defeat also underscored the necessity of closing ranks if organized labor wanted to defend union security; labor leaders could simply not afford to assume that their reputation as a powerful lobby would suffice. And furthermore, the division over strategies emphasized the problems of coping with a special interest issue when a large segment of labor was attempting to work primarily through one particular party.

For national and state right-to-work advocates, the victory infused confidence into their movement. Indiana was the first real success of a self-identified right-to-work committee; afterward no one could dismiss the presence of such a group lightly. "Business organizations here have worked long and hard to spread the gospel of conservatism," bragged INRTWC director William Book. "Our new right-to-work law could not have become a reality without such seed-planting." By planting those seeds early and gaining the unified cooperation of the business community, the INRTWC convinced the legislators and citizens of the Hoosier State that banning union security would somehow rid the state of its labor-management difficulties. And, of course, the NRTWC hoped other state business communities would emulate Indiana's. As *Nation's Business* advised, it was never "too early to get the wheels turning for right-to-work and other measures conducive to a good business climate."[10]

And indeed, the Indiana campaign had an impact well beyond the borders of the state. As expected, the success sparked the smoldering ambitions of other right-to-work partisans. Finding that labor lobbyists in most industrialized states did a good job of keeping legislative proposals in limbo, they confidently turned to the referendum technique, either by legislative submission or initiative petition, to place the restrictions on the statute books. They succeeded in a number of important areas, for by mid–1958 California, Idaho, Washington, Colorado, and Ohio had joined Kansas in placing the question on their electoral ballots for November. Moreover, congressional conservatives felt that they could use the momentum generated by Indiana and the McClellan labor racketeering hearings to drum up support for a national right-to-work law.

Pre-eminent among these national figures was Arizona Republican senator Barry Goldwater, who personally lobbied President Eisenhower on behalf of a national right-to-work bill. The right to work, he told the president in a February 1957 meeting, was a civil liberty that Congress should explicitly protect with a federal law. Only then would individual citizens' fundamental rights receive protection from compulsory unionism.[11] And Senator Goldwater was not the only conservative in Congress interested in pushing the idea. Several southern Democrats also jumped on the bandwagon, most notably Senator John McClellan of Arkansas, who used his investigation of labor racketeering as a springboard. In attempting to amend a civil rights bill, he offered a provision that would have functioned as a federal right-to-work law. However, this tactic failed, as many potential supporters in Congress thought his choice of vehicle improper and his strategy ill-advised.[12]

Obviously, by themselves conservatives could do little without the crucial active backing of the president, and here Secretary of Labor Mitchell worked throughout 1957 and 1958 to counteract their efforts. For instance, he lobbied hard against Goldwater's amendment bill to Taft-Hartley outlawing all forms of union security. "I fail to understand Senator Goldwater's reasoning," he wrote Sherman Adams. In every other area of law Goldwater insisted on the sanctity of states' rights. Yet when it came to labor legislation, the lawmaker contradicted himself and wanted to overrule the wishes of the people in those states that had not wanted such a law. "I think Senator Goldwater should be told," the secretary urged strongly, "that we do not favor such a proposal and if questioned about it we will publicly oppose it."[13] Furthermore, to lessen the political fallout that he felt could stem from Republican sponsorship of union security restrictions, Mitchell and his lieutenants in the Department of Labor carefully followed the progress of state right-to-work legislation, and, whenever feasible, quietly did what they could to prevent the Republican party from becoming identified as the party chiefly promoting right-to-work laws. As one of his aides reminded Mitchell during the Indiana campaign, a veto recommendation from a Republican secretary of labor to a Republican governor might carry some weight. "You might tactfully indicate to . . . [Governor Handley] the problems which you foresee if this bill does become law," wrote his assistant.[14]

Torn between these two factions, the president decided that while he could not make Mitchell's explicit opposition to right to work his own, he could exercise political caution and oppose a federal law. Personally, of course, he preferred Goldwater's position. "God damn it, Barry," the exasperated chief executive exclaimed to Goldwater during one of their meetings, "I believe as much in [the] right to work as you do, but I have to live with my Secretary of Labor!" To back Goldwater on a federal right-to-work bill would cause too many problems. Besides, he could always mitigate criticism from his more conservative business supporters by bringing up the hallowed subject of states' rights.[15]

The Indiana right-to-work victory also had an impact on many of the former CIO unions. Previously, union security restrictions had only marginally affected their power. In Indiana, though, there were hundreds of thousands of industrial union members. No longer could top industrial union leaders afford to continue to be complacent about labor law reform.

Right-to-workers had marched into their territory and this mandated a response.

This complacency had resulted from two factors: the previous inability to influence Democratic legislators on the subject of labor legislation and a realization that, to date, Taft-Hartley had not led to the predicted devastation of industrial unionism. The officers of the AFL-CIO's Industrial Union Department, the power center of former CIO unions in the newly merged federation, understood the building trades unions' continuing concern over the law, especially on union security. However, they were not willing to back ameliorating amendments limited to building trades unions which could then use the special exemption to raid the membership of industrial unions.

Nor were they willing to vigorously pursue amendment on behalf of the weaker and partially organized industrial unions. Although Taft-Hartley could create serious difficulties for unions dealing with centralized corporations, UAW president Walter Reuther admitted it was not "going to wreck our union." Similarly, right-to-work laws harmed those unions most in need of organizing and least capable of defending themselves against litigation. One management representative, for example, said that his state's right-to-work statute had "virtually eliminated organizational picketing" and, in some cases, even boycotts. The overall effect was a loss of will to undertake needed organization drives and other forms of self-help that would possibly subject the local's treasury to burdensome legal fees and damage suits. As a labor attorney in Tennessee informed AFL-CIO regional director Paul Christopher, "the real effect of . . . [these] statute[s] is seen in the daily practice of law, when unions call to request advice on what they can and can't do under the Open Shop Law."[16]

But even more importantly, industrial unionists realized that pushing the subject of national labor law reform—their preferred approach—cost them legislative credits with the Democratic leadership for other programs in which they had an interest. House Speaker Sam Rayburn and Senate Majority Leader Lyndon Johnson preferred to lead their party by orchestrating a consensus between its various factions, and labor legislation was simply too divisive a subject for their tastes. Nor did they appreciate being harangued about issues. For instance, when an education committee of a UAW local, in a publicly circulated letter to all senators, accused the Senate leadership of striking deals with big business, Johnson personally took Walter Reuther to task for the affront. "This is the sort of thing that to a tremendous extent has converted organized labor into a 'paper tiger' in politics," he wrote the UAW president. Arriving in the midst of heated debate, it made Johnson's task of controlling legislators all the more difficult. "I am not going to answer a letter of this character because I consider it insulting, threatening, and frankly, a little childish. Neither does it change my mind for acting prudently and soundly—rather than politically and wildly—in the field of labor legislation." This kind of behavior on the part of labor could do nothing but cause resentment. "Perhaps," the majority leader wrote sharply, "the Educational Commmittee of Local 501 needs some education."[17]

Thus, labor lobbyists faced a difficult choice. On the one hand, Johnson's middle-of-the-road approach displeased labor's liberal-minded legislative representatives. They believed that, even on many social-welfare questions, he would "run the Democratic Party . . . further and further from anything we can persuade our people to fight for," wrote UAW lobbyist Donald Montgomery to Roy Reuther. On the other hand, leaders such as Walter Reuther realized that Lyndon Johnson could occasionally rediscover his populist roots; and if labor people continued to berate him for his do-nothing attitude on labor law reform, they could make a vengeful enemy. As Johnson wrote Walter Reuther in April 1958, "you and I have had differences before," mainly because "you and I are [not] the kind of men who will ever permit others to do their thinking for them. But," the Democratic leader pointed out in consolation, "I believe that you and I can always work together on an issue that involves all of our people."[18]

INDUSTRIAL UNIONISM RESPONDS TO THE UNION SECURITY THREAT

Even before Johnson's correspondence, labor lobbyists had had a good deal of opportunity to learn that in the opinion of the party's congressional leadership, labor legislation was not a subject that "involved all of our people." For industrial unionism's political leaders, this lack of legislative influence along with the rural quarantine of right to work had led to inertia in the sector of American labor least affected by such laws. By mid–1957, however, they could no longer afford to ignore the growing agitation for legislation to outlaw union security.

For example, after the right-to-workers victory in Indiana the UAW found that the NRTWC even aimed at eventually capturing the powerful union's home state of Michigan. The committee sponsored ads that appeared in the state—as well as in many others—in the hope of attracting supporters. Joe Walsh, assistant public relations director of the UAW, wrote in September 1957 that the NRTWC was "quite obviously a growing organization. Not only has its advertising budget been increased substantially in the past year," he informed all UAW officers, "but it has opened a number of state and local offices throughout the country, always a firm indication of newly acquired wealth." What was even worse, the NRTWC had begun adopting the tactic of prominently featuring the names of disenchanted unionists— some of them UAW members—as a way of downplaying its strong ties to employers. "The group is always on the prowl for disgruntled union mem-

bers for exploitation" in its publications and ads, wrote Walsh. While no
one could foresee exactly how powerful the NRTWC could become, this
sophisticated use of public relations promised future trouble and required
a response in kind. "This is an organization that bears close watching," the
public relations director advised Autoworkers functionaries, "and one which
could conceivably visit serious harm." UAW activists should counter the
committee's propaganda wherever possible through letters to the editor, or,
in the event of a major campaign, through paid advertisements. Especially,
Walsh warned, since "the drive to enact right-to-scab legislation is also
being conducted on a more vigorous scale in highly industrialized and highly
unionized northern states."[19]

In 1957, however, Walsh's ominous warnings about the power of the
NRTWC were somewhat overdrawn. A look into the founding of the Illinois
Right to Work Committee (ILRTWC), for example, reveals that these state
committees had to draw mainly on their own resources for their work,
although the NRTWC gave some aid. One of the ILRTWC's founders was
Ira Latimer, a former Marxist who was now a self-described conservative
anti-Marxist as well as a lawyer and ordained Baptist minister. His anti—
union security group had close ties to the Conference of American Small
Business Organizations' Chicago office. Established in May 1957, Latimer's
organization first recruited business adherents and financial backers, and at
one point even hired a professional fund-raiser on commission. In addition,
as executive director, Latimer began to network with other state right-to-
work groups as well as the national organization in order to learn the
essentials of a successful campaign. The underlying motive, for the ILRTWC
at least, was that union security gave labor leaders more power that would
be used on behalf of liberal politicians and social-welfare issues. Even so,
at the end of 1957, the group had raised only $3,060.00 in corporate
contributions and $424.50 from individuals, leaving a net operating loss of
$23.38 for the year. In reality, in 1957 the right-to-work movement ap-
peared to be much more of a loose confederation than a monolith growing
more powerful each day.[20]

Nonetheless, the Indiana Right to Work Committee had shown what
could be done with proper commitment. Faced with a challenge on home
ground, industrial union leaders resolved to arouse and unify the labor
movement. Walter Reuther, president of the IUD, pressed AFL-CIO president George Meany to expand federation involvement in two areas. At a
meeting of the executive council in November 1957, he informed his staff,
he had won Meany's agreement "that during the AFL-CIO Convention we
would meet with a few key people . . . and set up a committee on the right-
to-work problem." In addition, shortly after the convention, Reuther persuaded the federation chief of the value of "setting up a national and state
committees of citizens groups which would send materials to unions combatting the propaganda of these right-to-work committees." Pursuing these

two strategies, Reuther believed, would buttress the AFL-CIO's revised public relations materials: a new pamphlet, a speaker's manual summarizing
anti-right-to-work arguments for various audiences, a number of canned
radio and television spots, and a fifteen-minute film documentary. In February 1958, the AFL-CIO executive council finally formed a high-level subcommittee devoted exclusively to fighting union security restrictions.
Chaired by Communications Workers of America president Joseph Beirne,
this subcommittee would monitor state right-to-work agitation, coordinate
defense efforts, and aid repeal drives.[21]

And this was not an easy thing to do, as the federation still suffered
adjustment problems two years after the merger—and many of them affected
legislative and political operations. Even though the two wings of organized
labor had joined, it was apparent that in many places the old craft-industrial
rivalries persisted. Throughout 1956 and into 1957, former AFL and CIO
functionaries did all they could to protect their turf. Wholehearted cooperation was a commodity in short supply in the early stages of the merger,
and it was not unusual for this reluctance to degenerate into petty personal
affronts. Carl Winn, director of Region 13, for example, could not get his
assistant director—the former AFL head in the region—to introduce him
to former AFL unionists if there was any way to avoid it. Similarly, former
CIO and AFL political leaders now serving as COPE directors undercut
each other for influence in the national organization.[22]

Moreover, former divisions also made the Legislative Department less
effective than it could have been. CIO lobbyists such as John Edelman of
the Textile Workers considered the merged organization's legislative operations inefficient, if not inert, and something of a closed club. "The AFL-
CIO legislative staff feels that *it* must direct and manage the efforts to push
all major legislative programs," he informed his union's executive board in
the fall of 1957. Legislative Director Andrew Biemiller, chosen by Meany
because of his ability to get along with both segments of the labor movement,
thus forced internationals and their Washington representatives—many of
whom were more knowledgeable on certain subjects than federation operatives—into a "subordinate role day after day and week after week."
Consequently, they understandably lost interest. Furthermore, Edelman
wrote to IUD director Al Whitehouse in July 1958, communication with
state and local labor movements was an "utter failure." "I can testify . . .
that the State Councils—merged and unmerged—just don't know what is
going on in the Congress. There is a distinct feeling that participation by
the State bodies is either not wanted or won't do any good or isn't important
enough." And worst of all, the lobbying methods used by the AFL-CIO's
Legislative Department were just plain amateurish. "What happens now is
that we rush in at the last minute with a lot of fuss and flurry and waste a
good deal of steam," Edelman reported, "that would have been used to
good purpose if employed over a period of time and in accordance with

careful planning and sufficient preparation." Implicit in Edelman's comments was the evaluation that the AFL-dominated Legislative Department did not always appreciate the involvement of former CIO lobbyists such as himself. "If we are to function as a labor movement—as distinct from a crew of labor bureaucrats—" he wrote once in frustration, "we must be willing and able to pool our efforts on matters of common concern irrespective of the identity of the union or the individual."[23] Thus, personal jealousies, power struggles, and differences in philosophies all worked against organizational integration and the successful functioning of any aspect of the merged federation's endeavors. This could be even more pronounced at the state level, as the experience of Indiana unionists proved.

By the end of 1957, however, one thing that virtually all unionists agreed upon was that defending union security should be the number one political priority for the next year. The activities of right-to-workers in Indiana, Kansas, Idaho, and several other states produced public discussion of national anti–union security legislation and a vigorous defensive reaction within organized labor. In particular, industrial union leaders rearranged their political priorities to emphasize the right-to-work challenge. They also suggested beginning a centralized response through national strategic planning and campaign funding, leading to the creation of the federation's first permanent organizational structure designed to deal with the right to work problem since it first appeared in the 1940s. With such a consensus behind them, the members of the special right-to-work subcommittee of the AFL-CIO executive council found their job much easier.

Indeed, the subcommittee did its work rather swiftly. Labor chiefs especially concerned over union security restrictions because of the relatively even dispersal of their memberships—Joseph Beirne of the Communications Workers, Albert Hayes of the Machinists, and James Suffridge of the Retail Clerks International Association—comprised the committee and began their work in mid-February 1958, making one of their first orders of business the preparation of adequate anti-right-to-work public relations material. By mid-April, they had developed "a thorough and detailed program of action," according to the report of the executive council. In order to expedite their work, George Meany assigned various national staff members to assist the subcommittee. In the beginning, Andrew Biemiller of the Legislative Department, Albert Zack of Public Relations, and Saul Miller of the Publications Department formed the core of the support group. Shortly thereafter, the AFL-CIO president added James L. McDevitt, head of the COPE operation, and Carl McPeak, state legislation representative, to round out the supporting staff.[24]

The task of the subcommittee and the state centrals was not going to be easy. Seventeen legislatures met in 1958, and the state organizations managed to stop legislative drives in Louisiana, Kentucky, Maryland, Rhode Island, and Delaware. Due to the 1957–1958 efforts of the opposition, however, organized labor found that, in addition to Kansas, its right-to-work antagonists had succeeded in placing referendums on the ballot in Ohio, California, Idaho, Colorado, and Washington. The federation subcommittee planned to stimulate the formation of state-level anti-right-to-work steering committees which would then encourage internationals and locals to do likewise, greatly increasing labor's readiness to respond to a referendum. AFL-CIO legislative director Andrew Biemiller made plans to include sessions on the state right-to-work problem at the federation's national legislative conference. Carl McPeak, as the state legislation representative, had the difficult job of coordinating the work and communications between the national headquarters and the multilayered structures at the state and local levels. In alliance with the National Council on Industrial Peace, the anti-right-to-work citizens group envisioned by Reuther and led by prominent liberals such as Eleanor Roosevelt and Senator Herbert Lehman (D-NY), the AFL-CIO subcommittee hoped to contribute strategic analysis, research support, and media professionalism to the various state campaigns.[25]

With this apparatus in place, in May 1958 the Industrial Union Department kicked off the national campaign against right to work by devoting its entire annual conference to the subject. Hoping to arouse industrial unionists to activism, IUD president Walter Reuther, United Steelworkers president David McDonald, and other leaders defined the union security problem as one of the forces of progessivism versus the forces of reaction. In fact, the IUD's title for the conference symbolized this whole approach: "Union Shop and the Public Welfare." Essentially, the top industrial union leaders charged, the right-to-work problem was a problem of partisan politics, for in the last analysis the attacks on union security boiled down to the difference between Democratic and Republican philosophies.

Reuther outlined his evaluation of the controversy in his keynote address. The modern right-to-work movement, he argued, owed its existence to much more than opposition to union security per se. If "you begin to look behind the scenes you will find very quickly what really motivates these people," he told his audience. In the IUD president's view, the widespread agitation resulted from organized labor's extensive lobbying for social-welfare legislation, a phenomenon now some two decades old. Labor's foes, he informed his brothers and sisters, preferred "a narrow labor movement that restricts itself to narrrow issues. They believe that they can manage that kind of movement." But because unions had become a force for the public good, "out of a conviction that labor's interests are inseparably bound together with the interests of the whole community," he said, ". . . at that point we become dangerous in the eyes of these men. That is why they would destroy us" by attacking the right of union organizations to exist.[26]

In Europe, Reuther pointed out, unions did not concern themselves with union security. Their social-democratic origins had made them an "important part of the economic, social and political fabric of the nation." In contrast, in "America we are being tolerated. We have not been fully accepted." Only by continuing to weave itself into America's political and social fabric would organized labor be able to fight off the attacks of right-to-work advocates such as Republican senators Barry Goldwater of Arizona and William Knowland of California. Unionists everywhere must oppose the temptation to look at the struggle as one of trade unionism, pure and simple. "It would be a tragic tactical mistake," Reuther cautioned, "to fight the 'right-to-work' conspiracy on a purely negative, defensive basis. We must make this fight on a positive basis in which we put all these issues in their proper relationship[,] one to the other[,] and then equate them with the forces pushing the 'right-to-work' laws."[27]

Thus, to Walter Reuther and to a lesser extent to the other labor leaders who spoke at the conference, an attack on union security had become important to conservative forces not only because of labor's collective bargaining finesse, but also because its political and social objectives ran counter to employers' laissez-faire ideology. As USWA president McDonald put it, the "real meaning of the 'right-to-work' drive is . . . a softening-up technique in a long-range drive to reduce unions to impotent groups so hamstrung by repressive legislation that their effectiveness on behalf of the individual will be drastically curtailed." It would be a disaster for both the labor movement and the public welfare if right-to-work proponents succeeded in sapping organized labor's power.[28]

Of that they were all sure. There was less assurance, however, on whether labor's political alliance with the Democratic party would produce the kind of commitment labor needed in the coming fight. In particular, for some time labor officials' unhappiness with the party's congressional leadership threatened to further disturb the relationship. While Reuther was content to throw in his lot with the Democrats by equating reaction and Republicanism, not every union leader shared his analysis. Old-line radical Mike Quill of the Transport Workers, for example, charged that Democrats like senators Eastland (MS) and McClellan (AK) were just as bad as the Republicans. Therefore, in order to mend political fences and smooth ruffled feathers, Democratic National Committee Chairman Paul Butler came to the IUD conference determined to repair the damage by laying the blame for right to work at the feet of the Republicans.

Of course there was no better way to do this than to point out that Republican sponsorship of Taft-Hartley started labor's current problems. In 1947, he asked the union leaders to recall, anti-labor Republicans passed a law that "cut away at organized labor's strength here and strengthened the hand of union-busters there. [And] they stuck in a scattering of booby-traps and set a number of time bombs that are still going off eleven years later." While Butler admitted that not "every Democrat is a friend of labor," he strongly affirmed that "day in and day out, year in and year out, the

4.1

Rice Index of Cohesion of Democratic and Republican Parties, in All State Legislatures, on Right-to-Work Measures, 1957

STATE/YEAR	TOTAL	INDEXES SENATE	HOUSE	BALLOTS CAST SENATE	HOUSE
DEMOCRATIC					
Indiana 1957	-75	-76	-74	17	23
Idaho 1957	-73	-84	-63	25	27
Kansas 1957	-64	-100	-58	6	38
Louisiana 1957	-	-52	NV	33	NV
REPUBLICAN					
Kansas 1957	84	82	85	33	82
Idaho 1957	76	79	75	19	32
Indiana 1957	43	52	40	33	73
Louisiana 1957	NR	NR	NR	NR	NR

Source: Appendix A
Key: NR-No Republicans, NV-No Vote
Index: +100(Totally Cohesive in Favor of Right to Work)
          -100(Totally Cohesive Against Right to Work)

Democratic average—the record of the party as a whole—on labor questions
is so much better than the Republican record there can be no doubt as to
which party really has the interest of the working man at heart."[29]

A review of the Rice Index of Cohesion scores for state legislative votes
on right-to-work measures in 1957 supports Butler's contentions. Table 4.1
gives both Democratic and Republican percentages in comparison. Indiana
Democrats tallied the highest overall pro-labor index with a −75. Idaho,
Kansas, and Louisiana Democrats followed with −73, −64, and −52,
respectively. In contrast, Kansas Republicans voted strongly for right to
work with an 84. Idaho GOP lawmakers came next with 76, and then
Indiana's with 43. The average for the Democrats was therefore a pro-labor
−70.6 percent while the Party of Lincoln averaged an anti–union security
percentage of 67.6. In all three states the Republicans were the majority
party, but each did have an active Democratic party capable of electing a
sizeable group of legislators.

Furthermore, Butler went on, the claim of prominent Republicans that
they designed their policies on behalf of working people was an insult—
and baldly contradicted by their support of right to work. "I suppose the
public is expected to thrill to the picture of...Barry Goldwater running
around protecting rank-and-file workers from Dave McDonald and Walter
Reuther and George Meany," the Democratic leader commented humor-

ously, "but somehow it just does not ring true." The simple fact was that the Republican party was the force behind anti-labor legislation like right-to-work laws. And its efforts were "backed with a tremendous amount of money and very competent propaganda and public relations people," he told his listeners. Just the kind of talent that was "highly skilled in making the public believe what they want the public to believe, whether it happens to be true or not."[30]

How could he prove that the Democratic party was any better? Butler, a member of the party's liberal wing, singled out the platform commitments of the respective parties. Since 1956 the Democratic party had officially opposed state right-to-work statutes and favored repeal of Taft-Hartley—a commitment Republicans certainly had plenty of opportunity to make but never did. And other than that, Butler could make no ironclad promises, for neither did the party dominate labor nor labor the party. The "Democratic Party believes that a political party can govern a nation wisely only when it is representative of the whole nation," he said in conclusion. "It does not believe in class government, [or] of single interest government. And because it refuses to be the tool of anybody it is the party best equipped to serve the interests of everybody."[31]

Butler's assertions, however, amounted to little more than what Democratic leaders had been saying for years. But by now, a relatively unified labor movement realized that it could not depend on its political friends to take the lead in defending its crucial interests. While Democrats might finally cast votes against inaugurating a right-to-work measure, most were clearly not going to lead the way on this issue. By the summer of 1958, the passage of the Indiana right-to-work law, the talk of a national bill restricting union security, and the right-to-work movement's successful efforts in six states—as well as the potential threat it posed in others—had roused all segments of organized labor. In short order, the political priorities of the industrial unions became symmetrical with those of the craft organizations. As IUD secretary James Carey wrote to the department's affiliates, virtually the entire liberal-labor community agreed that right to work posed a greater danger than any federal legislation on the horizon. By placing industrial unions under the pall of a union security attack, anti–union security agitators had provided the needed impetus for the national level of organized labor to rationalize its structure for fighting right to work. Now, the resources and expertise of the federation would be more available to state labor leaders who needed them. In the 1958 state right-to-work elections, organized labor aimed to win—with the help of its political allies, it hoped—but if not, then on its own.

THE 1958 STATE RIGHT-TO-WORK ELECTIONS

And in order to do so, organized labor's central organizations in each of the six states holding a referendum had to accomplish two tasks: they had to make sure that COPE registered union members and their families, in addition to apprising them of the danger to their unions, and they had to have some kind of campaign apparatus that could present the battle against right to work as a non-partisan election issue. By ensuring the highest possible labor participation and by reaching out to the general public with their side of the story, labor leaders felt they could foil the plans of their enemies. But, as with many endeavors, there was conflict about which aspect to emphasize.

From the beginning, IUD officials hoped the right-to-work elections would spark COPE activism well beyond the union security issue. Their interest even extended to subsidizing the AFL-CIO special per capita assessment levied at the executive council's April 1958 meeting. In July, the IUD executive committee, according to James Carey, "took a unique and unprecedented action" to help raise monies for these elections by agreeing to pay half of the five cent tax for its affiliates. By encouraging sufficient funding in this way, Carey wrote IUD member unions, the department would help prevent labor-management relations from reverting "to compulsory open shop chaos and the kind of industrial conflict and warfare that we believed had been put behind us forever."[32]

Industrial union political strategists saw the elections as an opportunity for injecting partisanship into the campaign—and worried about the proclivities of some labor leaders to focus exclusively on the threat to union security. "I am greatly concerned and disturbed about reports on some of labor's state campaigns against 'right-to-work' referendums," wrote the UAW's citizenship director, Roy Reuther, to his brother Walter in August 1958. These unionists were falling into a trap by concentrating too narrowly on the proposals as a purely trade-union-related issue. Public opinion surveys, he claimed, had proved that this approach had "failed to get its point of view over to either the general public or to many of its union members and their families." He thought it would be much better to try to expand the implications of the right-to-work agitation by placing responsibility where it belonged—with the Republicans. The same big-business-dominated administration that was responsible for unemployment and high inflation, he charged, was attempting "by trickery, deceit, and slick slogans to pass a law that would deprive every working man and woman of his only protection against ruthless and greedy employers." He had discerned a rising anti-Republican tide in many areas, and the labor movement could multiply Democratic victories by adopting this approach.[33]

So for better or for worse, organized labor faced the 1958 right-to-work elections united on the immediate ends if somewhat divided on the means and ultimate objectives. Those labor leaders who viewed the challenge as a strictly trade union question seemed mainly concerned about the integrity of their organizations, while more socially motivated unionists worried about the consequences for their broader purposes. As a confidential study of UAW organizing problems concluded in late 1958, there "are still some sections in our union where [the] union shop has not been achieved or is not legally permissible." Without being able to increase membership figures, the analyst noted, it "will become more and more difficult to influence the social, economic, and political life in the community and the nation . . . [than] it has [been] in the past."[34]

Thus, with COPE organizations rallying the troops it was not surprising the contest took on a partisan coloring—especially in California and Ohio where top Republican candidates made right to work a cornerstone of their campaigns. While Republican sentiment in the remaining states was generally supportive of right to work, candidates for office often shied away from the controversy if at all possible, or, if forced, opposed the referendum as did their Democratic opponents. The response of state Democrats ranged from neutrality to committed promotion of the labor position. Nevertheless, whether labor succeeded or not depended on a variety of factors besides the quality of aid rendered by political allies. In particular, the general political environment of the state, the proficiency of right-to-work supporters, the percent of workers organized, and the 1958 recession all affected the outcome.

The Colorado election exemplified how good planning and behind-the-scenes help from the state Democratic party could transform an anti-Republican swing into a victory for labor. In early 1958, the Colorado AFL-CIO quietly followed the activities of the newly formed Colorado Right to Work Committee in some detail while planning its counterattack. At the May 1958 convention of the newly merged Colorado Labor Council, President George Cavender outlined the federation's strategy for the election. A public opinion survey revealed that 57 percent of the respondents were for right to work, but were somewhat unclear as to exactly what the term signified. Middle-class voters and especially women seemed to be the strongest supporters. To overcome this startling disadvantage, Cavender told the delegates, the executive council was using the dollar per member right-to-work defense fund monies to retain a public relations firm to design materials for the election. In addition, the officers assisted in the formation of a citizens committee against right to work that would be the main group communicating with the non-labor public. And for this audience, they had decided, it was best to use a soft-sell approach, "rather than running around screaming and having cartoons showing labor in chains and that sort of thing."[35]

Furthermore, to date the Colorado labor movement had received excellent cooperation from its political allies—all due, no doubt, to the work of its COPE organization. As Cavender pointed out, the "Democratic Party, almost unanimously, is working with us, from the state level right on down." Even the Republican party seemed reluctant to take a stand against labor, and Colorado's labor leaders hoped to continue to prevent the Republicans "from getting themselves clear out on a limb." Making a special appearance at the convention, state legislation representative Carl McPeak urged the Colorado unionists to use the anti-right-to-work materials prepared by the national office in their fight and, in addition, pleaded with them to become more active in COPE. Someday, McPeak noted, labor wanted to put an end to this whole business by repealing section 14(b) of the Taft-Hartley Act, a job that would require 100 percent COPE participation. Until that time came, he informed his union brothers and sisters, "we must run scared in this campaign."[36]

Indeed, labor ran scared in all states where right-to-work backers had presented voters with a referendum. At the national level, though, AFL-CIO political strategists still saw the ultimate answer to these assaults as repeal of section 14(b). A COPE study of the right-to-work situation, presented to COPE's top administrative committee in late April 1958, outlined the tough electoral problems associated with these campaigns. First of all, labor was "always in a defensive position," forced to fight back "at the place and . . . at the time of our opponent's choosing." Moreover, each state's political environment differed slightly, making it impossible "to develop an over-all formula" and thus "no situation is exactly met." Finally, the de-centralized nature of the agitation spread labor's resources thin and led to an inability to accurately "anticipate where the next attack will come." The COPE report recommended a national campaign to repeal Taft-Hartley's right-to-work provision, arguing that it would place labor on the offensive, "put an end to the 'brush-fire' problem," nullify laws "in areas where chances of repeal are slight," lead to the establishment of a unified approach, and provide for a more economical use of resources. State AFL-CIO pres-idents should be notified of a coming campaign to repeal 14(b) in the next session of Congress, the report suggested. In addition, state labor movements and anti-right-to-work citizens committees should be instructed to explicity emphasize the inequities of 14(b) in public relations work. And lastly, all candidates for federal office seeking labor endorsements should be informed that 14(b) repeal was a top legislative priority and that labor suggested the candidates prepare the ground by discussing the issue in their campaign speeches.[37]

But for the time being, at least, at the center ring would be state politics. In Washington State, big business sponsorship of a right-to-work measure forced the state labor movement into organizing an encore performance of their 1956 right-to-work campaign. In agricultural Idaho, organized labor faced off against the farmers' groups that sponsored the vote and was joined by an unexpected ally—the *Boise Idaho Statesman*, the state's most influ-ential paper, which strongly editorialized against the proposed law. In these elections, even less so than in Colorado, major candidates of both parties did not allow the referendum to become a salient part of their campaigns.[38]

Such was not the case with the two most most populous states on the list. From labor's perspective, the elections in heavily industrialized and

Organized California and Ohio raised the possibility of a repeat of the Indiana humiliation. While the labor movements of these two states were more powerful than any of the others save Washington, labor leaders in both found their task complicated by the fact that prominent Republicans either campaigned for the referendum or gave it verbal support.

This was especially true in the California election where right to work had surfaced as a Republican intra-party factional dispute in the fall of 1957. Earlier in the year, cities in southern California responded to local business agitation by passing anti–union security ordinances; probably, a labor official thought, so that if these ordinances became widespread enough, proponents could present it to the California legislature as "something the voters evidently want." Local labor leaders carefully monitored events, and with the help of the chairman of the state Democratic party organization for southern California, they reminded state Democratic legislators of the party's platform promise to oppose right to work. Moreover, in response to this, both the State Federation of Labor and the Industrial Union Council, as yet unmerged, began to fight the ordinances through legal action.[39]

Matters became even more critical for California labor in late 1957 when Senate Minority Leader William Knowland resigned his seat in order to seek the Republican nomination for governor. To win the party's nomination he would have to defeat the incumbent Republican governor. Senator Knowland decided that his key issue would be strong support for a right-to-work law for California, a proposition that his opponent—Republican governor William Knight—adamantly opposed. Quickly, members of the state CIO's education committee outlined a general public relations and education program for the labor and non-labor public, channeled all legal activities through the state IUC's legal counsel, planned to start a defense fund, and resolved to coordinate all organization and education regarding right to work through COPE, which would get things underway with the "periodic calling of staff meetings in each area to mobilize leadership support and to stress [the] seriousness of [the] situation." The State Federation of Labor did much the same. It centralized all legal action, urged the establishment of local anti-right-to-work committees, established a campaign fund that could draw on the federation's organizing fund if contributions proved insufficient, assisted in all coordination and educational efforts, and convened a labor press conference with guest speakers from Washington state's successful 1956 publicity campaign.[40]

Evidently, Knowland's vigorous promotion of the right-to-work initiative played well to a significant number of California Republicans. By the spring of 1958, he had wrested the gubernatorial nomination from Knight, who then received the nomination for Knowland's vacant Senate seat as a consolation prize. More than any other single thing, the primary contest in the fall and winter convinced California's labor leaders that they were in for a no-holds-barred bout in November 1958. As AFL-CIO assistant regional director Irwin DeShetler wrote a colleague, because of Knowland's proselytizing "we'll have a real knock-down, drag-out fight here in the coming elections."[41]

And, labor functionaries also realized, one that would cost a lot of money because of the need to woo California voters. At a meeting of the state COPE executive council in February 1958, IUC political strategists discussed funding levels for their organization and the state federation. With a per capita tax of almost three cents, they reasoned, they could support a major media budget of $562,000: approximately $220,000 for advertising, $200,000 for television and radio, $22,000 for publications, $75,000 for subsidization of a citizens committee, and $45,000 for miscellaneous expenses. While this was less than the $740,000 target of the state federation, the AFL body had requested that both groups work cooperatively on this issue, and the expenditures would therefore complement each other instead of working at cross purposes. Furthermore, by attempting to push an initiative for a state income tax increase at the same time, state federation leaders thought they could divert conservatives' revenue sources away from the right-to-work initiative.[42] This was important because opinion surveys taken by the state federation's public relations agency revealed that while voters were split evenly into pros and cons on right to work, many had not yet decided how to cast their ballots.[43]

Paralleling the initiative campaign, in the spring of 1958 political activists in both of the state's central organizations screened candidates with special care. They wanted to make sure that as few politicians as possible would promote right to work in their campaigns or vote for restricting union security after elected. And in this they had some success, for in seeking to avoid labor's wrath, if not to win its support, many candidates affirmed— often under intense questioning—their opposition to union security restrictions. For example, Governor Knight and Lieutenant Governor Harold Powers, both Republicans, promised COPE functionaries they would not support right to work, and Knight even went so far as to insist he would vote for repeal of section 14(b) if elected to the Senate.[44]

Despite all the labor activism and relative cooperation between the two organizations, by late summer of 1958 there still remained a number of problems. Gettings politicians to promise not to vote for right-to-work measures was one thing; getting them to go out on the stump in opposition was quite another. With Knowland making right to work his keynote, top Democrats such as gubernatorial candidate Edmund Brown, the state's attorney general, could not avoid becoming a public advocate of the labor position. However, COPE activist Marie Bruce noted that at many campaign meetings, lower-level Democratic candidates seemed indifferent about publicly urging a negative vote on the proposition. In addition, funding for the campaign had fallen far short of expectations; the combined amount collected by both federations was only one-third of what they anticipated their opponents would spend.[45] And finally, President Eisenhower's personal intervention on behalf of Knowland provided the Republican candidate with a needed boost. Knowland *had* to win, according to the president, because if Democrats held control of the state's government the following year, when the legislature would reapportion districts, it would destroy California's Republican party, an event that would have national impact.[46]

To reinforce his personal promotion of the Knowland candidacy with California party regulars, the president even entered gingerly into the right-to-work dispute. In its advertisements, organized labor used Eisenhower's statements against a federal right-to-work law to imply that the president also opposed state union security restrictions. In September 1958, Eisenhower publicly released a letter to Senator Knowland in which he pointed out that "I have never expressed myself one way or the other whether any State should exercise this jurisdiction, feeling, as I do, that this should be determined by the citizens of each State." Though this was little more than a restatement of the president's split-the-middle justification for avoiding the controversy, he did want it to appear that at least he was not disagreeing with Knowland on the benefits of such a law.[47]

These setbacks, however, were only temporary. Money began to flow into the central organizations' coffers as the moment of truth approached, and state labor officials began to detect a shift toward their side. The penetration of the state federation's advertising campaign into geographic areas where labor support was weak had hurt the initiative by winning an edge in the undecided votes. Although the public opinion survey results showed that the initiative vote would be close, union political tacticians felt that if they stimulated a heavy turnout they would prevail on the referendum and defeat Knowland as well, for the Republican candidate admitted that his advocacy of right to work had forced labor leaders to get in "up to their necks" to elect his opponent. Moreover, state labor leaders wanted to send a message to their antagonists. "Remember," state COPE official John Despol wrote to California colleagues in late October 1958, "only a smashing defeat ... can prevent the same kind of fight from re-occurring in the 1960 elections."[48]

In Ohio, the campaign was similar. Ohio unionists faced a right-to-work initiative inspired by segments of the establishment/business community; and like California, that initiative received the support of one top state Republican candidate and the reluctant backing of a few others. At a meeting at the Columbus Athletic Club in late 1957, state Chamber of Commerce officials and several conservative manufacturers and retailers decided a successful drive was possible because of Ohio labor's recent political ineffectiveness in a wrangle over state unemployment benefits. By February 1958, they had borrowed money from several Ohio banks, reconstituted themselves as Ohioans for the Right to Work, and started circulating a petition, paying circulators a small amount for each signature obtained. Ohio businesses closely associated with the committee were General Electric, Timken Roller Bearing, Armco Steel, and Cincinnati Milling Machine.[49]

The political directors of the newly merged Ohio AFL-CIO were well aware of the activities of their fellow citizens. Representatives from the state federation, the Steelworkers, the Autoworkers, the Mine Workers, and the Railroad Brotherhoods met in late November 1957 to form an unofficial oversight committee. Later, this committee became known as United Organized Labor of Ohio (UOLO), a more formal, twelve-person steering committee charged with not only watching developments but also directing labor activities when needed. When it became apparent that the business group would garner the signatures necessary to put the question on the ballot, UOLO organized a February 1958 conference for 300 Ohio labor officials. At this gathering, state leaders explored campaign strategies and devised ways to increase the nearly $187,000 right-to-work defense fund that they had accumulated over the previous two months.[50]

Wisely, UOLO recognized the need for professional public relations assistance. It retained the services of Charles Baker and the Burr Agency, a Toledo public relations firm with a pro-labor orientation and ties to the UAW's publicity department. From early 1958 on, Baker directed the major aspects of the referendum response, subject of course to UOLO oversight. Afterward, the directors of Ohio labor's anti-right-to-work effort had to sell the idea of a centralized coordinating committee to the rest of the labor movement. It took some doing to convince suspicious internationals to allow their locals to respond to UOLO directives, and even the steering committee itself more than once experienced dissension. Nonetheless, the threat to union security kept most of Ohio labor unified.[51]

Yet the road ahead was difficult. The opposition had a good slogan, Baker noted, and one that blended well with the basic American value system. Besides that, a 1957 Gallup poll revealed that on a simplistic level, the public supported right to work by 2 to 1, so "we start out well behind the opposition," he informed UOLO director Walter Davis. Considering such general support, Baker believed that the political and social power structure would come out against the labor position unless the UOLO could "get to them with the arguments to which they are most receptive."[52]

Therefore, a winning campaign program would have to get out in front of its competition. Baker reasoned that labor should make right to work a public issue instead of a labor issue. If UOLO could round up the support of civic, fraternal, and religious organizations, it would put the opposition—and he anticipated the press would become a part of the opposition—in the position of criticizing respected community groups. The key to this was to try to avoid logical refutation of Ohioans for the Right to Work (ORW) propaganda. "Fact is," a researcher wrote Baker, "proponents of the 'right to work' law can—by skillful selection of the right years and by ignoring pertinent factors—'prove' anything they wish." The best approach, the public relations expert thought, would be to concentrate on the fact that the union shop was nothing more than industrial majority rule because this "puts us in the positive position of promoting American virtues." Even communications experts could not effectively explain the intricacies of labor law in a campaign atmosphere. Organized labor's public relations strategy would have to rely, for the most part, on "minimal explanation and maximum punch—threats and doomsday prophecy" predicting general economic loss to the whole state if the referendum passed. In short, Baker's cyncial but perhaps accurate conclusion was that he believed that "the winning combination is playing on . . . [public] doubts and fears and sugar-coating this with high-sounding rationalizations."[53]

But the other side aimed to win public acceptance too. ORW activists, however, put less emphasis on the media and more on forcing their political allies to tout their cause. Republican governor William O'Neill came to their aid by "conducting a marvelous campaign in face of opposition of the labor bosses," wrote Ohio industrialist Charles Hook to Secretary of Labor Mitchell in the fall of 1958. An ardent right-to-work supporter, Hook had worked diligently to get the backing of prominent Republican politicians.[54]

Despite the fact that the referendum had top-level Republican backing, press support, and a good slogan, by late September 1958, Ohio labor leaders suspected they would emerge victorious. Although the polls showed 31 percent against the referendum and 29 percent for, 40 percent of the voters still did not know how they would vote. There had been record voter registration, however, and, Baker wrote a friend, a "rank-and-file response that makes me feel like I'm working the West Side of Detroit." A state COPE worker wrote state central secretary Elmer Cope that "from all sorts of normally inactive places . . . there are reports of zip . . . [and] activity: loud speakers, trips into cities to pick up literature, crashing of [Republican] party meetings. . . . There's a *hell of a scrappy defensive action* [out] *there*," the functionary informed Cope, "*and make no mistake about it!*" Money began to flow in from the AFL-CIO national office: a promised $100,000 for the state organization and $60,000 for subsidization of a pro-labor citizens committee. In late October, right-to-work strategists confirmed labor leaders' feelings by launching into a strident attack against unionism in general. As Baker wrote a friend, "the right-to-workers have begun the expected attack on the [labor] corruption issue; they have bought a worker to say he was intimidated into opposing the right-to-work law; and the pattern of vilification is being shaped up."[55]

In Kansas, the Republican right-to-work faction rejected the tactics of Knowland and O'Neill, and for the first time in several years tried to separate the controversy from partisan politics. For Kansans opposed to union security, the proposed law capped four long years of educational and organizational work. This midwestern state had seen rifts within the Republican party, the state's dominant political party, for several years previous to 1958. Republican governor Fred Hall vetoed a 1955 right-to-work bill, causing the ascendant anti-labor faction within the party to deny him renomination in 1956. In that general campaign, Republican right-to-work advocate and gubernatorial candidate Warren Shaw made the issue a part of the party platform and his candidacy and he lost the race. Still unconvinced that they had been defeated, a coalition of business and conservative farm interests—the core of right-to-work support—turned to the constitutional amendment referendum route (by legislative submission) in mid–1957 because Democratic governor George Docking had assured all concerned he would veto legislation restricting union security. At that time, in the eyes of Kansas COPE functionary Gene Larsen, it looked as though the "Republican party in the State of Kansas has declared war" on labor.[56]

That was not the case in 1958. Learning from their past mistakes, the proposal's backers believed that since their efforts in 1958 depended on the voters directly, they would have the best chance of succeeding if they kept the campaign as non-partisan as possible. Though Kansas was largely Republican, the Democratic party and organized labor had some strength in urban areas such as Kansas City and Wichita, and votes in those districts could be crucial. It would be easier to secure passage, right-to-work strategists thought, if the issue did not get tangled up in partisan political loyalties as it had in the past.[57]

Thus, organized labor faced an uphill battle all the way: it did not have many members, had its closest ties to the state's minority party, faced general media opposition, and had an enemy that possessed energy, determination, and sophistication. Local unions in Kansas realized "what a Right to Work law will do to them," wrote the UAW's regional director to Walter Reuther in February 1958, "so they are reacting very well." In addition, the UAW's sub-regional director was Democratic county chairman in Sedgwick (the home county of industrialized Wichita) and COPE had offices in each of the state's congressional districts to facilitate its voter registration drive. Nevertheless, if it hoped to defeat the referendum, the Kansas labor movement would have to make its case to state farmers, a difficult proposition at best.[58]

All of these problems might have been surmountable had labor faced a lackadaisical opposition. Unfortunately, that was not the case. Kansas was not an easy place in which to compete electorally because of the vociferousness of its right-to-work activists. Their key strength, in the opinion of Kansans for Right to Work executive Reed Larson, who later went on to head the National Right to Work Committee, was that business leaders were willing to participate personally and that they had decided to keep the issue nonpartisan. Popular "support can be obtained in sufficient quantity only when business leaders come out from behind the cloak of anonymity afforded by business organizations to let it be known that they, as individ-

uals, believe in freedom from compulsory unionism," Larson later reported
to the National Right to Work Committee. The issue that observers had
declared dead after the 1956 elections was once again a raging public controversy because of the willingness of many Kansas executives to support
small businesspeople, farmers, and others from all walks of life.[59]

Corporations active in the Kansas campaign in the Wichita area were
Boeing Airlines, Cessna Aircraft, Vickers Petroleum, and the Coleman Company, among others. After the three-year education program of Kansans for
the Right to Work (KRTW) had placed the question on the ballot in April
1957, the advisory committees overseeing the local groups planned a fifteen-
month campaign schedule and met once a week for "more than a year to
guide the campaign." Local citizens committees organized by KRTW carried
the main burden throughout the state. They set up displays in over 50 county
fairs. They debated the question and presented programs, according to
Larson, "at every opportunity." Local finance committees conducted fund-
raising activities "directed toward businessmen" that were "extremely important in providing the necessary foundation" for the drive. The KRTW
also produced three right-to-work films and had 40 prints of the films
circulating for seven months before the election. Finally, in the last two
weeks prior to the vote, the KRTW blitzed the media with sponsored ads
and special showings of the films on television.[60]

The early start and the general unity of business, farm, and trade organizations helped right-to-work volunteers procure the only anti–union security legislation passed in 1958. Table 4.2 shows that Kansans voted
395,839 yes to 307,176 no to amend their state constitution, a 56 to 44
percent pro/con division. Eighty-nine out of 105 counties said yes, and only
14 of those 105 fell into the marginal column. Labor's face-off against a
vigorous opponent, its lack of allies, and its modest membership (about
131,050 or 23.7 percent of the labor force) led to the KRTW completely
rolling over Kansas unionists' countering efforts. According to AFL-CIO
right-to-work subcommittee member Albert Hayes, this showed that average
Kansans really had little understanding of the aims and aspirations of the
labor movement. If Kansas labor wanted to communicate, he told the delegates of a post-mortem convention in Wichita, it had to develop a statewide
labor press (since the establishment media had allied itself with labor's
enemies) and do a much better job of public relations.[61]

In the other five states, however, right-to-work evangelists did not fare
so well, as Table 4.2 also reveals. With the aid of the *Boise Idaho Statesman*,
Idaho labor's 35,700 members, or approximately 23.8 percent of the work
force, just barely defeated the proposal by 121,790 to 118,718 (49 percent
yes to 51 percent no). This mountain state's 45 counties split evenly on the
question, with 12 ending up marginal. In Washington State, unionists' efforts resulted in a repeat of their 1956 victory with 596,949 votes against
union security restrictions and 339,742 in support. Here, of course, labor

4.2
Public Right-to-Work Elections, 1958

STATE AND YEAR	YES RTW	NO RTW	TOTAL	%RATIO	COUNTY Y/N RATIO	# MARGINAL COUNTIES	% OF VOTE FOR HIGHEST OFFICE IN ELECTION	APPROXIMATE UNION MEMBERSHIP
Washington 1958	339742	596949	936691	36/64	6/33	3	106	380600(48.1%)
Ohio 1958	1160320	2001530	3161850	37/63	14/74	24	100	1072400(36.3%)
Colorado 1958	200319	318480	518799	39/61	23/43	19	97	120450(25.0%)
California 1958	2080020	3070870	5150890	40/60	5/53	20	101	1715100(37.2%)
Idaho 1958	118718	121790	240508	49/51	22/22	12	101	35700(23.8%)
Kansas 1958	395839	307176	703015	56/44	89/16	14	98	131050(23.7%)

Source: Appendix B, Cox, and Troy. See explanation in Appendix B as to the derivation of percent of state vote and union membership.

had much more voting strength since Washington's labor force was 48.1 percent unionized (380,600 members). Only 6 out of 39 counties said yes (with 3 being marginal) in the 64 to 36 percent victory. While Colorado labor's win was less spectacular, it was solid nonetheless. By a 61 to 39 percent split (318,480 no to 200,319 yes) Colorado voters nixed the right to work. Nineteen of the state's 66 counties were marginal; of those 66, 43 voted no and 23 voted yes. And this was in a state where the union movement represented 120,450 workers, or 25 percent of the work force.[62]

The labor movements in the two largest states, Ohio and California, also defeated the challenge to union security decisively. In these states, though, the issue had taken a strong partisan turn in that top Republicans made the question a focal point in their campaigns. The combined work of the California State Federation of Labor, the California Industrial Union Council, and their respective political arms yielded 3,070,870 no-votes against Initiative 198 in comparison to 2,080,020 yes-votes, for a 40/60 yes/no percentage split. The opposition had spent $907,000 on their campaign, according to documents filed with the California secretary of state. But organized labor—with a membership of 1,715,100 or 37.2 percent of the California labor force—far outspent its enemies with over $2.4 million going into their drive, half of which ended up in various advertisements. This was reflected in the county yes/no ratio with only 5 of the state's 58 counties voting yes (20 were marginal). It was an impressive showing, according to AFL-CIO assistant regional director Irwin DeShetler, and one that could not "be attributed to anything but the intense desire of the California labor movement—from top to bottom—to see . . . the defeat of the so-called right-to-work and its champion, Bill Knowland."[63]

Similarly, Ohio labor spent much more money to defeat the referendum than had the Ohioans for Right to Work. Besides the funds from the national office, internationals and other Buckeye State labor organizations raised about $1.4 million for the campaign, compared to the $776,000 raised by their opponents. As a result, labor's political strategists added 200,000 working-class voters to the registration rolls and ended up beating the initiative by a 63 to 37 percent vote (2,001,530 no to 1,160,320 yes). Ohio's 1,072,400 unionists (36.3 percent of the work force) captured 74 counties out of a total of 88, with 24 ending up marginal. Coalitions were especially helpful in defeating the measure. The support of minorities, respected community groups, and church leaders (particularly among Catholics) had been instrumental in producing such favorable results. A subsequent independent study of Ohio's right-to-work voting statistics substantiated this fact as well as coming to the conclusion that the election produced a general "economic class vote." Analyzing the counties along a number of variables, this study's author found that working-class and middle-class districts (even those that included non-union occupations and areas) voted against the proposal, "while only the very wealthy cast substantial majorities in its behalf." In fact, national and state COPE operatives found that Negro districts in Ohio—because of the work of black unionists—had produced the strongest opposition by tallying totals equal to 8 to 1 against the amendment. But the 3,150 hours put in by the Burr Agency and Charles Baker was perhaps the most crucial factor. As UOLO chief Walter Davis wrote to Baker, you "plotted the campaign, you called the shots and you deserve the credit." "We won a tough, dirty, no-holds barred fight," Davis concluded, "because we knew how to fight better than our opponents."[64]

In addition to the resounding defeat given the right-to-work referendums, the stimulus to the unions to become politically active elected many Democrats, a large number of whom were liberals. COPE-endorsed candidates won many major state offices and perhaps even more importantly, in the eyes of many of labor's political leaders, liberal congressional representation shot up as well. The two Republican gubernatorial candidates who ran on the issue of restricting union security—William Knowland in California and William O'Neill in Ohio—ended up badly beaten. In fact, the only Republican governor elected was in Idaho, where the Democratic candidate had supported an unpopular, unrelated issue. No doubt the increased registration of labor voters worked against the Republican party in many areas— and particularly when Republican candidates supported the issue. In addition, a COPE analysis for the AFL-CIO executive council by Director James L. McDevitt noted the unifying political potential of a right-to-work election on state labor movements. "More than anything else," an Ohio analyst wrote the national COPE director, "this campaign proved that when labor is aroused and forgets its differences it in turn can arouse the people" which could produce numerous benefits. As one Communication Workers of America official wrote in the wake of the 1958 results, it "might not be too bad if we could persuade our opponents to place . . . [right to work] on the ballot for every election."[65]

While facetious to a degree, the remark had something to it. Starting with the anti–union security agitation in Kansas, Idaho, and especially Indiana in early 1957, leaders of industrial unions began to sit up and take notice that right-to-work activists were no longer happy to have conquered areas peripheral to mass-production unionism. These events, combined with the confident talk of a federal right-to-work bill and referendum agitation in many states, pushed the IUD into providing the stimulus for a rationalization of labor's organizational structure to fight these special campaigns. As the president of the Idaho State Federation of Labor wrote to George Meany after his state's victory, about "one year ago I visted the National Headquarters to determine what assistance we could receive and I was frankly appalled at the lack of a coordinated program to counter-balance the serious attack which we were facing across the nation." The national AFL-CIO subsequently instituted a special subcommittee, contributed specialized staff talent through COPE and other departments where needed, produced anti-right-to-work materials in abundance, rallied the state leadership, and made more than token monetary contributions. State central organizations directed each individual effort with the help of national people, provided the bulk of the funding, reached a new sophistication in the utilization of professional media consultants, and received experience in building broad-based, liberal coalitions. The 1958 state right-to-work elections provided something for all unionists: successful defense of union security for the more conservative craft leaders, and political activism and Democratic victory for the more socially concerned unionists. The victory was well earned, and COPE's efforts had placed a good many liberal politicians in office.[66]

Thus, when IUD president Walter Reuther reviewed labor's political progress over the year and a half prior to the 1958 elections, he concluded that the movement had done its job well. Previously the pattern had been that Republicans generally supported right to work in the state legislatures, and Democrats normally voted against putting a statute in place. As a rule, though, neither group of politicians liked to exercise leadership in this area. Perhaps with the gains for liberals in the new Congress, this reticence on the part of the Democratic party would change. In January 1959, Reuther wrote his friends Eleanor Roosevelt and Herbert Lehman, co-chairs of the National Council for Industrial Peace, and thanked them on behalf of the labor movement for their group's "efforts to develop a better public understanding of the issues involved in the so-called right-to-work campaign." In fact, he wrote in reflection, much of the electoral festivities amused him, for the conservatives had him running as a "phantom candidate" in many states. "However," he noted humorously, referring to some of the opposition's well-known campaign literature showing Reuther's picture in every space on the Democratic ticket, "the Republicans in California, in their hour of desperation, outdid themselves and had me *running* for almost every place on the ballot." Actually, he thought, it was a tribute to his vision of the labor movement that right-to-workers got so upset about the power of unions. In fact, he was pleased that conservatives feared his attempts to raise unionism beyond collective bargaining and into politics and social-welfare issues. That, of course, was the real reason behind the growing right-to-work movement and why he frightened business leaders so much. Otherwise, they would not have bothered with him at all. Management, he wrote with self-satisfaction, "knows how to deal with labor leaders who have a price tag."[67]

NOTES

1. Reed Larson, "How Right to Work Was Adopted in Kansas," Special Report of the National Right to Work Committee, January 1959.

2. Appendix A, and Fred Witney, "The Indiana Right-to-Work Law," *Industrial and Labor Relations Review* 11(July 1958):507, 517.

3. Figures cited in Witney, pp. 507–512. Tables 7.1 and 7.2 of Troy and Sheflin cite the total Indiana membership for 1953 as approximately 587,000 (41.3 percent) but some slippage undoubtedly occurred as a result of the 1954 recession. With regard to the NRTWC, other founding members of the group were Edwin S. Dillard, president of the Old Dominion Box Company of Charlotte, N.C.; S.D. Cadwallader, a former railroad conductor from Cincinnati; P.M. French, president of the Southern Manufacturing Company, a Nashville clothing firm; Robert A. Englander, president of Dacam Corporation, a steel products firm in Lynchburg, Virginia; and Nathan Thorington, head of a Richmond, Virginia construction company. Another important member of the early NRTWC was William Taylor Harrison, a clerk with the Louisville and Nashville railroad, who became its executive secretary in 1956. See "The National Right to Work Committee," Special Investigation Report No. 12, 13 December 1962, Box 58, Irwin L. DeShetler Collection, WPRL; Political Action Report, Newsletter, "Reed Larson on the Right to Work" (June 2, 1979), NRTWC Reprint; Sybyl S. Patterson to Laurence C. Brown, 13 December 1956, Box 23, The Sligh Family Collection, BHL.

4. The second incident occurred in a different strike and the perpetrators were unknown; nevertheless, the public's wrath descended upon unions as instigators of this type of anti-social behavior. See Witney, "Indiana Right-to-Work Law," pp. 511, 514. "Here's Way to Sound Laws," *Nation's Business*, June 1957, pp. 42, 46.

5. Appendix A; Witney, "Indiana Right-to-Work Law," pp. 511–514; "Here's Way to Sound Laws," pp. 46–47; Memos, George Riley to President Meany, "Indiana State 'Right-to-Work' Legislation," 15 March 1957, Box 33, AFL-CIO President's Office: George Meany Files, GMMA.

6. "Here's Way to Sound Laws," p. 42.

7. Indiana State Federation of Labor, *Proceedings of the 72nd Annual Convention of the Indiana State Federation of Labor*, 11–13 November 1957, pp. 25–40, *State Labor Proceedings*, microform, Center for Research Libraries. Although the national structures of the AFL and CIO merged in late 1955, the integration of the various substructures of the labor movement took up to two years. Separate state central organizations affiliated with either the AFL or the CIO had to overcome their differences to join in a new state organization. This pattern was repeated in city central affiliates as well as international unions. In general, each labor entity had to propose merger at their scheduled convention and receive authorization from the delegates, a time-consuming process. Most state central organizations had merged by the end of 1958.

8. Ibid., p. 37.

9. Ibid., pp. 25, 32. For a discussion of Indiana labor's divisiveness and its right-to-work defense, see chapter 6 of Melvin A. Kahn's *The Politics of American Labor: The Indiana Microcosm* (Carbondale, Ill.: Southern Illinois University Labor Institute, 1970).

10. Quoted in Dempsey, *The Operation of Right-to-Work Laws*, pp. 23–24; "Here's Way to Sound Laws," p. 42.

11. Minutes, Diary, 4 February 1957, Box 8, "February 1957, Diary, ACW," Whitman Files, Ann Whitman Diary Series, DDEL.

12. "Amendment to Civil Rights Bill Offered by Senator Eastland Provides Federal Guarantee of 'Right-to-Work'; Amendment Offered by Senator McClellan,"

and "Democrats and Republicans Vie for Credit for Opposing 'Right-to-Work' Rider," *New York Times*, 30 April 1957, p. 1, and 7 May 1957, p. 30, respectively.

13. Secretary of Labor, "Memorandum for the Honorable Sherman Adams," n.d. [1957–1958], Box 24, "Staff Memo #1," Gerald Morgan Papers, DDEL.

14. Memo, Millard Cass to the Secretary [of Labor], "Proposed Indiana 'Right-to-Work' Law," 5 March 1957, with attachments, Box 37, "Secretary's Personal File, 1957, Confidential Miscellaneous (2)"; Memo, Stuart Rothman to the Secretary of Labor, 20 January 1958, Box 181, "National Legislation 1958: Department of Labor Program"; both James P. Mitchell Papers, DDEL.

15. Senator Barry Goldwater, Oral History Interview, p. 71, DDEL; Charles J. Graham to Sherman Adams, 30 December 1957; Adams to Graham, 14 January 1958; both Box 970, "126K–1 (1)," WHCF, General File, DDEL.

16. "Minutes of the Meeting of the Industrial Union Department Executive Board, AFL-CIO," 20 February 1957, Box 328; Memo, Paul Sifton to Walter P. Reuther, 6 March 1957, "A.F. of L. Legislative Meeting on Taft-Hartley Amendments," Box 208; both UAW President's Office: Walter P. Reuther Files, WPRL; Sanford Cohen, "Operating Under Right-to-Work Laws," *Labor Law Journal* 9(1958):577; George E. Barrett to Paul R. Christopher, 23 Janaury 1958, Box 23, AFL-CIO Region 8 Collection, SLA. Some of the legal problems generated by right-to-work laws are discussed by H.S. Brown, Director of Education, Texas AFL-CIO, "Ten Years of Folly: Compulsory Open Shop in Texas," n.d. [1957], copy in Box 2, Charles Baker Collection, WPRL.

17. Senator Lyndon B. Johnson to Walter P. Reuther, 28 April 1958, Box 373, UAW President's Office: Walter P. Reuther Files, WPRL.

18. Donald Montgomery to Roy Reuther, 5 July 1955, Box 63, UAW Washington Office: Donald Montgomery Files, WPRL; Senator Lyndon Johnson to Walter P. Reuther, 7 April 1958, Box 373, UAW President's Office: Walter P. Reuther Files.

19. Memo, Joe Walsh, Assistant Director of Public Relations, UAW, to all UAW Officers, Regional Directors, and Department Heads, Re: National Right to Work Committee, 24 September 1957, Box 11, UAW Citizenship Department: Roy Reuther Files, WPRL.

20. Ira H. Latimer to James W. Fifield, Jr., 23 February 1958, Box 72; Latimer to L.A. Hooser, 14 March 1957, Box 59; W.T. Harrison to Latimer, 5 April 1957, Box 61; Organizational Memo, Illinois Right to Work Committee, "Joint Appeal," 2 May 1957, Box 54; Dorothy B. Davis to Latimer, 12 August 1957, Box 60; Latimer to Carl W. Reinig, 20 August 1957, Box 60; Memo, Latimer to Cola G. Parker, 25 August 1957, Box 58; Latimer to James R. Mills, 5 September 1957, Box 53; Illinois Right to Work Committee, "Checklist for Employer Facing Union Organization Drives," 1957, Box 57; Illinois Right to Work Committee "Statement of Income and Expense," 31 December 1957, Box 54; all in the Ira H. Latimer Collection, Chicago Historical Society, Chicago, Illinois.

21. Minutes, WPR Staff Meetings, 26 November, 16 December 1957, Box 11, UAW Citizenship Department: Roy Reuther Files, WPRL; Memo, Henry C. Fleisher to Members of the Committee on Public Relations, "Memorandum on AFL-CIO PR Program," 21 November 1957, Box 323, UAW President's Office: Walter P. Reuther Files, WPRL; AFL-CIO, *Proceedings*, 1959, p. 193. For the views of other industrial union leaders on right-to-work offensives, see AFL-CIO, *Proceedings*, 1957, vol. 1, pp. 412–415.

22. Memo, Confidential, George T. Guernsey to Walter P. Reuther, 12 January 1956, Box 319; Carl Winn to Richard T. Leonard, 16 May 1956, Box 334; Confidential Memorandum, J.K. [Joseph Keenan], n.d. [1956] and Memo, Anonymous, "Two Outstanding Problems in COPE," 8 May 1957; both Box 318; all UAW President's Office: Walter P. Reuther Files, WPRL.

23. John Edelman, "Report of the TWUA Washington Office," 8 June 1957 to 1 September 1957, and November 1958, Box 8; John Edelman to Al Whitehouse, 9 July 1958, "Legislative Operations"; Richard T. Leonard to Edelman, 23 May 1957; both Box 77, all John W. Edelman Collection, WPRL.

24. AFL-CIO, *Proceedings*, 1959, pp. 193–196; Statement of the AFL-CIO Executive Council on "So-Called 'Right-to-Work' Laws," 11 February 1958, Box 187, CIO Secretary-Treasurer's Office: George L-P Weaver Files, WPRL. For the AFL-CIO national office's initial anti-right-to-work activities in late 1957 and early 1958, see Memo, Henry C. Fleischer and Andrew J. Biemiller to President Meany, 27 November 1957, Box 33; Oliver W. Singleton to William F. Schnitzler, 24 January 1958, Box 81; Memo, Andrew J. Biemiller to President Meany, "Legislative Conference," 3 January 1958, Box 33; all AFL-CIO Legislative Department Files, GMMA.

25. AFL-CIO, *Proceedings*, 1959, pp. 193–196.

26. AFL-CIO, Industrial Union Department, *Proceedings of the 2nd Annual Industrial Relations Conference: "Union Shop and the Public Welfare,"* 17–18 May 1958, (hereafter IUD, "Union Shop"), pp. 12–18, copy in Box 25, John W. Edelman Collection, WPRL.

27. Ibid.

28. Ibid., p. 96.

29. Ibid., pp. 66–68.

30. Ibid.

31. Ibid. Paul Butler's personal proclivities and the complaints of Democratic liberals had led the DNC chairman to challenge the party's congressional leadership on policy formulation after the 1956 election. Through the instrumentality of the Democratic Advisory Council, Butler wanted a centralization of policy formulation. By having a structural apparatus to pronounce authoritative Democratic positions—ideally liberal—Butler envisioned a diminution of the freedom of congressional representatives to buck the party's ideological majority. Within two years his plan had caused an "open breach" between the liberal wing and the congressional leadership. See Foley, *The New Senate*, pp. 23–25.

32. James Carey to all IUD Affiliates, 4 August 1958, Box 330, UAW President's Office: Walter P. Reuther Files, WPRL.

33. Roy L. Reuther to Walter P. Reuther, "Urge Reevaluation of Labor's Campaign Against 'Right-to-Work,' " 8 August 1958, Box 11, UAW Citizenship Department: Roy Reuther Files, WPRL; Walter Reuther, "Memorandum Re: WPR's Meeting with George Meany," 5 August 1958, Box 310, UAW President's Office: Walter P. Reuther Files, WPRL.

34. Memo, Confidential, "Organizing Problems Facing the UAW: A Suggested Program," October 1958, Box 177B, UAW President's Office: Walter P. Reuther Files, WPRL.

35. AFL-CIO, Colorado Labor Council, *Proceedings of the 2nd Biennial Constitutional Convention*, 8 May 1958, pp. 47–52; AFL-CIO, Washington State Labor

Council, *Proceedings of the 1st Annual Convention*, 14–17 July 1958, *State Labor Proceedings*, microform, Center for Research Libraries.

36. Colorado Labor Council, *Proceedings*, p. 53–56; George A. Cavender to William F. Schnitzler, 17 February 1958, Box 81, AFL-CIO Legislative Department Files, GMMA.

37. Memo, [James McDevitt], "COPE Administrative Committee Meeting," 30 April 1958, Box 15, AFL-CIO President's Office, George Meany Files, GMMA.

38. "Foes of Work Law Went Democratic," *New York Times*, 9 November 1958, p. 72.

39. William Rosenthal, Chairman of State Central Democratic Party for Southern California, to Irwin DeShetler, 17 April 1957, Box 50; Minutes of General Board Meeting, California Industrial Union Council, Box 60; both Irwin L. DeShetler Collection, WPRL; Philip Taft, *Labor Politics American Style*, pp. 240–242.

40. "Summary of Recommendations Made at State CIO Education Committee Meeting Held at the Statler Hotel, August 14, 1957," Box 60; Labor's League for Political Education, "1958 Pre-Primary Convention California Labor League for Political Education," Box 76; both Irwin L. DeShetler Collection, WPRL; "Right-to-Work Seen as Main Election Issue, Knowland-Knight Gubernatorial Campaign, California," *New York Times*, 22 September 1957, p. 52.

41. Lawrence E. Davies, "Knowland Stand on Labor Echoing," *New York Times*, 29 December 1957, p. 37; Irwin DeShetler to Harry Clark, 29 April 1958, Box 50, Irwin L. DeShetler Collection, WPRL.

42. Minutes, CIO COPE Executive Council Meeting, Alexandria Hotel, Los Angeles, 20 February 1958, Box 60, Irwin L. DeShetler Collection, WPRL. Because of craft-industrial jurisdictional rivalries, California's state federation and industrial union council did not merge until December 1958. See Taft, *Labor Politics American Style*, p. 245.

43. Taft, *Labor Politics American Style*, pp. 243–244.

44. Minutes, General Board, California CIO COPE, Fresno, California, 17–18 April 1958, Box 61; California LLPE, *Proceedings and Secretary Treasurer's Report: 1958 Pre-Primary Convention*, San Francisco, 14 April 1958, Box 76; both Irwin L. DeShetler Collection, WPRL.

45. Minutes, General Board, California CIO COPE, 8 September 1958; "Analysis of 'Right-To-Wreck' Initiative"; both Box 60, Irwin L. DeShetler Collection, WPRL.

46. Dwight D. Eisenhower to Charles S. Jones, Personal and Confidential, 22 August 1958, Box 35, Whitman Files, DDE Diaries Series, DDEL.

47. Dwight D. Eisenhower to William F. Knowland, 23 September 1958; Eisenhower to Vice-President Nixon, 29 September 1958; both Box 36, Whitman Files, DDE Diaries Series, DDEL.

48. Memo, John Despol, COPE, to all Directors and Staff, "Re: Last Available Election Poll," 21 October 1958, Irwin L. DeShetler Collection, WPRL; William Knowland Oral History, pp. 96–97, DDEL.

49. The Ohio right-to-work campaign of 1958 started with the support of important establishment leaders of the Ohio business community who sought to commit Ohio Republicans to the cause. Senator John Bricker (R-OH) and Ray Bliss, chairman of the Ohio state Republican party, appeared at the first strategy meeting and strongly advised Ohio business against promoting a controversial ballot on right to work. Reportedly, the business supporters of the idea denounced the Republican politicians'

lack of courage in no uncertain terms. See John Fenton, "The Right-To-Work Vote in Ohio," *Midwest Journal of Political Science* 3(1959):241–253. Also see Ed Heinke, "Right-to-Work Law Strategy Plotted by Four-Man Team," [*Cleveland Press?*], clipping in Box 1, Charles Baker Collection, WPRL, and Glenn W. Miller and Stephen B. Ware, "Organized Labor in the Political Process: A Case Study of the Right-to-Work Campaign in Ohio," *Labor History* 4(Winter 1963):51–67.

50. Michael J. Lyden, "Ohio Labor Fights Back," clipping in Box 1, National Council for Industrial Peace, "Ready Reference Facts on the 'Right-to-Work' Issue," n.d., attached to Robert G. Nixon, NCIP Director, to Walt Davis, 28 August 1958, Box 3; both in Charles Baker Collection, WPRL.

51. Memo, Burr Agency to UOLO, "Campaign Report," 18 November 1958; Memo, [Walt Davis?], "Miracle? The Victory Over the RTW Proposal in Ohio," n.d. [November 1958]; both Box 4, Sam Pollock Collection, WPRL; Memo, Charles Baker, "Campaign Summary," n.d. [November 1958], Box 4, Charles Baker Collection, WPRL.

52. Confidential Memo, Burr Agency to Walt Davis, "Tactics and Strategy," 1 August 1958, Box 3, Charles Baker Collection, WPRL.

53. Burr Agency to Walt Davis, "Tactics and Strategy," 1 August 1958, Box 3; Charles Baker, "Thinking File," and "Proposed Public Relations Aims and Strategy," Box 4, Charles Baker Collection, WPRL.

54. Charles R. Hook to James P. Mitchell, 28 October 1958, Box 970, 126-K-1, WHCF, General File, DDEL. Hook assailed Mitchell for speaking out against right-to-work laws in Ohio. The industrialist informed Mitchell that he constantly had to explain to Republican supporters of the initiative that the secretary's statements were private expositions and not official administration policy. Moreover, he charged, Mitchell's actions were hurting "Governor O'Neill and the other [Republican] candidates who have courageously expressed their opposition to compulsory unionism."

55. [Walt Davis?], Memo, "Miracle? The Victory Over the RTW Proposal in Ohio," n.d. [November 1958]; Memo, Burr Agency to UOLO, "Campaign Report," 18 November 1958; both Box 4, Sam Pollock Collection, WPRL; UOLO, "Steering Committee Minutes," 11 August 1958, Box 4; Charles Baker to Frank Winn, 25 September 1958, Box 1; Herman[?] to Elmer Cope, Ohio AFL-CIO Secretary-Treasurer, [November 1958], Roll 39, Elmer F. Cope Papers, microfilm edition, Ohio Historical Society, Columbus, Ohio. Burr Agency to Walt Davis, 13 August 1958, "Telephone Machine," Box 3; Charles Baker to W. J. Bassett, 16 October 1958, Box 1; all Charles Baker Collection, WPRL.

56. Kansas State Federation of Labor, *Proceedings of the 46th Annual Convention*, 23–25 May 1957, pp. 57–58, *State Labor Proceedings*, microform, Center for Research Libraries; Reed Larson, "How Right to Work Was Adopted in Kansas," National Right to Work Committee Special Report, January 1959. See also Leo Sandon, Jr., "When Kansas Said Yes to 'Right-to-Work,'" *Midwest Quarterly* 4(April 1963):269–281.

57. Larson, "How Right to Work Was Adopted in Kansas."

58. Russell Letner to Walter P. Reuther, 14 February 1958, Box 222, UAW President's Office: Walter P. Reuther Files, WPRL. Of course, this was almost the same context as in Idaho, but there labor had the support of the state's most influential paper and faced a less capable right-to-work opponent.

59. Larson, "How Right to Work Was Adopted in Kansas." Indeed, all state-level grass roots partisans of right to work generally agreed with this view. At a practicum co-sponsored by the U.S. Chamber of Commerce and the Missouri Chamber, held in St. Louis on June 3, 1958, right-to-work strategists from across the nation traded ideas on how to place such legislation on their state statute books as well as how to protect the laws from repeal once passed. Most activists echoed Larson's tactical views on the importance of business activism and nominal non-partisanism. See Memo, Confidential, "Report of Ira H. Latimer, Executive Vice-Chairman, to the Illinois Right to Work Committee, on June 3, 1958 'Right to Work Workshop,' " St. Louis, Missouri, June 1958, Box 50, Ira H. Latimer Collection, Chicago Historical Society, Chicago, Illinois.

60. Larson, "How Right to Work Was Adopted in Kansas."

61. Larson, "How Right to Work Was Adopted in Kansas"; AFL-CIO, Kansas State Federation of Labor, *Proceedings of Special Convention*, 13–14 December 1958, pp. 14–17, *State Labor Proceedings*, microform, Center for Research Libraries.

62. "Foes of Work Law Went Democratic," *New York Times*, 9 November 1958, p. 72. For a review of the 1958 elections in these states see Houston I. Flournoy, "The 1958 Knowland Campaign in California—Design for Defeat," *Western Political Quarterly* 12 (June 1959): 571–572; Curtis Martin, "The 1958 Election in Colorado," *Western Political Quarterly* 12 (March 1959):301–308; Boyd A. Martin, "The 1958 Elections in Idaho," *Western Political Quarterly* 12 (March 1959):339–342; Hugh Bone, "The 1958 Election in Washington," *Western Political Quarterly* 12 (March 1959):355–362; Sandon, "When Kansas Said Yes to 'Right-to-Work' "; and Fenton, "The Right-To-Work Vote in Ohio."

63. Taft, *Labor Politics American Style*, p. 244; Irwin DeShetler to Charles Heymans, 10 November 1958, Box 51, Irwin L. DeShetler Collection, WPRL.

64. Fenton, "The Right-to-Work Vote in Ohio," pp. 241–253; Miller and Ware, "Organized Labor in the Political Process," pp. 60–63; Memo, Philip M. Weightman to James L. McDevitt, 1 December 1958, "Report on Ohio Campaign Against 'Right-To-Work,' " 110–9–1–8, Texas AFL-CIO Collection, TLA; Walt Davis to Charles R. Baker, 20 November 1958, Box 1; Memo, Campaign Summary, Box 4; both Charles Baker Collection, WPRL; [Walt Davis] Memo, "Miracle? The Victory Over the RTW Proposal in Ohio."

65. Foley, *The New Senate*, pp. 25–26; "Foes of Work Law Went Democratic"; Memo, Weightman to McDevitt, 1 December 1958; Memo, James L. McDevitt, National Director, COPE, to AFL-CIO Executive Council, "1958 Congressional Elections," 6 November 1958, Box 27, AFL-CIO President's Office: George Meany Files, GMMA; W.A. Smallwood to All District Directors, CWA, 18 November 1958, Box 27, UAW Citizenship Department: Roy Reuther Files, WPRL.

66. Robert Lenaghen, President, Idaho State Federation of Labor, to George Meany, 6 November 1958, Box 38, AFL-CIO President's Office: George Meany Files, GMMA. Furthermore, in thanking Meany for the assistance the Idaho organization received in its campaign from special State Legislation Representative Carl McPeak, Lenaghen strongly recommended that the national office of the AFL-CIO establish a permanent department on state legislation to prepare for future battles. For a review of national AFL-CIO activities in the 1958 right-to-work elections, see AFL-CIO, *Proceedings*, 1959, pp. 193–200; AFL-CIO Education De-

partment, "Educate on 'Right-to-Work,' " *Education News and Views*, n.d. [1958], copy in Box 2, Charles Baker Collection, WPRL; General Correspondence,Box 50; Memo, William Schnitzler, "Debater's Kit on 'Right-to-Work' Laws," 20 September 1957, Box 65; both Irwin L. DeShetler Collection, WPRL.

67. Walter P. Reuther to Eleanor Roosevelt and Herbert Lehman, 21 January 1959, Box 560, UAW President's Office: Walter P. Reuther Files, WPRL. There was some legitimacy to Reuther's beliefs about the driving force behind right to work, as a review of Ira H. Latimer's Illinois Right to Work Committee papers suggest. For example, Latimer wrote on 25 June 1958: "The economic *base* of compulsory unionism is being used to grab political power to [*sic*] used to command control over the nation's economy." See Ira H. Latimer to Francis J. Dingel, 25 June 1958, Box 54, Ira H. Latimer Collection, Chicago Historical Society, Chicago, Illinois.

5

Campaign Promises

In particular, we call for the repeal of Section 14(b), the section of the Taft-Hartley Act that permits the infamous "right-to-work" laws to override the public policy of the nation on the union shop. The voters' repudiation of these laws is a clear mandate to the Congress to end this flank attack on organized labor.

—Statement by the AFL-CIO Executive Council on *Labor Legislation*, November 1958[1]

Between 1958 and 1963 AFL-CIO leaders experienced a political paradox regarding the union security controversy. COPE could achieve maximum electoral mobilization of the membership, as in 1958, only when direct threats, usually in the form of right-to-work initiatives, aroused state and local leaders and rank-and-file workers. On the other hand, AFL-CIO functionaries found it was precisely in the area of labor law reform, as manifested particularly in the effort to secure repeal of section 14(b) of the Taft-Hartley Act, that the congressional Democratic party proved most reluctant to follow labor's offensive priorities. In 1959, for example, faced with a public debate that continued to highlight alleged labor corruption, labor's legislative strategists soon found their agenda sidetracked and their relationship with key liberal supporters disrupted. At the state level, labor found the energy to launch repeal drives in Utah and Iowa, drawing a lukewarm Democratic response and strong Republican opposition. In New Mexico as well, state level Democrats provided a cool reception to labor's stance on a right-to-work proposal. Only in the Vermont and Wyoming legislatures did organized labor receive cohesive Democratic support; and these votes were in defense of the non-right-to-work status quo, with unionists winning in Vermont and losing in Wyoming. In fact, by 1963 these events, combined with their inability to induce sufficient numbers of congressional Democrats to support section 14(b) repeal, caused top level federation policy makers to feel their dashed expectations in full force, resulting in apathy and despair in AFL-CIO legislative planning on labor law reform.

Thus, from the highpoint of labor's victories in 1958 to the death of John F. Kennedy in 1963, AFL-CIO political operatives struggled unsuccessfully to find the formula that could transform electoral activity into labor law reform. Indeed, the passage of the Landrum-Griffin Act in 1959 was a stinging rebuke to the labor movement from the congressional Democratic party and a deeply disappointing denouement to its 1958 victories. Renewed efforts to shift the center of congressional debate to legal injustices directed at labor foundered first on the disruption in the labor-liberal alliance that stemmed from the Landrum-Griffin debates and then on the mathematical realities of the slim Democratic majorities in the early 1960s. Those efforts also reinforced the lesson that even with labor's increased electoral activity, at that point it simply did not command sufficiently widespread support in the party to attain its offensive objectives on labor law revision, especially in view of overwhelming Republican hostility. The narrowness of JFK's 1960 presidential victory and the small Democratic majorities that year and again in 1962 only drove home the point. Even labor's successes, as ex-emplified by its successful courtship of black voters in the 1958 right-to-work campaigns and afterward, pointed to the same conclusion: labor could be most successful electorally when it emphasized the threats to basic trade union rights; and legislatively (regarding its offensive goals) when it func-tioned as a broad, public-interest force. Therefore, even in these nominally productive years, repeal of section 14(b) receded into the background.

THE RESULTS OF THE 1958 ELECTIONS

After the 1958 elections, however, trade unionists were optimistic about section 14(b) repeal. The mobilization of all levels of organized labor in the six states holding right-to-work elections, plus the possibility of an assault in many others, had thrust the controversy into national prominence. This gave labor leaders the tool they needed to rally the rank and file to political activism, even in states not under direct attack. With their union security clauses threatened, state and local unionists clearly perceived the necessity of working hard to get members to register and vote. And as COPE func-tionaries hoped, Democrats, many of them liberals, proved to be the main beneficiaries of an increased working-class vote.

For example, in a confidential memo to President Eisenhower, Republican National Committee chairman Meade Alcorn outlined "the factors which brought defeat to so many of our candidates at national, state and local levels." In the 1956 elections, Alcorn wrote in his December 1958 report, "the Republican Party had cracked the labor vote wide open, winning from one-third to one-half of it in numerous Northern and Western industrial

Centers." That was before the right-to-work campaigns reversed the trend. Allies of the party, Alcorn asserted, pushed "this emotion-packed issue onto the ballot in several states and to the forefront of debate in the legislatures of many others." While he could not fault right-to-work supporters for their intentions, these people were by and large Republican. This fact gave the opposition the chance to brand the party as the originator and/or chief promoter of the measures, even though many prominent Republicans did not back such laws and many Democrats did. "The resources of labor were mobilized as never before in a political campaign. It was a double-barreled onslaught," Alcorn informed the president, "with one barrel trained on right-to-work and the other on Republican candidates. In both instances the aim was remarkably good." The chairman's considered opinion was that the party "lost scores" of races at every level "largely on the right-to-work issue." Whatever arguments there were for such laws, he noted, "a majority of voters said emphatically that they don't want" them. Moreover, Alcorn implied that in the future Republican candidates should be cognizant of the danger, for in the 1958 elections "the political careers of some of the nation's ablest public servants were shattered."[2]

Predictably, the Democrats were only too happy to benefit from the Republicans' mistakes. At the national level, Democratic control of the Senate increased by 28 votes, a gain of 16 for the majority with a loss of 12 for the Republicans, the largest gain/loss ratio of the century. In addition, the Democratic majority in the House of Representatives went from a 232 to 199 margin in 1957 to a 280 to 152 spread in 1959. More importantly, the party's composition changed, particularly in the Senate. The Eighty-sixth Congress would contain a much larger number of liberal-minded Democrats. For the first time the Senate's progressive wing had numerical superiority, 41 to 24, over its conservative counterpart.[3]

Considering such impressive gains, organized labor and the Democrats had reason to rejoice. And the Republicans, as one reporter observed, "had reason to be bitter about what . . . businessmen and non-union employers who backed the 'right-to-work' had foisted upon them." According to one such businessman, if they could sell "anything from soap to steel," they could surely sell the average worker on the importance of "the right to work when he pleases, where he pleases, for himself or whoever wants to hire him." Much to the chagrin of right-to-work advocates, that viewpoint received no support from the election returns. As John Edelman informed TWUA officers early in 1959, the 1958 elections "demonstrated, especially in the States where 'right-to-work' laws were on the ballot, that the rank and file could be roused" to support the leadership on this type of issue. And the Republican politicians who had believed right-to-work proponents stood corrected. President Eisenhower, for instance, wrote that in a post-election conversation with William Knowland, the former senator "talked much more objectively and sensibly after his defeat than he did before."

Indeed, the right-to-work referendums had been such a salient part of the 1958 elections that AFL-CIO leaders read the returns as signaling widespread voter support for national-level reform.[4]

Thus, at a meeting of the AFL-CIO's Industrial Union Department in December 1958, federation officers contemplated future action. General Counsel Arthur Goldberg accurately pointed out that the elections had produced only a defensive victory. As he told the assembled officers, fighting right to work at the state level was "a negative battle." "You will be fighting that battle for many years to come as the ebb and flow of political life takes place," he argued, "unless ... we re-establish the principle that federal legislation should control labor regulations." The best way to ensure the predominance of federal legislation over union security was to repeal section 14(b). Organized labor had tried this before as part of a broader Taft-Hartley reform package in 1953, and the resulting controversy had proved to be one of the major reasons the amendment drive stalled. But perhaps now, with labor unified and with the 1958 right-to-work votes to point to, a narrower, more concentrated approach would work. And craft union officers strongly seconded such a strategy. "We must get enough votes, somewhere, somehow, to take 14(b) out of Taft-Hartley," IBEW secretary Joseph Keenan had told the Colorado Labor Council in May 1958. "If we can take 14(b) out of Taft-Hartley, we have pretty much taken a great portion of the load off of us."[5]

AFL-CIO leaders labored under no illusions, however. The 1958 defeats of right-to-work referendums had not solved organized labor's problems in the area of union security. As continuing right-to-work agitation in New Mexico, Vermont, and elsewhere in early 1959 proved, anti–union security groups had no intention of going out of business. Unless labor could repeal section 14(b), trade unionists would face constant and expensive battles in the political arena. Even worse, some labor analysts believed that campaigns for right-to-work laws created an anti-labor atmosphere, making it much harder to organize in a state that had undergone such a contest. As more economic resources poured into the South and the Plains states, the inability of labor to organize in these new areas would lead to a decline in labor's overall power. Hence, some labor officials came to view the fight against right to work as a fight to secure labor's post-depression status in American society.[6]

EFFECT OF LANDRUM-GRIFFIN ON THE LABOR-DEMOCRATIC ALLIANCE

Therefore, the 1958 right-to-work campaigns, while indeed having national significance, only settled the issue in those states that had had elections. As the U.S. Chamber of Commerce's journal *Nation's Business* editorialized, in a way the elections "sharpened, rather than blunted, the controversy. Both sides are analyzing and trying to benefit from the results in planning their future course and strategy." To labor, the outcome indicated that it was time to launch an offensive attack at the national level. And the coming session of Congress would be a test of the loyalty of the lawmakers elected or re-elected by the large turnout of union voters in 1958.[7]

As always, however, organized labor faced the challenge of how to turn campaign promises into reality. After the glow of victory faded, labor's legislative leaders assessed their chances for repeal in a somewhat harsher light. Immediately following the opening of the first session of Congress, it became apparent that public concern over union corruption would control the legislative agenda on labor law matters. In the preceding Congress, the AFL-CIO responded to issues raised by the McClellan investigations by pushing the Kennedy-Ives bill, a moderate regulatory proposal aimed at controlling alleged union dishonesty and undemocratic practices. Federation strategists quickly realized that they would have to dispose of this issue before they took up section 14(b) repeal.

In this climate of opinion, though, there was little likelihood that many congressional Democrats would push for union security reform. Clearly, many legislators increasingly perceived that a vote to repeal section 14(b) would be popularly regarded as a vote for increasing the power of union officials. And most of the public, as manifested by the continuing concern over guaranteeing union members' democratic protections, seemed to believe that labor leaders had too much of that already. Consequently, the crisis over union regulatory legislation not only temporarily sidetracked the section 14(b) repeal drive, but over the next two years it also eroded whatever political capital labor had on deposit with the Democrats as a result of the 1958 elections.

The Industrial Union Department's chief lobbyist, Robert Oliver, made much of this clear to Walter Reuther in a December 1958 memo. The strong possibility of congressional legislation dealing with labor corruption and union electoral practices, Oliver noted, had led to difficulty in composing a program for labor law revision. Currently, the AFL-CIO's legislative leaders were discussing three alternatives. They could try to keep the corruption and Taft-Hartley amendment separate; they could include major amendments to Taft-Hartley, such as section 14(b) repeal, in the same bill dealing with corruption; or they could simply place non-controversial amendments to Taft-Hartley in the corruption bill. President Meany favored the latter approach, as did Oliver, for a House straw-vote analysis revealed "a substantial majority" of legislators, Democratic and Republican, would not back a repeal effort. Of the chamber's Democrats, 106 would vote against labor, 96 of them from the South. Moreover, the federation "would be lucky to get" 10 of the 153 Republicans to vote repeal, and thus the probable vote on removing section 14(b) would end up 250 for to 186 against.[8]

The AFL-CIO's officers still hoped, however, that if the corruption bill, or at least the version they supported, could be taken care of quickly, there might be a chance for favorable Taft-Hartley reform later in the session. In fact, a special subcommittee of the AFL-CIO executive council adopted such a program including, according to Legislative Director Andrew Biemiller, repeal of section 14(b). But by May 1959, the wide range of internal regulation proposals started to tear at labor unity. The building trades representatives insisted on taking up section 14(b) immediately, and other unions wanted a large-scale review of Taft-Hartley and its administration by the NLRB. As UAW lobbyists Victor Reuther and Paul Sifton wrote to Walter Reuther, there were "heavy cross currents" playing within the AFL-CIO. Meany wanted a reform bill that was not punitive, but felt the House had no liberal Republicans to which labor could pitch its arguments, and southern Democrats would not follow the party line on labor legislation. In the future, Biemiller told Reuther and Sifton, organized labor would "have to rely more and more on young Democratic leadership" if it wanted to get anything done.[9]

What did get done by the end of the first session exasperated George Meany. Over the course of the summer, the Democrats' desire to appear "responsible" to the public began to dissipate the AFL-CIO's influence. There were several bills regulating the internal affairs of unions being considered by Congress; some, proposed by conservatives such as Philip Landrum (D-GA) and Robert Griffin (R-MI), were stringent; others, submitted by labor's Democratic allies, were more moderate. In one way or another, though, all the bills dealt with union fiscal affairs and members' electoral rights within the union. Fearing the popularity of harsh regulations, labor lobbyists initially attempted to prevent any regulatory bills from coming to the floor, a strategy quickly undermined by moderate and non-labor liberal elements in the Democratic party. At one crucial point, for instance, a small group of non-labor-oriented liberals on the House Labor Committee refused to go along with labor's attempt to bottle up all proposed regulations. Increasingly, the Democratic politicians' reading of public sentiment indicated that an overly pro-labor position would not benefit their political fortunes.

The bill finally passed by Congress—as the Landrum-Griffin Act—did so over the federation's strong objections and incorporated a union member bill of rights, financial reporting regulations for labor organizations, and several minor amendments to Taft-Hartley. What had appeared as a great election victory for labor in 1958 now seemed more like a resounding defeat. For all of its heralded political clout, organized labor could not even get the type of reform bill it wanted, much less launch a 14(b) repeal drive.

Some noteworthy trade unionists bitterly denounced the perfidy of the liberal Democrats and explicitly charged AFL-CIO complicity. The secretary-treasurer of the Machinists, for example, charged that except for 2 liberal senators and 52 liberal congressmen, who stood steadfast, many "of the phony liberals, including numerous ones aspiring to become candidates for the presidency," betrayed labor. In a blistering letter, he bitterly assailed Biemiller's decision to "release" some politicians from commitments to vote with labor on the final ballot on the bill. Other union officials blamed the desire of every trade union to protect its own turf for having hampered effective AFL-CIO leadership. Robert Oliver, the IUD lobbyist, wrote George Meany that disunity had led to the failure to place concentrated rank-and-file pressure on legislators—in sharp contrast to what the business lobby accomplished. "The employer efforts on the Landrum-Griffin bill," he informed the federation president in early 1960, "resulted in the most effective mobilization of 'Main Street, America' that I have ever seen." Faced with that kind of outcry, no wonder Democrats went with the flow of public opinion. Oliver advised Meany to be blunt and tell international union officers to stop paying lip service and support the federation's legislative program.[10]

But what else had gone wrong? AFL-CIO leaders discussed just that question at the federation's convention in late 1959. Specifically, the federation's officers examined the value of COPE in light of the legislative results of 1959. All delegates agreed that starting out the year contemplating section 14(b) repeal and finishing it saddled with a major piece of unwanted legislation was not an impressive accomplishment. In the official view of AFL-CIO political analysts (meant for general comsumption, of course), the votes on Landrum-Griffin indicated that in truth labor's liberal friends had not betrayed the movement. Of the 95 Democrats who voted against the labor position, 92 came from the South or the Plains states. There were only 3 Democratic legislators out of 174 from the North and West who cast their votes for the new labor law. Perhaps more importantly, in 1958 COPE endorsed 181 federal lawmakers, and only 16 went against the federation; and of those, 14 were from conservative areas. And of the 52 first-term congressmembers endorsed by the AFL-CIO's political arm, a mere 4 voted for Landrum-Griffin. All in all, federation leaders concluded that organized labor was electing the right type of people but just not enough of them.[11]

No matter how the AFL-CIO Legislative Department and COPE manipulated the figures, there could be no doubt that labor experienced Democratic defection during the Landrum-Griffin episode. While this defection was not as devastating as it had been during the passage of Taft-Hartley, the Rice Index of Cohesion scores were lower than in both the drive to repeal Taft-Hartley in 1949 and to amend the union shop provisions of the Railway Labor Act in 1951. Table 5.1 indicates that, overall, Democrats

5.1

Rice Index of Cohesion of Congressional Parties, on the Landrum-Griffin Act, 1959

LEGISLATION	AGAINST LABOR	FOR LABOR	TOTAL	PERCENT AGAINST	PERCENT FOR	RICE INDEX
Landrum-Griffin Act 1959						
House						
D	95	184	279	34	66	-32
R	134	17	151	89	11	77
Senate						
D	15	44	59	25	75	-49
R	32	2	34	94	6	88
Both Chambers						
D	110	228	338	33	67	-35
R	166	19	185	90	10	79
Total	276	247	523	53	47	6

Source: Congressional Quarterly, <u>Congress and the Nation, 1945-1964,</u>
          (Washington, DC: Congressional Quarterly Service, 1965).
Index: +100(Totally Cohesive Against Labor)
          -100(Totally Cohesive in Favor of Labor)
          Rice Index Rounded to Nearest Integer.

in Congress scored a relatively weak pro-labor −35 Rice Index in 1959. In 1949 and 1951 the comparative index for Democrats was −45 (Table 2.5) and −58 (Table 3.1), respectively.

The official AFL-CIO analysis, though, proved more comforting to federation officials, for it implied that problems surrounding thorny labor law issues could only be solved by sufficient electoral activism—primarily at the local level. Federation leaders could therefore logically rededicate themselves to increasing the Democrats' margin in the next election even as they struggled to bring the subject of repeal to the forefront of the Democratic agenda. However, labor's political strategists had ignored how the battle over union regulatory legislation had fractured party support for national union security reform.

With liberal Democrats from industrialized areas, such as Senators Hubert Humphrey of Minnesota and Pat McNamara of Michigan, labor lobbyists usually had no problem. These legislators had a close relationship with labor and depended on its political support for reelection. In fact, Senator McNamara, a former union official, had taken the lead in introducing section 14(b) repeal bills since he first won office in 1954—and he never hesitated to publicly defend labor's need for union security. For example, a Michigan right-to-work supporter criticized the senator's stand in September 1957. Right-to-work advocates, this businessman argued, were "in favor of GOOD unions." They saw no reason, however, for allowing employers and unions to negotiate union security clauses that would force employees to pay "tribute" to labor leaders in the form of union dues. The senator responded that he was glad his correspondent did not want to destroy unions and favored "good" ones. "However," he replied tongue in cheek, "I am afraid that others who might say they are in favor of GOOD unions only mean, to paraphrase an old frontier saying, that the only good union is a dead union."[12]

Not all liberals would so quickly come to the movement's defense on union security. In particular, if a liberal hailed from a right-to-work state, local supporters of the law could make the legislator pay a personal political cost for opposing the concept. Arizona Congressman Morris Udall's situation typified the problems facing such liberal Democrats throughout the 1950s. In those years the subject of union security "was a crucial political issue in most statewide and congressional elections in Arizona," Udall later recalled. The Arizona press and the Republican party, fearing repeal of the state law, constantly "belabor[ed] Democratic candidates . . . on this issue in light of the repeated approval of the Right to Work principle by Arizona voters." Consequently, if Democrats failed to support repeal of either the state law or section 14(b), they risked losing labor backing; if they adopted labor's position, they handed the opposition a "damaging" electoral issue. "This posed a painful dilemma for most major Democratic candidates," Udall concluded.[13]

Indeed, the events of 1959 had revealed the limited character of the Democrats' commitment to labor law reform. Organized labor and the party could be allies in this area only insofar as labor's objectives imposed little political cost. John F. Kennedy's handling of section 14(b) repeal during his campaign for the presidency only further emphasized this point.

Throughout the presidential campaign of 1960, Senator Kennedy gave rhetorical support to section 14(b) repeal, though clearly he regarded his words as a campaign necessity and not an ironclad promise. As was the case in his leading role during the Landrum-Griffin debates, his affirmation of labor's position on union security had much more to do with his presidential aspirations than any other factor. This made it easier for him to abandon his support in short order if necessary.

For example, when powerful conservative Democrats threatened public opposition to his candidacy if he pushed repeal, Kennedy quickly backtracked. At the party's convention, Democratic Senators James O. Eastland (MS) and Harry F. Byrd (VA) strongly objected to the party's section 14(b) repeal plank. Shortly afterward, in August 1960, Byrd made certain that both Kennedy and Lyndon Johnson, the vice-presidential candidate, knew that trouble lurked ahead if they meant to pursue the party's promise to organized labor. Since carrying the South was perceived as crucial to any Democrat's hopes for election, the nominees evidently believed they could not afford influential southern Democrats' active opposition. Therefore, according to the *New York Times*, Kennedy and Johnson told Byrd that if elected they would not push for repeal.[14]

Furthermore, acrimony stemming from Landrum-Griffin harmed the AFL-CIO's working relationship with liberals on the House Labor Committee. Several liberals refused to go along with the federation's attempt to stall regulatory legislation, and organized labor applied heavy pressure against these defectors. As a consequence, the legislators became resentful, and by the election of 1960 federation lobbyists had little influence within the committee. According to UAW lobbyists Paul Sifton and Ralph Show- alter, there was "bad blood" between important liberals on the committee and the federation. This made it "at best awkward and perhaps impossible for AFL-CIO interest[s] to be taken into account." The UAW chief could more effectively "represent the views of the labor movement" to the com- mittee members. "If the matter is left to other labor people," they wrote, organized labor's views "will never be given proper audience."[15]

Sifton and Showalter's memorandum pointed out a source of growing difficulty between organized labor and non-labor progressives. By the early 1960s, many middle-class liberals felt that the labor movement had little reason to be regarded as a force for beneficial social reform. As Jacob Clayman, adminstrative director of the IUD, wrote to Walter Reuther, "with the passing of every new day" liberals seemed to believe that labor took "on more and more of the appearance and habits of its business counter- parts." Therefore, when labor lobbyists pressured liberal congress members on strictly trade union issues, like right to work, they often found goodwill and a cooperative attitude in short supply.[16]

A tremendous Democratic victory in 1960 might have mitigated these problems, but the narrow Democratic margin only sharpened them. Al- though Kennedy's election owed much to the voter registration stimulated by COPE, Democratic congressional representation slipped. The Senate stayed the same, but the House margin declined by 43 members for the Eighty-seventh Congress. This made the ostensibly liberal Kennedy admin- istration even more dependent on the party's conservative wing for enact- ment of its own legislative program. And with the exception of civil rights legislation, nothing would have been more divisive to the party than an offensive against section 14(b).[17]

In order to secure repeal, then, organized labor found that even with a Democratic president it would have to mobilize liberal forces without the help of the White House. Through 1961 the AFL-CIO made halfhearted moves toward labor law revision. Given the state of organized labor's re- lationship to the political structure, its operatives made little progress.

In fact, labor's influence was so anemic that in March 1961 UAW lobbyist Ralph Showalter went so far as to suggest to his strongly partisan principals the need to cultivate stronger ties with liberal Republicans. In a report to UAW leaders, he argued that the labor movement could do more to try to understand the needs of liberals in the opposition party. In any event, he noted, if organized labor wanted its program to get off the ground, it simply needed the votes. "I think labor lobbyists should be instructed to discretely study the possibilities for votes among the liberal Republicans and as discretely and precisely [*sic*] plan how to corral them," Showalter wrote. "This requires top direction of our legislative forces and soon."[18]

Even with that top direction it would have been difficult to bring section 14(b) repeal to the forefront of public discussion. For in addition to an unfavorable voting balance, the differences with non-labor-oriented Democrats, and the lack of influence on liberal Republicans, AFL-CIO political strategists seemed confused, and at times apathetic, about their chances to secure any type of labor law reform. While liberal Democrats did not relish putting themselves on the line for section 14(b) repeal, they did not object to cooperating on less visible issues. For example, in the spring of 1961 Congressman Roman Pucinski (D) of Illinois agreed to chair an oversight committee investigating the administration of the National Labor Relations Act by the NLRB. Many smaller unions, such as the Textile Workers, had found the conservative "Eisenhower" board's interpretations of Taft-Hartley slanted toward management, and for years had lobbied hard for just such an inquiry. Once Pucinski's subcommittee began the investigation, however, it became apparent that the AFL-CIO's uninterest had led to a "woeful lack of preparation" on the part of the labor movement. According to IUD attorney David Feller, only the Textile Workers had a complete case for presentation and that was not enough to carry a full-scale investigation. Moreover, Feller informed IUD president Walter Reuther, "an investigation of the Board at this time, conducted in a cursory manner in which it is apparent this investigation will be conducted, is not a desirable thing." If union officers did not have enough facts to back up their charges, it would look as though labor leaders had been exaggerating their complaints against the board.[19]

Both Showalter's concern for cultivating liberal Republicans and federation uninterest in the NLRB hearings indicated the troubled state of the AFL-CIO's legislative program on trade union issues. Clearly, in early 1961, the federation was drifting on the legislative front. The most desired objective, repeal of section 14(b), was no longer a possibility. The experience since 1958 suggested that even when the more progressive brand of Democrat won in considerable numbers, conservatives retained enough obstructive power—through public relations onslaughts as in the McClellan investigations, or through skilled parliamentary maneuvering—to defeat labor's legislative offensives. Once again, organized labor's only workable answer to the stalemate was to reintensify its electoral activities in the hope of winning an overwhelming victory that would crush the opposition once and for all. But now, though, virtually all top AFL-CIO leaders began to realize that if labor sincerely wanted to liberalize American politics and secure favorable union security reform, labor needed help in breaking the back of conservatives' power. With the opposition thus weakened, COPE-endorsed Democrats would surely commit to and advance labor's agenda on labor law matters.

COPE AND COALITION BUILDING

One of the main reasons for this decision stemmed from the problems the federation experienced in trying to politically activate international and local labor leaders. At this level, union officials seemed interested in politics only when confronted with an immediate threat to trade union rights. Otherwise, COPE had trouble generating sustained commitment. The federation's political strategists constantly tried to relate the two, but unless the challenge was glaringly apparent they had little success.

For instance, in June 1960, state legislation representative Carl McPeak warned the officers of all state organizations to be on guard against complacency. The electoral success of 1958 had led to the "general feeling in many segments of the labor movement that the 'right-to-work' issue is a dead one. Unfortunately," he pointed out, "this is not true." The National Right to Work Committee, the U.S. Chamber of Commerce, and the Farm Bureau Federation were still active in promoting anti–union security legislation in many states. The movement's newest trick was to agitate for constitutional amendments to buttress state statutory legislation, thus making it harder for labor to win repeal. "You can see they have not slackened their pace," McPeak informed unionists, "they have just changed their tactics."[20]

In addition, in order to make the most out of local labor leaders' anti-right-to-work sentiment, the AFL-CIO's top officers chose to amplify partisan themes. In mid–1960, the Beirne right-to-work subcommittee, charged by the executive council with overseeing right-to-work matters, shaped its report to the council along these lines. Right to work, the report pointed out, was now a national issue and one that generally paralleled party philosophies. The Democratic party's platform, and its presidential candidate, John F. Kennedy, had both "unequivocally" pledged to work for repeal of section 14(b). Republican candidate Richard Nixon and his party, by their failure to support repeal, implicitly supported union security restrictions. Although in a number of states Republicans opposed such laws, in many more right to work is "an issue on party lines." In the coming elections, Republicans did not want to repeat the mistake of 1958 and seemed content to keep the issue off state ballots. But, Beirne argued in a summary of the subcommittee's report published in the *American Federationist*, the opposition party wanted to elect enough Republicans at the state level to pass new right-to-work laws and stop labor's repeal drives. No doubt Republican politicians also hoped to add enough congressmembers to block the AFL-CIO's campaign to repeal section 14(b). Thus, according to the CWA's Beirne, the political stakes in 1960 were far greater than in 1958, for the scope of the battle was now national.[21]

From 1959 to 1961, right-to-work floor votes at the state level partially substantiated Beirne's contentions. As Table 5.2 shows, in the three states where anti–union security measures were being proposed, Vermont, New

5.2

Rice Index of Cohesion of Democratic and Republican Parties, in All State Legislatures, on Right-to-Work Measures, 1959–1963

STATE/YEAR	TOTAL	INDEXES SENATE	HOUSE	BALLOTS CAST SENATE	HOUSE
DEMOCRATIC					
Indiana 1961	–	-92	NV	26	NV
Vermont 1959	–	NV	-90	NV	39
Wyoming 1963	-67	-82	-58	11	19
Iowa 1959	–	NV	-38	NV	48
Utah 1959	–	NV	-24	NV	42
New Mexico 1959	–	4	NV	25	NV
Mississippi 1960	71	63	73	38	126
REPUBLICAN					
Iowa 1959	–	NV	100	NV	59
Indiana 1961	–	92	NV	24	NV
Utah 1959	–	NV	90	NV	21
Wyoming 1963	66	88	57	16	37
New Mexico 1959	–	0	NV	8	NV
Vermont 1959	–	NV	-4	NV	190
Mississippi 1960	NR	NR	NR	NR	NR

Source: Appendix A
Key: NR-No Republicans, NV-No Vote
Index: +100(Totally Cohesive in Favor of Right to Work)
         -100(Totally Cohesive Against Right to Work)

Mexico, and Mississippi, the indexes indicate substantially differing party responses only in Vermont, where Democrats in the House ran up a pro-labor −90 index compared to the Republicans much weaker −4. In the New Mexico senate, Democrats actually tallied an anti-labor score of 4 and Republicans bettered them slightly with 0. Unsurprisingly, Mississippi Democrats compiled a 71 on a bill for a right-to-work constitutional referendum. In repeal drives in Indiana, Iowa, and Utah, the parties clearly differed in their cohesion. Republicans in the Iowa and Utah house chambers scored anti-labor indexes of 100 and 90, respectively. Their Democratic counterparts, in turn, responded with a pro-labor −38 in Iowa and a −24 in Utah. Indiana Democrats in the state senate, on the other hand, put together a much stronger −92 to match their Republican colleagues' anti-labor 92. Thus, while there was a significant divergence in party cohesion in four of these states, Democratic scores in favor of labor's position tended to be less cohesive on a repeal ballot in the Plains states and in the West.

Obviously, given the arguments outlined in Beirne's article, labor's top officers had come to use right to work as one of their most effective electoral rallying cries. But despite COPE's best efforts, the subterranean nature of right-to-work agitation in most states after 1958 hindered a repeat of organized labor's political performance at the national level. After an initial spurt of interest on the part of the old AFL unions, 1960 electoral commitment tailed off and the former CIO unions ended up carrying most of the burden for political spending.

COPE functionaries realized, therefore, the necessity of supplementing their efforts to politicize union members. Intermittent interest in defense of trade union rights would not produce a Congress committed to section 14(b) repeal. In the context of the 1960s, this meant forming a coalition with the civil rights movement. By activating other forces likely to vote for pro–civil rights (and expectedly pro-labor) progressives, labor's political strategists hoped they could break the power of the Republican-southern Democrat coalition. Increasing minority registration in Republican urban districts would lead to Democratic gains. And relatedly, the political activization of the southern Negro community would provide a sorely needed liberalizing force.

To a large degree this strategy evolved from what national COPE workers discovered during the 1958 Ohio right-to-work campaign. In a December 1958 report to COPE director James McDevitt, coordinator Philip Weightman outlined the crucial role that black voters played in defeating right to work and electing an overwhelmingly Democratic slate. After overcoming the doubts of some Ohio state central board members about Negroes' interest in the issue, minority COPE operatives launched an extremely effective registration, canvassing, and get-out-the-vote program in heavily black urban areas across the state.[22]

After this intensive voter registration drive, Weightman and his colleagues targeted the rest of their activities to defeating the referendum and found that "our biggest obstacle to offset was the matter of discrimination within some of the unions." Therefore, in addition to using tried-and-true public relations techniques, COPE representatives designed their literature to refute the opposition's claims that a right-to-work law would end employment discrimination. In fact, later in the campaign Weightman successfully exposed right-to-work backers as being the chief opponents of state fair employment practices legislation.

Throughout the fall, Weightman and his staff worked diligently at convincing Ohio blacks that right to work would hurt them and their standard of living. In November, an 85 percent turnout of registered black voters rewarded their efforts by rejecting the right-to-work referendum by overwhelming margins. Returns for wards with a high density of Negroes in

Cincinnati, Cleveland, Youngstown, Akron, Dayton, and Toledo indicated that blacks voted against the measure by 8 to 1, with the margin being as high as 20 to 1 in some places.

Clearly, the Negro community's support of labor had been an important factor in the resounding defeat of right to work *and* the extensive Democratic victory. "It would be a real pity," Weightman advised McDevitt, "if we were to lose the gains we so carefully made during the campaign." And that could happen if labor again isolated itself from the black community. The political contacts made during the struggle promised continued victory, but only if labor took steps to "end discrimination within its ranks[,] and thereby repay the loyalty of the Negro people." The message to McDevitt was unmistakable. Black voters could help organized labor achieve its political agenda on many issues—even such a presumably narrow trade union concern as right to work.

Thus, in 1960 and afterward COPE incorporated this strategy by targeting minority registration. In his November 1959 field report, Weightman recommended mass registration drives "where the potential strength of labor and the Negro vote is sufficient to elect a president in 1960." Black voters, he informed COPE director McDevitt, would buttress labor's efforts to elect liberal candidates.[23]

And while Negro voters were an important liberalizing force in the North's urban areas, they were even more crucial to labor's political objectives in the South. In a November 1961 report to the national office, COPE southern director Daniel Powell asserted that a labor-Negro political alliance would greatly ease the federation's burden. Organized labor provided most of the financial support for liberals in the South—sometimes up to 75 percent—because the area lacked other organized liberal forces. Powell pointed out that the South's labor movement had almost no contact or cooperation with southern black leaders. Any effective political effort in the South, Powell implied, mandated closer cooperation.[24]

Indeed, labor's political leaders were not the only ones who saw an advantage in building an electoral-legislative coalition. The enlistment of an ally in the struggle to mobilize black voters in the South benefited civil rights leaders as well. In his address to the 1961 AFL-CIO convention, Dr. Martin Luther King reminded the delegates that the only southern state to repeal union security restrictions was Louisiana. "This was achieved," said the civil rights leader, "because the Negro vote in that state grew large enough to become a balance of power, and it went along with the [state federation's] effort to wipe out anti-labor legislation" by electing a favorable legislature. If given the vote, Dr. King argued, Negroes "will vote liberal and [with] labor because they need the same liberal legislation labor needs."[25]

Therefore, if the labor and civil right movements could fashion a workable electoral coalition, a significant and potentially powerful political force could break the strength of southern conservatives. For civil rights activists, this meant they would receive the aid of labor's poltical arm in their struggle to open up black political participation in the South through voter registration drives. And for labor, this could lead to a concurrent liberalization of the southern legislatures and Congress. Consequently, labor leaders hoped, right-to-work advocates would have a more difficult time at the state level. And eventually, the House and Senate would have enough liberals to repeal section 14(b) as well as enact long-sought social legislation.

This embryonic alliance took on added importance as state-level right-to-work agitation heated up just as the national offensive sputtered and died. Before the 1960 elections, according to the Beirne subcommittee's convention report, the federation's "activity was designed to counteract the efforts of 'right-to-work' state committees to purge legislators who had opposed" union security restrictions in 1958. Afterward, AFL-CIO functionaries noticed new wrinkles in the tactics of right-to-work proponents. As Legislative Director Andrew Biemiller warned readers of the *American Federationist* in August 1961, one new method was to have allied legislators attach "sleeper" right-to-work provisions to state civil rights bills or labor codes. Or, as AFL-CIO monitors were now finding, advocates would push constitutional amendments or enabling legislation in right-to-work states that did not have both. Table 5.3 shows the results of such a referendum in Mississippi in 1960. By a 69 to 31 percent margin (105,724 yes to 47,461 no), 51 percent of the Mississippi voters voting in that election agreed to anchor their right-to-work statute firmly in the state constitution. In a state with approximately 48,200 union members (11.9 percent of the labor force), the proposal carried in 78 out of 82 counties, with only 2 of those falling in the marginal column. In this way, according to Biemiller, right-to-workers could make repeal attempts harder and enforcement more vigorous. While Mississippi labor lost its effort to keep such a provision out of the state constitution, state federations in fifteen other states stopped all attempts to extend or strengthen restrictions.[26]

But for how long would labor be able to fend off such agitation? According to Andrew Biemiller, a November 1961 opinion poll suggested considerable public support for an individual's right to refrain from joining a union. Evidently, the restructuring of the National Right to Work Committee in the wake of 1958's losses had had some effect. In 1959, the NRTWC's board of directors hired Reed Larson, mastermind of the Kansas right-to-work victory, to oversee the national group. In the same year the organization raised $480,000 for its activities, most of it from business contributions. The 1960 victory of a president ostensibly committed to section 14(b) repeal caused the group to redouble its efforts. By 1961 the NRTWC claimed 15,000 members and activity of some type in all 50 states. In addition to retaining Reed Larson as executive vice-president, the group's directors expanded the organizational structure. The NRTWC now employed Lafayette Hooser, a former railroad unionist, as director of employee

5.3
Public Right-to-Work Elections, 1960

STATE AND YEAR	YES RTW	NO RTW	TOTAL	%RATIO	COUNTY Y/N RATIO	# MARGINAL COUNTIES IN ELECTION	% OF VOTE FOR HIGHEST OFFICE IN ELECTION	APPROXIMATE UNION MEMBERSHIP
Mississippi 1960	105724	47461	153185	69/31	78/4	2	51	48200(11.9%)

Source: Appendix B, Cox, and Troy. See explanation in Appendix B as to the derivation of percent of state vote and union membership.

membership; Glenn Green, a conservative journalist, as director of information; Charles Bailey, a public relations professional, as director of state activities; and Jane Bottorff, a personnel administrator, as director of the women's division.[27]

Furthermore, in late 1961 the U.S. Chamber of Commerce formally aligned itself with the right-to-work movement by forming a special committee on voluntary union membership. In 1959 the chamber had engaged a private research organization to study what it took for a successful right-to-work campaign. According to the organization's journal *Nation's Business*, such a drive needed long-term commitment, good organization, skilled educational and public relations programs conducted by local people, and sufficient money. These observations paralleled the judgement of NRTWC strategists, and it was clear that an important increase in business commitment was needed to promote right-to-work legislation wherever possible.[28]

Throughout 1962, therefore, the national federation's right-to-work monitors kept watchful eyes on the activities of their enemies. Carl McPeak investigated the sources of the NRTWC's financial backing and conveyed whatever useful information he could to AFL-CIO people at the state level. Federation officials also commissioned and distributed an extensive research report on the NRTWC which, James McDevitt informed state COPE activists, "tears the veil of respectability" off right-to-work supporters by exposing their ties to right-wing extremist groups such as the John Birch Society. And finally, in August 1962, George Meany urged affiliates to be militant in fending off the new right-to-work campaign. Barry Goldwater's recent screening of a NRTWC film for his legislative colleagues indicated the necessity to be vigilant, wrote the federation president. Meany recommended that affiliates use the public relations materials prepared by the national office to counter the propaganda of the opposition. It was the only way, he said, to deal with the "mounting campaign against not only the unions which make up the labor movement but the people whose hands and hearts make up [the] unions."[29]

Despite such considerable activity on the part of the federation, COPE could not keep the secondary leadership in a constant political frenzy over *future* threats to union security. For example, California labor had nineteen local COPE committees active in the 1958 elections; by 1961 the number had fallen to seven. Many other state labor movements experienced a similar drop in political interest. "Must the labor movement have to have a right-to-work fight in which it gets its back to the wall" [in order to sustain political activity?], angrily asked Roy Reuther at the California state central's 1962 convention.[30]

In this context, the incipient coalition between COPE and minority registration took on added significance for the 1962 elections. "We will have to bolster our Negro-labor alliance if any liberal candidate is to have a chance of re-election," recommended COPE staff member Earl Davis to

James McDevitt in early 1962. And cautiously, AFL-CIO officials lent resources to struggling civil rights groups trying to register black voters in the South. The combined efforts showed some results, but certainly not the imposing victory for which COPE leaders hoped. In the fall congressional elections, Democrats gained two seats in the Senate. The margin in the House, however, declined by only one member, reversing the usual trend of dilution of majority party strength in non-presidential elections.[31]

RISING STATE AGITATION AND NATIONAL STALEMATE

Unfortunately for labor, the intensification of state right-to-work agitation during 1962 started to produce results. Wyoming unionists battled a vigorous drive for anti–union security legislation for much of the year. And in Oklahoma, it appeared as if anti–union security activists would be able to secure a public referendum on the issue in the near future.

In 1961 the Oklahoma AFL-CIO had stopped such a move in the state legislature. Now, at the beginning of 1962, anti–union security activists turned to the initiative petition route, for which they needed nearly 136,000 signatures within 90 days in order to place the question on the next statewide ballot. The state central organization immediately started an effort to make sure union members did not unwittingly sign the petitions. When the opposition filed the collected signatures in April, the state federation challenged their validity in court. And according to Oklahoma labor's legislation representative Len Yarborough, at "the time we started this contest the AFL-CIO, on a National level, made money available to the state organization."[32] With these funds, the state organization then hired five full-time workers to begin a signature challenge operation. Collaterally, volunteers from COPE's women's activities department scanned the petitions in an effort to find one of the 46 reasons to invalidate signatures. Through August 1962, some 35 people worked on this project for the Oklahoma AFL-CIO. And as a by-product they produced an alphabetical card file of voters likely to back the measure—useful information for targeting labor's resources in the event of an election. When the Oklahoma secretary of state ruled the petitions valid, the state AFL-CIO appealed the decision to the courts after consultation with the federation's national office. By late 1962, the state federation had spent approximately $65,000 to fight the drive, with nearly $17,000 of that amount coming from AFL-CIO headquarters in Washington. Yarborough estimated total costs, with the incorporation of volunteer time, to be in the area of $250,000.[33]

Nor did things improve much at the state level in the ensuing months. In early February 1963, Wyoming passed a right-to-work statute—the first state to do so since 1958. Lloyd Tagart, president of a Caspar construction company, was the moving force behind the Wyoming Right to Work Committee. Beginning in August 1961, the group began using NRTWC educational materials to shape public opinion. Group members represented the traditional business proponents of union security restrictions: the Farm Bureau Federation, the General Contractors Association, the Retail Merchants Association, the Trucking Association, the Stock Growers, and the Grange. After laying the groundwork, the WRTWC took advantage of a union-inspired dairy boycott to arouse the legislature to action. Table 5.2 lists the Rice Index of Cohesion for the two parties in Wyoming on the 1963 vote. The Democrats in both chambers supported labor with an index of −67. The Republicans opposed the Wyoming labor movement with an anti−union security score of 66. Thus, in short order, the formula of a united and dedicated business leadership directed by a single-purpose organization, as well as enough money and time to conduct educational activities, had resulted in success for Wyoming right-to-work activists with Republican respresentatives.[34]

At the same time as the events in Wyoming, the Oklahoma Supreme Court ruled the right-to-work initiative petitions valid and ordered them placed on the state's primary election ballot for 1964. Immediately, Oklahoma AFL-CIO president Roy Tillman called the state federation's officers together to plan a response. They recommended the appointment of a full-time coordinator to head anti-right-to-work activities. State federation leaders then put together a statewide program of action designed to increase affiliation and establish anti-right-to-work committees at the county level. To oversee the county activities, the Oklahoma AFL-CIO created a state organization composed of state central officers, international union directors, national COPE staffers, and the AFL-CIO regional director. The county groups would draw their membership from county council officers, state officers residing in the district, full-time union representatives residing in the county, and members of the county council's women's auxiliary. Even with good organization, though, Oklahoma labor faced a difficult task. At a special state convention in March 1963, officers informed delegates that preliminary polls showed voter sentiment running 4 to 1 against labor.[35]

Once again, to many union leaders it seemed as if the momentum on right to work was again shifting in favor of their enemies. At a 1963 meeting, IUD officers vented some of their anger at the constant struggles over union security in general, and at the national stalemate in particular. Department president Walter Reuther argued against pressing for reform on labor legislation at the present time, especially when there was so much that labor needed to do in the field of social legislation. If organized labor insisted on giving top priority to ending union security restrictions, though, Reuther thought it should be certain it could win outright or at least ensure a veto of an unacceptable bill. Other members of the executive committee believed that there was a cost to such a cautious approach. Al Hartung of the Woodworkers insisted that labor "in the South will never be able to organize [sufficiently] unless . . . Section 14-B is amended or repealed." And Textile

Workers president William Pollock noted the political consequences of continued timidity. Many union leaders, according to Pollock, were in a "bad position with their membership, who after contributing money to elect liberal legislators, are later told that we must be cautious about amending anti-labor laws."[36]

It was a familiar predicament. As Oklahoma unionists girded themselves for battle, the twenty years of constant frustration on this issue had finally taken their toll on national AFL-CIO leaders. They would help their state brethren defend union security; they could do no less. Labor leaders' difficulties with national politicians, however, had by now drained them of much of their desire to resurrect section 14(b) repeal. In the spring of 1963, the executive council re-energized the Beirne right-to-work subcommittee to study the opportunities. But by May 1963, Andrew Biemiller informed Washington labor lobbyists, the subcommittee was "of a mind to forget the whole thing." "The wavering attitude of the AFL-CIO will . . . mean that no money or effort will be put into this right-to-work repealer drive from headquarters," wrote a disappointed John Edelman to his union's president. This timidity disheartened the Textile Workers lobbyist, particularly because he sensed a changing political climate. For one thing, the rift between the AFL-CIO and some liberal congressmembers—especially in the Senate—had had time to heal. "A group of liberal Senators," he noted, "have introduced on their own hook a 14(b) repealer and have launched a series of speeches to call attention" to what the provision has done to labor-management relations. Obviously, concluded Edelman, "there is a group of dedicated men in the Congress who are ready to go to bat on this issue, which we in the labor movement have been quiet about for too long a time."[37]

Therefore, it was necessary to light a fire under the leadership. "Certainly I realize we won't pass such a law this year; but surely you will agree that we just can't stall and stall in starting a determined move," he wrote TWUA president William Pollock. "There is no ideal 'right' moment for this thing to begin," the lobbyist counseled. We must "gradually create the climate we need." Perhaps if the IUD took the lead the AFL-CIO would get off dead center. In any event, Edelman recommended that Pollock press George Meany and Walter Reuther on the issue, "and that we get going now and mean it on a repealer effort." "After all," he pointed out, "we are committed anyway because these liberals in the Senate have made their move. We just can't hang back now or we look quite foolish."[38]

Feeling foolish was something that the AFL-CIO's legislative leaders could not afford much more of; by May 1963 the failure of almost every national initiative on union security had aroused deep self-doubts. In the 1958 elections, organized labor mobilized the largest Democratic electoral victory in a decade. Interpreting the voting results as a "clear mandate" to Congress on union security, labor's political strategists avidly hoped they could parlay their electoral partisanism into removal of section 14(b). Immediately after the opening of the new Congress, however, public pressure for labor legislation dealing with union corruption derailed repeal efforts. After the passage of the Landrum-Griffin Act, the AFL-CIO found it increasingly difficult to organize a repeal drive. The conservative coalition and lack of influence on liberal Republicans remained continuing problems. Only now, a severely strained relationship with some liberal Democrats in Congress further wore down labor's legislative efficacy.

The fallen expectations had side effects, though. It was true that right-to-work measures usually evoked divergent party responses; it was also true that, as presently constituted, the Democratic party's highest pro-labor cohesion occurred in opposition to proposals that would *worsen* the labor law situation on union security. To be effective offensively, at the state level and nationally, would require much more electoral success than occurred in 1958. To accomplish this task, COPE leaders began to seek out new sources of political strength in an effort to break the impasse. Unless right-to-work activists posed a visible threat to union security, many international and local union leaders ignored COPE's entreaties for electoral activism. Therefore, in order to create a more potent liberalizing force, the AFL-CIO's strategists quietly broadened voter registration efforts. The 1958 Ohio right-to-work campaign provided important evidence that black voters—if approached correctly—would support labor not only on social legislation but on trade union issues. Thus, in the 1960 and 1962 elections COPE tried to strengthen an incipient electoral coalition by concentrating on voter registration in both working-class and minority districts.

Nevertheless, through the middle of 1963 this involvement was still in a gestation period. For the time being only northern, labor-oriented liberals gave section 14(b) repeal more than rhetorical commitment. Yet, even as the federation's crisis of confidence delayed unified action, some experienced labor lobbyists sensed opportunity when a few liberal legislators initiated attacks on the state union security provision of Taft-Hartley. A combination of hard work in the legislative and electoral spheres could prepare the ground for a serious offensive in the next Congress. But reliance on an increased minority vote would not be enough. Organized labor itself must participate as never before. Ultimately, in John Edelman's analysis, the "success of the drive will depend almost entirely on whether the officers at the local level[,] and their membership[,] will respond wholeheartedly and get into this fight with energy and determination." To find out if the secondary leadership would, however, AFL-CIO officers had to wait, as they had so many times before, for the outcome of the next election.[39]

NOTES

1. AFL-CIO, Statement by the AFL-CIO Executive Council on *Labor Legislation*, Washington, D.C., 6 November 1958, Box 27, UAW Citizens Department: Roy Reuther Files, WPRL.

2. Confidential Memo, Meade Alcorn to the President, 15 December 1958, Box 1, "Alcorn, Meade," Whitman Files, Administration Series, DDEL.

3. Foley, *The New Senate*, pp. 5–31.

4. Wayne Phillips, "Labor Dazzled by Ohio Victory," *New York Times*, 6 November 1958, p. 15. Industrial spokesman quoted in Los Angeles County Labor Committee, "Save Our State," n.d. [1958], Box 2, Charles Baker Collection, WPRL; John Edelman, "Report of the TWUA Washington Office," 27 January 1959, Box 8, John W. Edelman Collection, WPRL; Dwight D. Eisenhower, "Memorandum for the Record," Confidential, Box 37, "DDE Dictation, 12/58," Whitman Files, Administration Series, DDEL. For the AFL-CIO's official policy statement on the significance of the 1958 elections, see note 1.

5. Interestingly, the IUD and its affiliates provided over 75 percent of the monies in the AFL-CIO's 1958 right-to-work campaign fund. Out of the approximately $589,000 collected, the IUD and its officials contributed nearly $478,000. Walter Reuther felt this failure of the building trades to contribute their fair share for a bread-and-butter trade union issue had no excuse, and indeed, paralleled these unions' failure to fund COPE. More than likely, however, old-line craft unions probably used their own channels of political spending rather than the federation's. See "Transcript, Meeting of the IUD, AFL-CIO, Washington, D.C.," 10 December 1958, pp. 41–52, 92–94, Box 328; Joseph Beirne, Albert Hayes, James Suffridge, "Report of the Subcommittee of the Executive Council on So-Called 'Right-to-Work' Activities," 18 May 1959, Box 313; Walter Reuther to George Meany, 10 December 1958, Box 310; all UAW President's Office: Walter P. Reuther Files, WPRL; AFL-CIO, Colorado Labor Council, *Proceedings of the 2nd Biennial Convention*, 8–10 May 1958, pp. 15–17, *State Labor Proceedings*, microform, Center for Research Libraries.

6. For example, see Solomon Barkan, "American Trade Unions' Most Pressing Challenge: Renewal of Growth," Report for the Fund for the Republic, December 1959, Box 4, John W. Edelman Collection, WPRL; Robert Oliver to Walter P. Reuther, 28 October 1959, Box 340, UAW President's Office: Walter P. Reuther Files, WPRL.

7. "Right to Work: Bigger Battle Coming," *Nation's Business*, January 1959, pp. 40, 41, 46; "Notes taken of Morning Session, Legislative Conference, 12/3/58," [AFL-CIO] Box 85, AFL-CIO Legislative Department, GMMA.

8. Memo, Robert Oliver to Walter P. Reuther, "Kennedy-Ives Bill," 15 December 1958, Box 340, UAW President's Office: Walter P. Reuther Files, WPRL.

9. Andrew J. Biemiller to Joseph Rourke, Colorado State Labor Council, 23 December 1958, Box 36, AFL-CIO Legislative Department, GMMA; Paul Sifton to Walter P. Reuther, "Legislative Priorities," 30 December 1958, Box 10; Memo, Victor Reuther and Paul Sifton to Walter P. Reuther, "AFL-CIO Policy, Position, Strategy and Tactics on Labor Reform Bill in the House," 4 May 1959, Box 14; both UAW Citizenship Department: Roy Reuther Files, WPRL. The best study of labor's response to the Landrum-Griffin Act is Alan K. McAdams, *Power and Politics in Labor Legislation* (New York: Columbia University Press, 1964).

10. McAdams, *Power and Politics*, p. 145; [Paul Siemiller?] to Andrew J. Biemiller, 1 December 1959, Box 33, AFL-CIO President's Office: George Meany Files, GMMA; Robert Oliver to George Meany, "Re: Legislative Conference," 5 January 1960, Box 340, UAW President's Office: Walter P. Reuther Files, WPRL.

11. Convention discussion cited in Alan Lloyd Draper, "A Rope of Sand: The AFL-CIO's Committee on Political Education, 1955–1967," (Ph.D. diss., Columbia University, 1982), pp. 164–168.

12. Edwin Olney Jones to Senator Pat McNamara, 11 September 1957; Senator Pat McNamara to Edwin Olney Jones, 17 September 1957; both Box 662, Senator Pat McNamara Collection, WPRL. The Senate leadership never gave 14(b) bills much attention; for example, they were never assigned to a subcommittee for hearings. See Enoch D. Chase to Walter C. Wallace, Executive Assistant to the Secretary of Labor, "Senate Bills of the 86th Congress dealing with Section 14(b) of the National Labor Relations Act," 12 August 1960, Box 182, James P. Mitchell Papers, DDEL.

13. Morris Udall to Michael Wade, 21 July 1972, quoted in Wade, *The Bitter Issue*, p. 108; clipping, *Phoenix Arizona Republic*, reprinted in National Right to Work Committee, "Loopholes in their Logic" (Washington, D.C.: NRTWC); W. Don Ellinger, Director, COPE Area 8, to Walter P. Reuther, 27 October 1958, Box 318, UAW President's Office: Walter P. Reuther Files, WPRL.

14. Foley, *The New Senate*, pp. 37–42; "Byrd Defies Foes of Role in Senate," *New York Times*, 4 December 1960, p. 48. For Byrd's specific objections to his party's platform plank on right to work, see the *Congressional Record*, 18 August 1960, 106:16647–16648.

15. In the crucial House vote to forestall regulatory legislation, eight Democratic liberals refused to follow the AFL-CIO's strategy. They were Carl Elliot (AL), Edith Green (OR), Frank Thompson (NJ), Stewart Udall (AZ), James O'Hara (MI), Dominick Daniels (NJ), John Brademas (IN), and Robert Giaimo (CT). Labor also had a strained relationship with Richard Bolling (MO) and Lee Metcalf (MT), coordinators of the House Democratic leadership's effort to write a balanced labor reform bill. See McAdams, *Power and Politics*, pp. 145–156; Memo, Paul Sifton and Ralph Showalter to Walter P. Reuther, 15 November 1960, Box 10, UAW Citizenship Department: Roy Reuther Files, WPRL.

16. Jacob Clayman to Walter P. Reuther, 11 June 1962, UAW President's Office: Walter P. Reuther Files, WPRL.

17. Draper, "A Rope of Sand," pp. 169–184.

18. Ralph Showalter to Walter P. Reuther and Victor Reuther, 20 March 1961, Box 11, UAW Citizenship Department: Roy Reuther Files, WPRL.

19. Memo, David E. Feller to Walter P. Reuther, "Re: House Subcommittee Investigation of NLRB," 28 April 1961, Box 332, UAW President's Office: Walter P. Reuther Files, WPRL.

20. Carl McPeak, State Legislation Representative, to Presidents and Secretaries, All AFL-CIO State Bodies, 14 June 1960, Box 110–9–1–8, Texas AFL-CIO, TLA.

21. The Beirne/Hayes/Suffridge Subcommittee reported to the AFL-CIO Executive Council in May 1960. The conclusions of the committee's deliberations can be found in Joseph A. Beirne, "The Right-to-Work Issue," *American Federationist*, October 1960, pp. 21–24; Agenda, AFL-CIO Executive Council Meeting, 3 May 1960, Box 314, UAW President's Office: Walter P. Reuther Files, WPRL.

22. Philip M. Weightman to James L. McDevitt, "Report on Ohio Campaign Against 'Right-To-Work,' " 1 December 1958, 110–9–1–8, Texas AFL-CIO Collection, TLA. Unless otherwise noted, all information on COPE's right-to-work campaign in Ohio is from Weightman's memo.

23. The fifteen states mentioned by Weightman were California, Connecticut, Illinois, Indiana, Kentucky, Maryland, Michigan, Missouri, New Jersey, New York, Ohio, Oklahoma, Pennsylvania, Tennessee, and Texas. See Memo, Philip M. Weightman, Field Director, COPE, to James L. McDevitt, "Minorities Report for 1959," 10 November 1959, copy in Elmer Cope Papers, Roll 41, microfilm edition, Ohio Historical Society.

24. Daniel Powell to Al Barkan, 23 November 1961, cited in Draper, "A Rope of Sand," pp. 202–213.

25. AFL-CIO, *Proceedings*, 1961, p. 287.

26. AFL-CIO, *Proceedings*, 1961, pp. 176–180; Andrew J. Biemiller, "Right-to-Work Forces Try 'Back-Door,' " *American Federationist*, August 1961, pp. 5–9.

27. Ralph Showalter to Victor Reuther, "Report on lst 1962 AFL-CIO Administrative Committee Meeting," Box 208, UAW President's Office: Walter P. Reuther Files; National Right to Work Committee, "The Right to Work National Newsletter," 18 November 1960; NRTWC, "The National Right to Work Committee: What it is, Who it is, Where it's going," (Washington, D.C.: NRTWC, 1961); copies in Box 58, Irwin L. DeShetler Collection, WPRL.

28. U.S. Chamber of Commerce, News Service Press Release, 18 September 1961, copy in Box 58, Irwin L. DeShetler Collection, WPRL; "New Trends in Right to Work," *Nation's Business*, August 1959, pp. 69–71.

29. "On file in Office of C. A. McPeak, AFL-CIO, Washington, D.C., Letter from the Following Companies Soliciting Funds for the National Right to Work Committee," 7 November 1962, Box 58; Irwin L. DeShetler to Carl McPeak, 31 October 1962, Box 51; James L. McDevitt, "Distribution of 'Right-to-Work' Report," 17 December 1962, Box 58; all Irwin L. DeShetler Collection, WPRL; Circular Letter, George Meany to All National and International Unions, State and City Central Bodies, 28 August 1962, Box 311, UAW President's Office: Walter P. Reuther Files, WPRL.

30. Roy Reuther quoted in Draper, "A Rope of Sand," p. 156.

31. Earl Davis, staff member COPE, to James McDevitt, 31 January 1962, quoted in Draper, pp. 216–218.

32. Oklahoma State AFL-CIO, *Special Convention Proceedings*, 21 March 1963, pp. 2–7, *State Labor Proceedings*, microform, Center for Research Libraries.

33. Ibid.

34. Herbert Livingston, "How Wyoming Achieved its Right to Work Law," (Washington, D.C.: NRTWC Reprint), copy in Box 635, UAW President's Office: Walter P. Reuther Files, WPRL.

35. Oklahoma State AFL-CIO, Minutes of Executive Board Meeting, 1 February 1963, with attachments, 33–2–1, COPE Area 8 Collection, TLA; Oklahoma State AFL-CIO, *Special Convention Proceedings*, 21 March 1963, pp. 8–13, *State Labor Proceedings*, microform, Center for Research Libraries.

36. Minutes, Executive Committee Meeting of the Industrial Union Department, AFL-CIO, Pan-Am Room, Statler Hilton, Washington, D.C., 15 January 1963, Box 330; UAW President's Office: Walter P. Reuther Files, WPRL.

37. Memo, J. A. Beirne, Chairman, Right to Work Committee to Lane Kirkland, Executive Assistant to the President, 24 April 1963, File 4.1.2., Box 48, AFL-CIO Legislative Department, GMMA; John Edelman to William Pollock, 21 May 1963; John Edelman to TWUA Officers, Joint Board Managers, and Staff, "Right-to-Work

Repealer Introduced in Senate," 27 May 1963; both Box 3, John W. Edelman Collection, WPRL.

38. John Edelman to William Pollock, 21 May 1963, Box 3, John W. Edelman Collection, WPRL.

39. John Edelman, "Notes for Marcia Smith for *Textile Labor*," John W. Edelman Collection, WPRL.

6

Extended Discussions

The record after sixty-four proves that Johnson came through on practically every-thing. . . . He knew Congress; he knew the workings, how
everything went. He knew who was on every subcommittee and every
committee. . . . He was an expert on legislation; he knew more about
the workings of Congress than any [other] President I have ever known.
—George Meany[1]

In 1965 and 1966, capitalizing on a reversal of political momentum, the
AFL-CIO finally pushed the congressional Democratic party into a serious
but unsuccessful offensive against section 14(b) of the Taft-Hartley Act.
More than anything else, this defeat uncovered the limitations inherent in
labor's attempts to exercise national political influence on behalf of its
narrow organizational interests—limitations previously obscured either by
Republican legislative dominance or obstructive Dixiecrats. Even with labor's progressive allies in control of Congress, the Johnson administration
pursued repeal with a notable lack of zeal and vigor. While President Johnson did eventually propose and lobby for the proposal, when faced with
the possible disruption of his own political agenda as a result of a potentially
bruising legislative battle, the president declined to exercise the full power
of his influence on behalf of labor. As Johnson realized, however upset
union officials might be with his administration, the Democratic affinities
of labor's top directorship guaranteed that any breach would be of short
duration. In the final analysis, despite all of its heralded electoral activism,
the AFL-CIO did not wield the kind of social clout necessary to command
full commitment from the national party.

Although right-to-work politics seemed bleak to labor's legislative plan-
ners in late 1963, the outlook reversed itself in short order. Beginning in
1963, and continuing throughout 1964, the growing civil rights crisis

brought Democrats, unionists, and black voters into a closer alliance; and COPE officials believed the May 1964 defeat of Oklahoma's union security referendum, due in large part to a strong anti-right-to-work vote from the Sooner State's black precincts, provided further proof of the utility of the coalition approach for labor. In addition, the Republicans' nomination of ardent right-to-work advocate Barry Goldwater gave COPE strategists the perfect foil to mobilize union leaders on behalf of the Democrats in the coming presidential election. By November 1964, widespread fear of the Goldwater candidacy had activated even normally inert levels of labor leadership and led to a responsive rank-and-file turnout. Moreover, federation officials' related interest in expanding black voting coincided nicely with Democratic leaders' desires to secure both the labor vote and channel civil rights protest into electoral participation. All of these factors had now converged to produce the greatest liberal Democratic victory since the depression.

With reform-minded Democrats in effective control of Congress, AFL-CIO officers now felt justified in *insisting* that the party repay its electoral debts. The Democrats' handling of the repeal campaign, though, revealed that the party's chief decision makers doubted the federation's ability to inflict direct retribution—and indeed, whether the AFL-CIO had any realistic alternatives to the Democratic party. Thus President Johnson, who once likened labor's power in national politics to that of a "paper tiger," thought he could conduct a pro forma repeal effort and still keep the allegiance of top AFL-CIO executives—a perception strengthened to some degree by the accession of Walter Reuther and George Meany to the president's initial strategic decisions concerning the legislative agenda for the Eighty-ninth Congress. Despite mighty endeavors, when the federation failed to overcome Senator Everett Dirksen's (R-IL) final filibuster against repeal in early 1966, the AFL-CIO's political chieftains were left with uncomfortable evidence that, even under the best of conditions, their Democratic alliance had limitations previously unknown to them.

FACTORS REVERSING THE STALEMATE ON SECTION 14(B)

Though AFL-CIO officials' apathy on possible repeal of section 14(b) remained pronounced through 1963, some of the elements responsible for reversing the right-to-work momentum were actually present at that time. For one thing, state-level agitation once again aroused wider union interest in the positions of candidates, and consequently somewhat greater attention to the issue from Democrats. For example, President Kennedy appeared at the AFL-CIO's convention in November to reiterate his rhetorical support; and more importantly, Secretary of Labor Willard Wirtz publicly attacked the Arkansas law, an event which the NRTWC charged presaged the start of a joint COPE-Democratic party repeal blueprint for all twenty right-to-work states. Also indicative of growing union interest was a 1963 convention proposal to create a permanent right-to-work department at federation headquarters to give permanency to previously ad hoc arrangements.[2]

For both organized labor and the Democratic leadership, though, it was the civil rights movement that served as the linchpin of their increasing cooperation. The militant demonstrations and racial violence that punctuated most of 1963 convinced the Kennedy administration's Justice Department of the need for vigorous efforts to broaden the black franchise. Therefore, COPE's growing involvement in stimulating minority voter registration, especially in the South, took on added importance for party executives. While federation political strategists became involved in minority registration because of frustration over failures to effect labor law reform, they also desired many of the broad social goals that a victorious progressive alliance could win. Therefore, as early as mid-1963 the Democratic National Committee and COPE developed voting profiles for selected cities and states with high minority populations. In addition, COPE functionaries increasingly invited black leaders of voter registration drives to the organization's political conferences.[3]

These forces fused further in 1964. After John Kennedy's assassination, the new president, Lyndon Johnson, personally sought the AFL-CIO's lobbying expertise in the seething congressional civil rights battle, and its subsequent electoral aid in winning the presidency in his own right. In the summer of 1964, COPE's hard-hitting concentration on the threat to union security posed by the Goldwater candidacy generated widespread electoral interest in union ranks, even as civil rights protest itself shifted to the enfranchisement of southern blacks. It began to look as if COPE's increasing emphasis on minority voter registration was fortuitously well placed to advance a progressive swing, especially considering the recent political events in Oklahoma.

Indeed, AFL-CIO leaders judged the surprise defeat of the Oklahoma right-to-work referendum in May 1964 as proof of the potential effectiveness of their strategy and its utility to organized labor.[4] From the beginning, the national AFL-CIO played an important role in the Oklahoma state federation's efforts. Labor's tacticians divided the state into seven districts, and in each district the national office arranged for a full-time national representative to work on the state federation's "Program of Action." The national representative was responsible for facilitating cooperation among unionists within the district. If district union officials did not unite, the representative would report the problem individual to state officers and the relevant international union officials. Such an arrangement promoted broad activity on the part of the state labor leadership.[5]

The Oklahoma AFL-CIO supported its campaign by passing a relatively large $5 per member assessment in January 1964. From that point until the election in May, COPE coordinators and volunteers from the Women's

Activity Department worked their assigned districts to generate registration and coordinate get-out-the-vote efforts. State legislation representative Carl McPeak also spent a good deal of time organizing electoral activities in the eastern part of Oklahoma.[6]

The hard work paid off. As Table 6.1 indicates, on May 5, 1964, Oklahoma voters rejected the proposal by a 52 to 48 percent margin (376,555 no to 352,267 yes). The county yes/no ratio ended up at 34 to 43, with 25 of the states's 77 counties yielding marginal percentage divisions. And, according to state central president Roy Tillman, black voters were instrumental in the defeat. With the cooperation of the Reverend Ben Hill, a respected black leader, Oklahoma unionists and their allies turned out a large anti-right-to-work vote in districts with a high percentage of black citizens. In total, 78 percent of voters casting ballots in this primary election also expressed their desires on the issue. To Tillman, the coalition strategy showed the desirability of a "closer alliance" between labor and minorities, "not only when we have a crisis come up, but the year round." To be fair, organized labor's ability to capture the votes of senior citizens and small farmers, in the latter case brought about by a good working relationship with the National Farmers Union, aided the campaign as well. The key to victory, though, proved to be the successful activation of Oklahoma's 104,100 union members (representing about 15.2 percent of the work force), along with a highly successful registration and get-out-the-vote program in minority areas. New national COPE director Alexander Barkan informed all of labor's political leaders of the achievement. Oklahoma's anti-right-to-work formula "can be applied to every election campaign in every state," he wrote in a widely circulated letter. "I hope that the Oklahoma experience will inspire the AFL-CIO in each state to redouble its efforts to achieve the kind of organization and cooperative effort" found in Oklahoma's right-to-work contest.[7]

The Oklahoma success story gave national AFL-CIO officials renewed confidence that their struggles to build a broad liberal coalition would in fact produce results—not only in the sphere of social welfare, but also on issues of special concern to trade unionists. Nevertheless, there were many difficulties in getting an organization such as the AFL-CIO, with its many divisions, to act cohesively as part of a liberal coalition. For example, in states such as Texas, building trades unionists objected to the state federation's endeavors to build a close political association with minorities and other Democratic-leaning groups. State officials H. S. Hank Brown and Roy Evans complained in a June 1964 letter to Building Trades Department official C. J. Haggerty that they simply could not understand why some union leaders had "such a strong dislike and contempt for their Negro and Latino brothers" as well as "resentment and suspicion of liberal and intellectual groups." A divided labor movement would not only be ineffective politically, it would eventually fail to organize minorities for collective bar-

6.1
Public Right-to-Work Elections, 1964

STATE AND YEAR	YES RTW	NO RTW	TOTAL	%RATIO	COUNTY Y/N RATIO	# MARGINAL COUNTIES	% OF VOTE FOR HIGHEST OFFICE IN ELECTION	APPROXIMATE UNION MEMBERSHIP
Oklahoma 1964	352267	376555	728822	48/52	34/43	25	78	104100(15.2%)

Source: Appendix B, Cox, and Troy. See explanation in Appendix B as to the derivation of percent of state vote and union membership.

gaining purposes. Such divisions made it easy for establishment politicians to ignore, even scoff, at labor. Hence, they argued, Texas Democratic Governor John Connally knew he could keep some labor support even as he publicly appealed to retain the state Democratic party's pro-right-to-work platform plank. "If labor had been united," the state officers contended on this subject near and dear to the hearts of building trades leaders, "we would not have had to suffer this insult."[8]

But in the short run, such difficulties remained in the background, as union leaders at every level sensed that repeal of section 14(b) was no longer only a remote possibility. As a COPE functionary told Maryland laborites, "it was amazing the battle we put up" in Oklahoma. "And the tragedy of the whole thing has been the simple fact that we were waging a defensive fight." However, more and more unionists were eager to go on the offensive. For example, a special COPE report to the AFL-CIO executive council in May 1964 noted that the union security controversy would play a major role in the coming national elections. The political education committee's analysts maintained that to repeal section 14(b), organized labor's friends needed to win four toss-up Senate contests while other labor endorsees had to gain three new seats. In the House, federation allies had to keep 37 seats that were in danger while also winning half of the remaining contests. "Repeal of 14B creates enthusiasm and activity, particulary on the part of union officials," the COPE report asserted. It also had "broad appeal among the membership where there is knowledge of the expensive, strength-sapping campaigns waged in individual states to fight right-to-work legislation or referenda."[9]

Indeed, unionists' feelings on the issue were intense, so intense that one COPE organization insisted on a loyalty oath pledging a repeal vote on section 14(b) in exchange for its endorsement. Then, when the Republican party nominated longtime right-to-work promoter Barry Goldwater as their presidential standard-bearer in July 1964, GOP officials handed COPE strategists the perfect opportunity to hang the primary responsiblity for anti–union security agitation on the Party of Lincoln. From that point onward, trade union leaders' interest in and active commitment to the 1964 elections climbed to new levels. COPE director Barkan toured 48 states during the year and everywhere stressed the threat. The election of Goldwater, Barkan argued over and over again before his labor audiences, would lead to a national right-to-work law, for it was well known that such a proposal had been a pet project of the Arizona senator's since the 1950s. As a result of COPE's work, unions' financial backing of federation electoral activities on behalf of Democrats rose dramatically. In urban areas the committee had no trouble staffing voter-registration teams, producing a larger pool of potential Democratic voters. Even stalwart Republican union presidents Maurice Hutcheson of the Carpenters and James Suffridge of the Retail Clerks International Association rejected their party's top candidate and underwrote national COPE. As Barkan later reflected, "we have never been able to arouse our [affiliated union] staff people as we did in those states where we faced a right-to-work fight." Now COPE had been given a chance to simulate those conditions, to an extent, during a presidential election.[10]

Democratic officials noted this avid electoral participation. Over the last year, President Johnson had sought to cultivate a mutually beneficial relationship with the AFL-CIO. "You see," commented George Meany, LBJ "was one President who realized more than... any other President the tremendous influence that organized labor has... on Capitol Hill." During early 1964 the new chief executive had needed labor lobbyists' assistance in pushing through civil rights proposals. And Johnson could use influential liberal labor leaders such as Walter Reuther as an important communication link with House liberals, a group with which he had had little contact.[11]

More than anything else, however, the president wanted to enlist labor's electoral troops in helping him win reelection to the presidency in his own right. In fact, his actions at times bordered on transparent manipulation. Concerned that Goldwater was making inroads into the conservative South, for example, LBJ carefully used union leaders to counterbalance the Arizonan's popularity. In Georgia, Johnson political operatives identified Atlanta and nearby northern counties as crucial to carrying the state. Georgia Democrat Philip Landrum, whose co-authorship of the Landrum-Griffin Act hardly qualified him as a friend of labor, recommended that Walter Reuther of the Autoworkers and Al Hayes of the Machinists—whose unions had large locals in the area—cooperate with him in heading off noticeable Goldwater sentiment among the rank and file. As presidential adviser Larry O'Brien wrote in a September 1964 memo, Landrum "was convinced that a program of this nature can result in a pickup of 40 to 50 thousand votes in north Georgia which he feels at this time could make the difference." Johnson personally instructed O'Brien to arrange the necessary details between the labor leaders and Landrum. Similarly, in many other areas the personal involvement of union executives strengthened the highest Democrat's campaign.[12]

In November, the AFL-CIO's electoral aid contributed to a landslide victory for Lyndon Johnson and the Democrats. Not only did the president trounce his opponent, his coattails brought many of the party's candidates to Washington with him. The party division for the Eighty-ninth Congress ended up at 68 to 32 for the Democrats in the Senate, and 295 to 140 in the House. It was not only an impressive electoral achievement for the party quantitatively; more importantly, many reform-oriented Democrats captured Republican seats in the North and Midwest, giving progressive Democrats the upper hand at setting the legislative policy agenda. In this victory, there could be little doubt that labor's registration efforts in working-class and minority districts helped increase the percentage of blue-collar and black voters by 9 percent and 11 percent, respectively, since the last presidential election. Moreover, each group's Democratic loyalty increased; blacks voted 99 percent Democratic (up from 72 percent in 1960), and 80 percent of union members and their families pulled the Democratic lever (up from 66 percent four years earlier). The president's advisers willingly voiced their appreciation of labor's crucial role. In reviewing "our mutual political activity," Larry O'Brien wrote Walter Reuther the day after the election, "I wanted to tell you how impressed I have been with Labor's performance this year." As director of campaign organizing, O'Brien had traveled extensively with the UAW president's brother, Roy Reuther, to political meetings all across the country. According to the presidential aide, COPE director Barkan also did an "excellent job," as did all the federation's regional directors. To "a man [they] were on the ball," the campaign manager informed Reuther. Overall, "I could not have been more impressed and I made note of my impressions repeatedly to the President."[13]

Understandably, COPE's top leaders were proud of the labor movement's performance as well. The victory was a vindication, they reasoned, of the correctness of the coalition approach. Now that reform-minded Democrats had swept the election, they could see no impediment to repeal of section 14(b). "It wasn't so long ago that I congratulated you on your splendid victory" in Oklahoma, Barkan wrote Roy Tillman in mid-November 1964. "My cup of political joy overflowed when we got the news" that not only had the Johnson-Humphrey ticket carried Oklahoma, but that the COPE-endorsed Senate candidate, Fred Harris (D), had won too. And, there could be no doubt that that Harris realized he owed labor a political debt. "You would be interested," Barkan informed Tillman, to know that Harris "called the office last week while I was out and left word for us not to worry about [his vote on] 14(b)."[14]

ORGANIZED LABOR LOBBIES THE JOHNSON ADMINISTRATION

The AFL-CIO's position in November 1964 was, to a good degree, novel. For over two decades, labor politicians strove to build an alliance with the Democratic party and from within that alliance tried to shape party policy, particularly on labor legislation. During those years, most union political analysts believed, either the party's conservative wing forestalled their efforts or a generally unsympathetic Republican party dominated the political environment. Now, with the reelection of a president who had explicitly sought to utilize the federation's political energies in the promotion of his administration's program, as well as the advent of what most observers contended would be a "reform" Congress, AFL-CIO leaders anticipated harvesting their long-cherished goal of repealing section 14(b) and thereby invalidating some twenty state right-to-work laws. In this kind of climate, organized labor's chieftains expected much more than lukewarm commitment to its primary legislative objective.

AFL-CIO officialdom understood, however, that a critical ingredient to victory in this area lay in winning presidential commitment to making it an "administration" goal as well. Without the top Democrat's coordination and backing, without the chief executive personally making it a part of his program for reform, too many legislators might find it convenient to forget their pre-election promises to labor. Moreover, from labor's perspective, none of the former counterforces preventing presidential endorsement and promotion existed. Johnson had actively solicited the AFL-CIO's lobbying and electoral aid in the 1964 congressional session, and the enactment of the rest of his Great Society proposals hinged on continued effective co-operation. In addition, the president was aware—to some degree at least—of how COPE had used the issue as a rallying cry, suggesting that future participation of the lower echelons of the labor movement depended on effecting repeal. In the final analysis, Johnson could simply not contend, as had President Kennedy, that the conservatives in the party were still too powerful. The liberal and moderate wing clearly had enough votes to repeal section 14(b) of the Taft-Hartley Act.

That is not to say that top federation strategists thought President Johnson would take up their cause without substantial pressure. The AFL-CIO's legislative directors knew that at best the former Senate majority leader was a political opportunist, and at worst tended to be conservative on labor issues. "I had a lot of suspicions" about the president, George Meany later recalled. "I knew Johnson...was a tough politician. I had worked with him to a certain extent, but I didn't trust him; I just didn't trust Johnson."[15]

Still, they expected that the president would pay his debts, for after all, he was above all else a consummate politician. Labor lobbyists recognized that Johnson's leadership style emphasized balancing interests by putting together a legislative consensus, and they hoped that their insistence on repeal would make it one of the foremost interests of the Democratic co-alition that the administration would have to satisfy to keep its legislative influence at peak efficiency. Unionists who claimed to know Johnson well believed the president accepted, more and more over the course of time, organized labor's arguments against legislative restrictions on union security. Thus, H. S. Hank Brown, president of the Texas AFL-CIO, discussed the issue with his fellow Texan many times. "I think Johnson, the longer he stayed" in Washington, Brown recalled, "seemed to be more in accord with the A.F. of L.-CIO's position that the right-to-work was a bad scheme that really pit labor against management."[16]

Besides all this, the president's renowned skill as a legislative tactician provided a further reason to secure his personal commitment. As Senate majority leader, Johnson had proved himself a talented strategist and tac-tician. Moreover, if needed, he could cultivate both conservative Democrats and liberal Republicans better than either liberal congressmembers or the AFL-CIO. By concentrating on winning proposals, negotiating with congressional elites, engaging in discreet liaison contact, engineering coalition votes privately, and timing his battles perfectly, the former majority leader had won many close victories in the Senate. "Johnson in close contact," said IUD legislative director and fellow Texan Robert Oliver, "was one of the most persuasive people there ever was, just absolutely almost irresistible."[17]

Thus, President Johnson's position as party leader and his leadership skills made it imperative that AFL-CIO leaders win the administration over to active participation in the anticipated 14(b) repeal drive. Most unionists, though, also realized that moving the president to do so would require serious self-assertion on the part of the highest echelon of the federation. At a November meeting of the IUD, Walter Reuther informed the department's officers that the failure to convince successive presidents of the need for labor law reform had been a long-standing weakness of the labor movement. At his last meeting with President Kennedy, in fact, Reuther said he had told the chief executive that the "labor movement had not been tough enough in the [legislative] in-fighting" within his administration, "and that there were times when we should have pushed him" further on matters of particular interest to labor. Kennedy, he claimed, had agreed. The IUD chief argued that if labor sincerely wanted to repeal 14(b), it was going to have to be hard-nosed about it. Labor's legislative leaders would have to apply pressure to "the people who control the power structure [and] make the decisions." We "have never learned to bargain with the government" on these kinds of issues, Reuther insisted. We just simply "get taken in."[18]

Labor's top leaders could not afford to "get taken in" on this kind of question once again. COPE functionaries had made repeal of section 14(b) the most salient part of their appeal to the secondary leadership, and ostensibly received a positive response. Additionally, COPE endorsees had won and won big. In a way, at least in the short run, future political activism on the part of this tier of the labor movement, which was the only way the AFL-CIO could reach the ordinary union member, depended on federation officials' ability to translate the victory into *positive* legislative gains that could be appreciated by union officials closest to the collective bargaining system.

In the past, it was not unusual for the national AFL-CIO's officers and lobbyists charged with legislative responsibilities to have somewhat divergent perceptions about priorities. They dealt with politicians on a day-to-day basis on a wide range of issues and thus had to maintain a cooperative and continuing relationship. This made it appear that at times they were more willing to see a legislator's point of view than their constitutency's. Liberal attorney Joseph Rauh, for example, thought that Robert Oliver was "more Lyndon Johnson's lobbyist to the labor movement than he was ever the labor movement's lobbyist to Lyndon Johnson." Rauh admired Johnson's ability to have the person who was "supposed to tell you to go farther

go back and tell the other side that they really don't want to go that far
and that he's getting them the best deal possible."[19]

In 1964, though, no matter how much top AFL-CIO officers felt a convergence of interests with the president on Great Society goals, they knew
many AFL-CIO people would be severely embarrassed if the president did
not undertake the leadership necessary to achieve labor's primary legislative
goal. Through the first part of November George Meany, legislative director
Andrew Biemiller, and COPE director Alexander Barkan analyzed the election results, contacted state labor leaders, and conferred with legal staff,
close political allies, and international union lobbyists in the preliminary
effort to structure a 14(b) repeal program. But as some labor leaders suspected, it soon became apparent that the Johnson administration was less
than enthusiastic about giving this measure priority status. At a session of
the AFL-CIO's executive council meeting on November 24, Secretary of
Labor Willard Wirtz informed the council that labor's legislative priorities,
as they applied to the submission of proposals, did not coincide with the
administration's schedule for the new Congress. In a December summary
of his executive council remarks, the secretary privately wrote the president
that he had "pressed strongly and bluntly . . . the position that the timing
of any Administration action regarding Section 14(b) should and must be
left *entirely* a matter of Presidential determination." According to Wirtz,
George Meany and Walter Reuther were agreeable; however, IBEW leader
Joseph Keenan as well as legislative director Andrew Biemiller argued for
an early submission, fearing delay would give the opposition time to marshall their resources and dilute the Johnson administration's commitment.
"There is unquestionably sharp division on this within the AFL-CIO Council," noted the secretary. For the time being, though, Wirtz asserted that
the two most powerful AFL-CIO officials had acceded to the president's
wishes to press ahead with other proposals early in the session. Ultimately,
Wirtz pointed out, the administration *would* have to bring the matter up
and give it full backing. "If there is such support, there will be no problem,"
he judged. "If there isn't, there will be a *strong* adverse reaction" by union
leaders against the administration.[20]

Wirtz's reticence on behalf of the Johnson administration posed a dilemma
for George Meany. Both he and Walter Reuther identified strongly with the
president's social-welfare goals. By this time they had reached the stature
of labor statesmen; their legislative vision was cast over a broader range
and hence they were more willing to allow President Johnson some leeway
in pursuing repeal. Nevertheless, Meany had to reassure executive council
members who were answerable to others further down in the labor movement that the president would deal with the problem by giving it the kind
of backing labor felt it should have. Thus, he confronted Johnson about
repeal, emphasizing the AFL-CIO's part in his reelection. To provide further

substantiation of 14(b)'s importance to organized labor, as well as to make a political demonstration of his own, Meany brought an AFL-CIO delegation to the president on December 14 to reiterate the federation's concerns. They received a presidential commitment on 14(b) repeal, but LBJ advised them that there were "several other matters of unfinished business" that "should have priority."[21]

The conversations had their intended effect of elevating the importance of 14(b) repeal within the Johnson administration. In late December, Wirtz recommended "that repeal be proposed by the Administration at such time during the First Session, as is deemed consistent with over-all legislative objectives." Noting that the Democratic platforms of 1960 and 1964 promised repeal and that from 1961 to 1964 Democratic administrations had not submitted repeal bills, the secretary believed this administration should move forward with his recommendation. Wirtz felt that the president now had to determine to what extent he should publicly back the proposal and whether the bill should be a formal administration submission.[22]

In early January 1965, Johnson settled the proposal and mitigated AFL-CIO criticism. He explicitly, if curtly, acknowleged his administration's support of 14(b) repeal in his state of the union message. Concurrently, liberal Democrat Frank Thompson, Jr. (NJ) introduced a repeal bill in the House. Nevertheless, even these moves were not actions the president undertook with any alacrity. The president did not care to risk his legislative credits by bringing such a controversial matter to the boiling point early in the session. He made sure, however, that his aides maintained close personal contact with the federation officers planning the eventual assault. Vice-President Hubert Humphrey, in particular, had the confidence of a broad range of laborites and served as the keynote speaker at the federation's January 1965 legislative conference. But during the first half of 1965, while Great Society proposals wended their way through Congress, President Johnson postponed legislative action on labor law reform.[23]

Meanwhile, right-to-work matters at the state level veered in a pro-labor direction as well. Indiana laborites avenged themselves by repealing the state's 1957 anti–union security statute and even Wyoming unionists made a serious try at overturning their 1963 law. In both these states in 1965, Democrats closed ranks behind labor in *offensive* thrusts, something that did not happen too often. The Democrats in Indiana were the most impressive: 35 state senators and 73 house representatives scored a perfect, pro-labor −100 index of cohesion, as shown in Table 6.2. Their Wyoming counterparts in the house tallied a strong −89. Republicans, though, united in the opposite direction, compounding a 78 index in Indiana (60 in the senate and 91 in the house) and a somewhat less solid 68 in Wyoming.

Thus, with the political winds blowing in labor's favor at both the state and national levels, perhaps it did not seem as critical to Meany and Reuther to be "hard-nosed" about repeal with the president, and of course their

6.2

Rice Index of Cohesion of Democratic and Republican Parties, in All State Legislatures, on Right-to-Work Measures, 1965–1967

STATE/YEAR	TOTAL	INDEXES SENATE	HOUSE	BALLOTS CAST SENATE	HOUSE
DEMOCRATIC					
Indiana 1965	-100	-100	-100	35	73
Wyoming 1967	-	NV	-100	NV	28
Wyoming 1965	-	NV	-89	NV	35
REPUBLICAN					
Indiana 1965	78	60	91	15	22
Wyoming 1965	-	NV	68	NV	25
Wyoming 1967	-	NV	64	NV	33

Source: Appendix A
Key: NV–No Vote
Index: +100(Totally Cohesive in Favor of Right to Work)
          -100(Totally Cohesive Against Right to Work)

desire to remain administration intimates facilitated the chief executive's scheduling. After having satisfied himself that Johnson would, at least at some point, work for repeal, Meany looked favorably on administration arguments that AFL-CIO lobbyists had to undertake sufficient liaison contact to prepare the way for a smooth legislative course. Congressman Frank Thompson had introduced a repeal bill, H.R. 77, in January, with Senator Pat McNamara (D-MI) doing likewise in the upper chamber with S. 256. Laborites descended on their legislative representatives after the AFL-CIO legislative conference, and from January through mid-May the liaison work continued. Contact between Meany and Biemiller, the president and his aides, and key legislative players occurred frequently, with the AFL-CIO obviously taking the initiative in most instances. Real progress, however, awaited the president's decision to move ahead. With Reuther, especially, Johnson administration officials could play on his somewhat stronger social-welfare sympathies and point out the importance of passing Great Society legislation first. Indeed, according to Willard Wirtz, Reuther told him that he personally felt that any AFL-CIO pressure aimed at bringing 14(b) repeal up before the Democratic coalition had accomplished its social-welfare agenda was "a serious mistake."[24]

Given these assurances, the president had clearly succeeded in stalling for time without damaging his relationship with labor. By May 1965, however, the administration's agenda had progressed to the point where the president could no longer afford to put off the repeal drive. After the AFL-CIO executive council meeting in April, union leaders' demands for action escalated. Even the unaffiliated Teamsters were placing heavy pressure on members of Congress. As some of labor's political strategists had warned, a recent congressional poll by Andrew Biemiller indicated that many of the representatives now did not relish having to vote on 14(b) repeal. If the president did not soon take action, the "strong adverse reaction" Wirtz had warned of earlier was likely to occur.[25]

Under the leadership of Larry O'Brien, administration lobbyists tested congressional sentiment. In mid-May, after having Wirtz clear matters with Meany and Biemiller, the president signaled the launching of the joint administration-labor repeal drive by including 14(b) repeal in his labor message to Congress. "These words from you—'I recommend the repeal of Section 14(b)'—will be the only seven *words* that will have any effect at all in this whole business," Wirtz counseled the president on May 20. He advised Johnson to stay above the fray and to avoid debating the merits of repeal publicly. "This issue is not going to be settled by reason," wrote the Secretary of Labor, "but on a stand-up-and-be-counted basis."[26]

THE JOHNSON ADMINISTRATION'S EFFORTS TO SECURE 14(B) REPEAL

For the first time since 1949, the AFL-CIO had convinced the Democratic leaders to actively pursue beneficial labor law reform. President Johnson's considerable success with other issues during the first session of the Eighty-ninth Congress indicated that the legislative momentum was on the side of organized labor. That very success precluded party leaders from arguing that the president and the party did not wield effective legislative control. During the ensuing months, however, the contentiousness of the issue continued to strain the Democrats' commitment to 14(b) repeal. Nevertheless, the battle over repeal in the House proved that the Johnson administration was willing to expend resources and time, once the president's major proposals had been taken care of, in order to keep organized labor's political support.

After the president's labor message signaled the official go-ahead, Congressman Frank Thompson's subcommittee on 14(b) repeal took up hearings in earnest in late May 1965. Tactically, both the administration and the AFL-CIO concentrated on the House first because it was there that they believed they would have the harder fight. The Thompson subcommittee's first witness, Secretary of Labor Wirtz, presented the administration's official case for repealing the provision; George Meany quickly followed and rendered the AFL-CIO's formal objections. Afterward, assorted civil rights leaders voiced their backing. In this way labor's political strategists thought they could heighten the impression that a broad coalition of citizens groups supported the proposal. Then, to further buttress organized labor's attempts to make the issue appear less special interest oriented, the president of the National Farmer's Union, a liberal agricultural group often allied with labor on progressive causes, informed legislators that his organization supported labor's position. The subcommittee also heard the complaints of groups opposed to repeal, with the National Right to Work Committee most prominent among them.[27]

As Willard Wirtz had commented, though, repeal was a "stand-up-and-be-counted" issue on which the hearings of the subcommittee would have little persuasive effect other than to provide the rationale for Thompson's bill. Meanwhile, under the direction of Larry O'Brien, Johnson administration operatives lobbied legislators on behalf of the measure. The administration had concocted a plan to win the votes of representatives from the agricultural Midwest: their votes for 14(b) repeal in exchange for eastern legislators' backing of an unpopular farm subsidy proposal. Despite the "tremendous struggle" that would be necessary to win, predicted Hubert Humphrey to Walter Reuther in late June 1965, "we intend to be victorious."[28]

Also in June, the AFL-CIO and affiliates stepped up their efforts to apply local pressure on legislators. The Texas AFL-CIO, for example, exhorted its affiliates to provide financing for a citizens coalition. Through the public relations activities of this group, and with the help of state central financing, Texas labor leaders hoped to influence the votes of eleven representatives in the state who claimed they still had open minds on the subject. Prompted by the national office, AFL-CIO officials in other states undertook similar campaigns.[29]

In June, the bill hit a snag when Adam Clayton Powell, a black congressman from Harlem who chaired the House Labor Committee, threatened to stall progress until the House passed fair employment amendments to the Civil Rights Act. Shortly, though, Democratic leaders prevailed upon Powell to bring the legislation to the floor. By late July, arm-twisting by labor lobbyists reached a peak. Vice-President Hubert Humphrey continued cultivating rural representatives. Even the president participated by securing a handful of votes no one else could win. On July 28, the House passed Thompson's repeal bill, H.R. 77, by a 221 to 203 margin. As Table 6.3 shows, 138 House Republicans adopted an anti-labor position on the question and scored a Rice Index of Cohesion of 70. Their 286 Democratic colleagues tallied a pro-labor -40 cohesion index overall: 190 northern representatives recording a strong -92 in favor of repeal, with the conservative, southern contingent of 96 members nearly equaling the Republicans in their opposition by totaling an anti-labor 63.[30]

The AFL-CIO and the Johnson administration had emerged victorious in the first round. According to COPE's Alexander Barkan, labor received "particularly strong support . . . from the new congressmen who were elected in 1964." Still, mindful of the vagaries of the legislative process, Barkan

6.3

Rice Index of Cohesion of Congressional Parties, on Repeal of Section 14(b) of the
Taft-Hartley Act, 1965–1966

LEGISLATION/YEAR	AGAINST LABOR	FOR LABOR	TOTAL	PERCENT YES	PERCENT NO	RICE INDEX
H.R. 77 1965						
House						
D						
Northern	8	182	190	4	96	-92
Southern	78	18	96	81	19	63
Total	86	200	286	30	70	-40
R	117	21	138	85	15	70
Senate 1965						
D Cloture						
Northern	5	36	41	12	88	-76
Southern	16	4	20	80	20	60
Total	21	40	61	34	66	-31
R	26	5	31	84	16	68
Both Chambers						
D	107	240	347	31	69	-38
R	143	26	169	85	15	69
Total	250	266	516	48	52	-3
Senate 1966						
D Cloture						
Northern	5	40	45	11	89	-78
Southern	17	5	22	77	23	55
Total	22	45	67	33	67	-34
R	26	6	32	81	19	63
Total	48	51	99	48	52	-3

Source: Congressional Quarterly, _Congress and the Nation, 1945–1964_
          (Washington, DC: Congressional Quarterly Service, 1965).
          Congressional Quarterly, _Congressional Quarterly Almanac, 1965,_
          1966 (Washington, DC: Congressional Quarterly, 1965,1966)
Index: +100(Totally Cohesive Against Labor)
          -100(Totally Cohesive in Favor of Labor)
          Rice Index Rounded to Nearest Integer

cautioned state-level leaders not only to thank the new members warmly
for their votes but also to withhold criticism of those representatives who
did not side with labor this time. Affiliates should be informed, the political
chief wrote Oklahoma AFL-CIO president Roy Tillman, "but please do not
issue any public statements attacking ... Congressmen ... or threatening any
reprisals. Let the vote speak for itself at this time."[31]

THE LIMITATIONS OF LABOR'S INFLUENCE IN A PARTISAN ENVIRONMENT

Facilitating labor's conquest of conservative forces in the House of Representatives had been strenuous and costly—in terms of the time expended
by administration officials—but did not pose any fundamental obstacle to
President Johnson's leadership in other areas. As the focus of action shifted

to the Senate, however, the cost of 14(b) repeal escalated as mounting opposition from repeal foes raised the legislative ante. These forces, led by Senate minority leader Everett Dirksen (R-IL), with whom LBJ had always had a constructive relationship, blocked Senate repeal with filibusters on two separate occasions by early 1966. Only by being as determined as Dirksen could the president have chipped away enough votes to prevail. However, a bitter and divisive fight in the Senate would not only have threatened the remaining facets of the Great Society program, it would also have hampered the president's conduct of foreign policy, which, because of Vietnam, drew more and more of his attention. When presented with the choice of alienating Dirksen or angering organized labor—whose support in domestic and foreign policy matters he would in all likelihood keep anyway—the president chose the latter course. Thus, even at the height of liberal Democratic control, the Senate struggle over 14(b) repeal revealed the limitations of labor's influence with the Democrats. In the president's estimation, labor leaders such as George Meany and Walter Reuther would never long abandon his administration.

Of course, at the start of the Senate's repeal hearings in late June, the future difficulties were not apparent. Speaking for the AFL-CIO, Legislative Director Andrew Biemiller put forth the federation's position, basically reiterating George Meany's testimony. Subsequent to the hearings, further progress in the Senate stalled until the House vote in late July, after which LBJ personally called George Meany and urged immediate action in the Senate. In mid-August, the upper chamber's subcommittee handling the repeal hearings voted to recommend removal of 14(b) to the full Senate Committee on Education and Labor. At this point, the activities of repeal opponents finally began to produce meaningful results.[32]

For most of 1965, the National Right to Work Committee had been desperately promoting an extensive public relations program designed to forestall repeal. The NRTWC's three goals were specific and limited: to convince the public that the fight would be close, that no one wanted repeal except devious labor leaders, and that President Johnson's actions were a blatant political payoff to Big Labor. National Right to Work Committee lobbyists believed they could capitalize on general industry and media opposition to 14(b) repeal and thus generate some committed conservative support in the Senate. By arousing public opinion against repeal, NRTWC strategists hoped to show that the battle had not been lost. According to the committee's executive vice-president, Reed Larson, while "union lobbyists were moving their bill as quietly as possible in the House, in order to avoid public controversy, we were endeavoring to create controversy and thereby focus public attention on the issue." In this effort, the ardent editorial opposition of many newspapers provided a useful public relations tool. A careful NRTWC study of newspaper reaction to the proposal indicated that the nation's editorial writers strongly opposed the repeal of section 14(b) from the Taft-Hartley Act. The major thrust of the organization's campaign, therefore, would be to try to promote as much adverse editorial comment as possible and funnel it to key conservative legislators. Thus, NRTWC press releases aimed at stimulating adverse editorial position taking. And the group also worked hard, according to Director of Information Hugh Newton, "to keep editors informed of what other editors were saying about Section 14(b), thereby generating even more comment on the issue."[33]

In addition, the NRTWC opened a temporary office near the Capitol. Under the direction of Legislative Liaison Ed Nellor, a former newspaper reporter, committee lobbyists conducted research for pro-right-to-work congressmembers and held luncheon meetings for their aides. Nellor and his lieutenants distributed ample copies of the committee's anti–14(b) repeal material to all legislators.[34] But most importantly, as a result of these activities, NRTWC officials enlisted the generalship of Senate Republican Minority Leader Everett Dirksen in a last-ditch attempt to prevent repeal. "At our initial meeting with the Senate Minority Leader in July," said NRTWC Information Director Newton, "the Illinois Republican was not optimistic about waging a successful fight for 14(b)." He believed the public cared little about what was going on and that labor's legislative allies had the votes needed. Shortly thereafter, Newton returned armed with 3,000 editorials from 1,500 newspapers, most of them opposing repeal. "The change in Senator Dirksen's attitude toward the issue was immediate," observed Newton. "Victory had become a definite possibility."[35]

Moreover, the success of Republican senator Paul Fannin (AZ) in securing a respectable number of conservative senators willing to filibuster repeal further convinced Dirksen. With the cooperation of southern Democrat A. Willis Robertson (VA), by mid-August Fannin, a former Arizona governor and Barry Goldwater's replacement in the Senate, forged a coalition of Republicans and southern Democrats. "Without question, Senator Fannin's role was a vital one in assembling the forces necessary for the successful defense of Section 14B of the Taft-Hartley Act," recalled NRTWC chief Reed Larson. "His efforts led to the enlistment of more and more Senators, laying the base of support necessary to encourage Senator Dirksen to assume leadership in the Senate debate."[36]

Since 14(b) repeal opponents thought that the Senate's labor supporters had enough votes for passage on a straight vote, the only recourse open was to stop the measure from reaching that point. Now sensing serious trouble, AFL-CIO strategists beseeched Democratic leaders to bring the measure up for a quick vote, but with little success. Senator Wayne Morse (D-OR) informed Mike Manatos, White House Senate liaison, that "there is tremendous pressure from Labor to lay away [the] Higher Education [bill] until after 14(b)." By early September, Dirksen had gone public with his threat to lead the filibuster, and the Senate Labor Committee sent the repeal bill on to the whole chamber. Still, Senate Majority Leader Mike Mansfield (D-MT) refused to accelerate the scheduling for floor debate. On September 2, the majority leader told Manatos that he would have the president's "must" legislation—the farm, immigration, highway beautification, and vocational education bills—on the calendar within a week. "All of these, as you know," Manatos wrote to Larry O'Brien, "are practically within our grasp." The section 14(b) repeal bill, however, would come after. "Mansfield does not want to be in the position of having 14(b) on the calendar all by itself," the Senate liaison wrote. "It would then be impossible for him to avoid scheduling it. Despite all of the pleas from Labor, Mansfield will remain firm in his contention the President and country will be better off if we pass" the other bills first. "There is no doubt in his mind," Manatos informed O'Brien, "that this bill will be in for very tough sledding."[37]

The administration thus proceeded with its own agenda—to the dismay of labor. AFL-CIO leaders then escalated their pressure on the president, insisting that the chief executive and his aides become more actively involved. This approach yielded some success, as the administration stepped up its efforts to lobby the Senate. As Larry O'Brien wrote Manatos in mid-September, administration representatives wanted to be sure that "we can validly claim we have made our share of contacts..." in case they were questioned by Biemiller. In addition, the president talked to Dirksen but without much success. He "called me a time or two about it," the minority leader later recalled. "And then I called him, and then I went to see him, and I made it, I thought, abundantly plain, first that we had enough troops on both sides of the aisle to stop that sort of thing, that it just couldn't win and [he] might just as well withdraw it." In this exchange, the president's renowned persuasive powers seemed notably absent.[38]

The president was in an increasingly uncomfortable position. In general, Johnson's relationship with Dirksen had been good and the senator had contributed bipartisan support on many issues. And, according to Manatos, he "could be persuaded on the basis of logic and justice that his course was wrong." Both Johnson and Dirksen had crossed swords on occasion, but with little lasting ill feeling. The president and his aides knew, however, that if the minority leader carried through with his threat to filibuster, only the harshest kind of political tactics would win the day.[39]

Unfortunately for the Johnson administration, George Meany knew it too. In a September 21 memo to Larry O'Brien, Andrew Biemiller outlined the results of his and Meany's visits with the liberal and moderate Senate contingent. Clearly, Biemiller designed the thrust of his comments to convince LBJ's aide that the federation had sufficient Senate support to meet Dirksen's filibuster head on, hoping to nudge the administration into using hard-nosed tactics. According to the legislative director's report, all senators surveyed were willing "to take on the hardships involved in an attempt to break the threatened filibuster." They believed, furthermore, that round-

the-clock sessions would be needed and doubted that the Republican minority leader's "filibuster group was as potent as Dirksen claimed." The
senators also promised "to notify the Majority Leader of their views on this
question." Biemiller pointedly added Senator Warren Magnuson's (D-WA)
opinion about the possible adverse consequences for the party. In his role
as Senate campaign committee chairman, Magnuson asserted that he would
"tell the [majority leader] it is imperative [this] issue be settled this year,
not next[,] for benefit of Senators up in 1966 and many House members
including new members from Washington."[40]

Not unexpectedly, Johnson administration officials preferred to downplay
their responsibility and shift the major burden for securing passage to the
federation—Wirtz told a September 20 executive council meeting that repeal
was "in labor people's hands." Meany and Biemiller knew, from an earlier
meeting with Dirksen, that the minority leader's price for dropping his
opposition was too high.[41] According to Biemiller, "Meany loathed Dirksen
and all those honey-toned speeches," but at that time he felt compelled to
try to persuade the minority leader that it was unfair and undemocratic not
to allow the measure to come to a vote. "George," Dirksen said, "you're
not going to get a straight up-and-down vote." "You're in a fight; you're
fighting me and I'm fighting you. When I fight I use everything," said the
Illinois senator. As Biemiller recalled the confrontation, the Illinois Republican was "pontificating all over the place about a man's principles," but
intimated that he would drop the filibuster if labor dropped its opposition
to his pet project of trying to undo the Supreme Court's ruling on legislative
reapportionment. Meany refused. The "Senate Minority Leader and all his
anti-labor stooges can filibuster until hell freezes over before I will agree to
sell the people short for that kind of deal," the labor chief later told the
1965 AFL-CIO convention. Meany accepted the liberal contention that
reapportionment would add political representation to urban areas and by
decreasing the power of conservative ruralists prospectively lead to more
progressive policies. Such an agreement with Dirksen would only have hurt
labor's political abilities in the long run, he believed, even on trade union
issues.[42]

Thus, unable to prod the Democrats' top leadership into taking harsh
action against the filibuster, supporters of 14(b) repeal fought Dirksen's
delaying tactics as best they could. Mansfield's public comments about the
forthcoming struggle certainly did not cause the filibuster group to doubt
the viability of their challenge. In late September, news sources quoted the
majority leader as stating he would not "pursue exercises in procedural
futility" such as round-the-clock sessions. Unfortunately, this made Dirksen's task easier and removed a psychological variable. The minority leader
began his filibuster on October 4, and over the course of the next week
federation leaders did their utmost to marshall the necessary two-thirds
votes to pass cloture. On October 11, when Senator Mansfield called for a

vote on cloture, the Dirksen forces prevailed. By a 17 vote margin, 45 to 47, Senate Democratic leaders failed to obtain the two-thirds vote needed to invoke cloture. Table 6.3 lists the index of cohesion for the 41 northern Democrats as a pro-labor − 76—in sharp contrast to the 20 representatives of southern wing who compiled an anti-labor 60. Twenty-six like-minded Republicans went along with the southerners with an index of 68. Thus, the total Democratic pro-labor cohesion of − 31 was not enough to defeat the Republican-Dixiecrat coalition.[43]

The defeat terribly embarrassed the AFL-CIO's political leaders. In the immediate aftermath of Dirksen's victory, they searched for answers as to why their cherished legislative goal became the first major casualty in the president's program. The most obvious explanation, at least to many in the labor movement, was the quality of presidential leadership. If one thing became clear in the ensuing weeks, it was that organized labor's top executives were not willing to let the administration off the hook so easily. Federation leaders realized that if 14(b) repeal did not pass in the Eighty-ninth Congress, it might be a long time before political conditions were again ripe for such a change. Additonally, almost every high-level official now knew that failure to have a Democratic-controlled Congress produce reform would severely undermine their efforts to keep secondary level labor leaders active in politics.

For its part, the Johnson administration concerned itself less with the defeat than with how the AFL-CIO leadership was reacting to it. The day after the failed cloture vote, Hubert Humphrey talked with George Meany "and found him surprisingly amendable [sic]." Humphrey told the president that Meany said "we've had a wonderful Congress … altho [sic] I am very disappointed about 14-B." Meany indicated that the federation would like to bring the matter up in the next session, but was uneasy about how Senator Mansfield intended to schedule the measure. For that reason, the AFL-CIO chief wanted to talk personally with the president. Humphrey noted, however, that Meany was in no way "vindictive or vexed unreasonably."[44]

Given this, one could not blame Johnson for judging that national AFL-CIO chieftains, with some exceptions, were "not reacting to [sic] badly about 14B," as a White House aide phrased it. With this knowledge in hand, the president decided that although he would have to continue to make it appear that administration commitment on repeal was substantial, any breach between himself and organized labor would not be irreparable. Consequently, Wirtz appeared at a special 14(b) repeal strategy session of the AFL-CIO executive council on October 28, mainly to reassure the labor executives that repeal was still a high presidential priority. In addition, the president sent a personal message to the November IUD convention thanking labor for contributing the "special shock troops" necessary to enact the Economic Opportunity Act and other administration proposals. "We have made significant progress in 1965 toward the long-sought goal of repealing

Section 14(b)," wrote the president. "Just as we had to come back last year
to finish the unfinished battle for Medicare, we will come back in the next
session to remove this divisive provision from the law."[45]

Despite these presidential assurances, the cloture defeat had stunned the
federation's political leaders into confusion, forcing them to reconsider their
strategy. This was particularly evident at the executive council meeting in
late October. At the April 1965 executive council meeting, federation officers, acting on the suggestion of IBEW secretary Joseph Keenan, formed
a subcommittee to study the wisdom of proposing broader labor law reform.
Unfortunately, the subcommittee, chaired by Walter Reuther, had put off
the work in confident anticipation that there would be little trouble with
14(b) and the federation could work on broader amendments the next
session. With the Dirksen victory came renewed demands that repeal should
have been worked into a more inclusive labor law reform package, particularly since it now appeared as if the battle would be resolved under the
glare of intense publicity.

Many labor officials agreed. Industrial Union Department general counsel
David Feller, Reuther's designated representative on the subcommittee
studying broader Taft-Hartley revision, informed the IUD president on October 27 "that it would be a great mistake to insist" that 14(b) continue to
be the sole objective. Repeal of that provision, Feller argued, would not
help the labor movement where it was weak. "If the labor movement is to
remain static and simply seek to protect what it has, it makes sense to regard
the repeal of 14(b) as our sole or primary objective." Removal of the clause
would "have psychological value, no doubt, but that is all." Being able to
negotiate union security clauses would not help most organizing campaigns;
indeed, revisions dealing with the rights of strike replacements, NLRB de-
lays, and liberal interpretations of employer free speech rules were much
more important. "The image of the labor movement created by the 14(b)
fight is the image of a strong labor movement, able to negotiate union-shop
contracts with employers and desirous of picking up dues from the minority
of employees in such situations who do not join the union." Feller advised
Reuther that an attempt to combine repeal with revisions designed to show
how "the overwhelming strength of employers" constantly crushed infant
unions would counterbalance labor's poor public relations image. In fact,
by combining repeal with changes restricting employer campaign tactics and
speeding up NLRB procedures, the AFL-CIO could get the kind of amendments it needed to organize the unorganized as well as 14(b) excision.[46]

Feller's suggestions, however, did not go far. At the October 28 meeting
of the executive council, it was clear that most officers regarded a switch
in direction at this point as capable of doing more harm than good. Nevertheless, the special meeting generated two objectives. The federation had to
hold the votes it had in the Senate until Congress reconvened in January
1966. In addition, it now had to conduct a public relations campaign of

sufficient intensity to break loose some of the votes of the anti-cloture senators. A special 14(b) repeal subcommittee, again chaired by Reuther, would direct these activities.[47]

While such a campaign was indeed important now that public opinion had become a crucial tactical factor, it would accomplish little if the AFL-CIO could not get the critical help it needed from the Democratic leadership. In mid-November, Reuther and other executive council members lobbied with Hubert Humphrey for three hours on 14(b), resulting in the vice-president's personal commitment to work more closely with labor lobbyists on the next assault. Most of the federation's political strategists had been upset at Majority Leader Mansfield's reluctance to press forward with 14(b) repeal during the previous session, and set out to convince the administration to prevail upon Mansfield to pay greater heed to labor's strategic game plan. Whenever Meany or Biemiller had a conference with the senator from Montana, the federation's legislative director recalled, "Mansfield wouldn't say a damned thing when we talked to him, he'd just sit there and puff on that pipe." Especially exasperating was the majority leader's continued refusal to counter Dirksen's unusual tactic of leading a filibuster by adopting the equally unusual tactic of round-the-clock Senate sessions. According to Reuther, Mansfield personally disliked the kind of arm-twisting that was necessary for a measure like 14(b) repeal. Hubert Humphrey's intercession through the Senate's Democratic Policy Committee, which met in December, "made some real progress" according to the vice-president, in convincing the majority leader to place 14(b) on the agenda at the beginning of the next session.[48]

Meanwhile, the AFL-CIO's public relations campaign materials went into distribution. By this point, though, the NRTWC's propaganda thoroughly dominated the media for it had been working at blocking repeal for most of 1965. In addition to the AFL-CIO's publicity efforts, a special group of union representatives targeted 33 states for individualized lobbying activity. Until Congress started again, they concentrated on visits with the senators from their state, began rank-and-file letter-writing drives, and sought to secure additional coalition assistance.[49]

The federation's legislative department also planned a counterstrategy for Dirksen's second "extended discussion," as the Illinois Republican euphemized his filibustering. The Senate minority leader had again promised he would not shrink from the task in the next session. AFL-CIO spokespersons in the Senate thus decided to keep their speech time to a minimum, forcing Dirksen's group to shoulder a greater portion of debate time. Moreover, until the last minute, AFL-CIO chiefs continued to hold out hope that the Democratic leadership would extend the hours of debate.

During the AFL-CIO's preparatory period in early January, President Johnson promised his assistance. The president, however, refrained from personally entering the battle, preferring to let the Senate Democratic leadership and his aides handle as much as possible. And in this, administration functionaries were much more interested in political appearances than in the fulfillment of commitments to labor. Wirtz and presidential assistant Bill Moyers, for example, concocted a plan they hoped would help the president politically on two fronts. Moyers recommended to the chief executive that the administration submit a bill allowing federal intervention in public service strikes such as the one currently disrupting the transit system in New York City. "If a way can be found," the assistant wrote, "why not tie it to repeal of 14(b), which short of some miracle is dead this session." "While some labor noses would be tweaked, Wirtz points out that Labor has to stay with you and the loss in that corner would more than be compensated for by gains with Mr. Average American," Moyers closed.[50]

However, it was now crucial that the president intervene personally if the measure was to have any hope at all. As Senate majority leader, Johnson had used round-the-clock sessions on occasion. Moreover, he had never been particularly intimidated by a filibuster. "The trouble with you guys is that you don't realize that you can beat the filibuster," Johnson once told liberal advocate Joseph Rauh. "You can always beat a filibuster if you've got fifty-one strong enough people" on hand to keep a quorum. In addition, he had options other than insisting Mansfield hold extended sessions. He could try harder to convince Dirksen to drop the filibuster. Alternatively, he could put his renowned persuasive powers to work and get enough of his former southern Democratic colleagues from right-to-work states to vote for cloture in the interests of democracy. Afterward, they could vote against repeal if they wanted to protect themselves from conservative criticism.

The president, however, chose to do none of these; he would not put his personal legislative influence on the line. "I don't know that the President ever tried to overcome my conviction on the subject," Dirksen later recalled, "but I remember occasions when I undertook to overcome his." Nor, according to Mansfield, did Johnson intervene directly with the majority leader and ask him to forgo his normal predilections for Senate scheduling. Nor did he try to dissuade any of the southern Democrats from cooperating with Dirksen. In weighing the costs of alternative courses of action, the president evidently decided that labor's displeasure was less encumbering than the legislative debts he would incur by ardent personal intervention.[51]

Therefore, for most of the month of January, the success of 14(b) repeal hinged on organized labor's ability to convince the president and the Senate's Democratic leaders that it had enough power to make failure extremely unpalatable. As federation strategists requested, Mansfield would bring the measure up early in the session, but in his own way. By late January, it was apparent that the AFL-CIO's public relations campaign had not substantially altered the position of either the Democrats or the Republicans. With the president personally distancing himself from the coming fracas, it began to look more and more like Dirksen's second filibuster, begun on January 24, 1966, would also thwart labor.

In desperation, AFL-CIO operatives made one last attempt to threaten reprisals in the 1966 elections if the party failed to use its full power to break the filibuster. In a meeting with liberal senators on February 3, during the midst of Dirksen's second "extended discussion," COPE director Alexander Barkan told the senators and administration representatives that state and local COPE leaders were withholding contributions for 1966 because of the party's pallid response to Dirksen's tactics. According to administration liaison Mike Manatos, who attended the meeting, Barkan said his "funds are $250,000 shy of what they ought to be." Manatos informed President Johnson that many COPE leaders had begun asking Barkan if Dirksen was running the Senate. Many of the liberal senators agreed that more should be done. "We ought to go to around-the-clock sessions and the Leadership and the White House ought to cooperate," said Senator Jennings Randolph (D) of West Virginia. Nevertheless, neither the majority leader nor the president was willing to go beyond scheduling evening and weekend sessions. On February 8, Mansfield called the roll on cloture and found that at 51 to 48 he was still far below the two-thirds margin. The 1966 cohesion scores, as Table 6.3 shows, were quite similar to the vote in October. Northern Democrats ended up at a pro-labor −78 and their southern brethren at an anti-labor 55, for a total cohesion index of −34. Republicans had a bit more anti-labor cohesion than the Dixiecrats with a 63 total. Two days later the majority leader announced his last attempt to bring the bill to the floor, stating that if cloture failed once more, he would put H.R. 77 back on the calendar with the "letters R.I.P. beside it." Predictably, right-to-work forces won by 50 to 49. Repeal of section 14(b) in the Eighty-ninth Congress was no longer a realistic possibility. "Thank God for the majority leader," commented Dirksen at the close of battle. "He can really sweat you some, but that's never Mike's way."[52]

DISRUPTION OF THE LABOR-DEMOCRATIC ALLIANCE

The final defeat of 14(b) repeal in early February 1966 caused a temporary rift between organized labor and the Johnson administration. For several months, the frustration and anger of the secondary leadership forced national leaders to criticize the Democrats. During this period, top AFL-CIO officials did their best to exonerate the president and to mute the criticism. By mid–1966, administration officials found that labor still supported the president, although with a good deal less enthusiasm. Ultimately, the president's analysis of the limited political options open to labor seemed to have proved correct.

At first, the secondary echelon of labor leadership reacted to the failure with considerable anger. "The cloture vote on 14(b) confirms the lack of the Administration's sincere interest in repeal," wrote Texas AFL-CIO president H. S. Hank Brown to George Meany on February 11, "a lack strongly suspected when last session did not take up consideration until too late." To Texas labor, Brown wrote, 14(b) repeal was "must" legislation "if we are to continue to give active support to the Democratic Party." Similarly, local union official James Ferrace complained to the AFL-CIO president that the Johnson-Mansfield efforts reflected an ineffectiveness that bordered on duplicity. Everyone knew that there would be Republican opposition from the start. What, other than betrayal, could account for such inept management of the fight?[53]

In addition, much as Barkan had feared, COPE functionaries soon had to answer uncomfortable questions regarding the utility of electoral action and ultimately labor's alliance with the Democrats. "We worked hard on that, hard and long," recalled IBEW secretary Joseph Keenan of the 14(b) lobbying. "Everybody took hold for themselves on that one, because they're all affected. But we looked to the AFL-CIO for leadership." Thus, the fallen expectations almost ensured that federation political operatives would have difficulty in quieting criticism of the Democrats. At the federation's executive council meeting in Miami in late February 1966, for example, Barkan arrived a bit late, and according to Democratic National Committee functionary Cliff Carter, "by the time he visited with some of his state COPE leaders, their anger over the failure of 14-B to be repealed had been whipped into a frenzied hostility." To redirect their anger away from the president and the AFL-CIO, Barkan lamely intimated that the DNC should have rendered more aid.[54]

By now, President Johnson himself seemed fed up with the whole business. When a political adviser urged that "visible White House participation" on other legislation of special interest to labor would help rebuild the administration's hurting image among unionists, the president angrily shot back that he was "sick of having to offset any image." Nevertheless, in his meetings with George Meany during February and March of 1966, the chief executive confidently expected to waylay any serious criticisms. In particular, legislative liaison Henry Wilson recommended that the president could claim the high ground for the congressional party by placing the onus on the Republicans. "I have turned the figures around several ways," Wilson wrote the president, "and concluded that you can make a far better case explaining the wrong Democratic votes on the basis of which states have right-to-work laws." While it was true that many Democrats in those states voted against labor, he noted, a minority of the Democrats in them *did* support repeal. "The point to stress is that not a single Republican in either House or Senate from a state with right-to-work laws voted with organized labor," Wilson advised. The president could thus make a plausible case that, relatively speaking, the Democrats were still far better labor supporters than

6.4

Rice Index of Cohesion of Congressional Parties, by Geographic Areas, on Repeal of Section 14(b) of the Taft-Hartley Act, 1965–1966

LEGISLATION	EAST	SOUTH	MIDWEST	WEST
House				
H.R. 77 1965				
D	-97	63	-91	-72
R	18	100	86	91
Senate				
H.R. 77 1966				
D	-88	57	-85	-71
R	20	67	100	56

Source: Congressional Quarterly, <u>Congress and the Nation, 1945-1964,</u>
          and Congressional Quarterly, <u>Congressional Quarterly Almanac,</u>
          <u>1966</u>(Washington, DC: Congressional Quarterly Service,1965,1966)
Index: +100(Totally Cohesive Against Labor)
          -100(Totally Cohesive in Favor of Labor)
          Rice Index Rounded to Nearest Integer

Republicans. Moreover, this would get around the severely embarrassing fact that in the president's home state, 18 of the 22 Texas House members cast their ballots against repeal.[55]

And it was true that in all geographic areas save the South Democrats sided with labor to a significant degree. Table 6.4 lists the Rice Index of Cohesion for both congressional parties by regions. Democrats in the East, Midwest, and West tallied strong cohesion scores in both the House and Senate, ranging from −71 to −97. Only in the South did Democrats sharply abandon organized labor; House members compiled an anti-labor 63, while southern Senators came almost as close with a 57. In contrast, in no region of the country did Republicans approach a pro-labor total. Their sums ranged from 18 through 100, with the weakest anti-labor cohesion scores occurring in the East.

Armed with such information, the president would have an easier time convincing Meany, Reuther, and other high-level labor officials that the administration had worked hard for 14(b) repeal. For others in the labor movement who occupied leadership positions, though, the *quality* of presidential commitment *was* an issue, and the defeat thus touched off at least some political disaffection. Presidential labor adviser George Reedy recognized the role 14(b) had played in disrupting the administration's relationship with labor, but he thought the difficulties would be of short duration and were manageable. The AFL-CIO was happy with the social-welfare legislation of the Great Society, Reedy told the president, but "no purely 'Labor Bill' has passed Congress in many years." Indeed, because organized labor's influence was not what it once was, labor leaders had developed "something of an inferiority complex. They feel that they carried the hod for the Democratic Party during the long, lean years of the Eisenhower regime and now they want a measure that recognizes them as something special. . . . This is the reason for the tremendous emotional display on 14-B." But, according to Reedy, the lasting political impact of the administration's current problems with the labor movement was hard to predict accurately. He felt, however, that it would be minor; mainly, he wrote the president, "because there is a very real question of how much political influence organized labor can exercise and how many alternatives Labor has to the Democratic Party."[56]

Thus, key presidential advisers believed that little long-term harm had resulted and that organized labor would return with commitment to the Democratic fold by the 1966 elections. The major problem, in economic adviser Gardner Ackley's estimation, was that union chiefs were realizing "that labor's political power is not what they thought or hoped it was. And they don't like to contemplate their apparent weakness." By mid–1966, the main fallout seemed to have settled. Secretary of Labor Wirtz attended four national union conventions in May, including the UAW's, and found that "14(b) is being mentioned very little." In short, Wirtz felt there was support but a shortage of enthusiasm. The "reasons for the shortage are 5% 14(b)" and the rest other issues.

Still, this lack of enthusiasm led to a falling off of political activism on the part of labor in 1966. When Walter Reuther invited President Johnson to kick off the fall congressional campaigns in Detroit on Labor Day—as Democratic presidents had traditionally done—Johnson met an unimpressive crowd of unionists. And, according to a reporter, the "eagle eye of the old campaigner" spotted an unused truckload of "Welcome LBJ" signs. The apathy of Michigan Democrats and laborites "visibly miffed" the president. On the way back to the airport, Johnson lectured UAW president Reuther. "There's a lot of legislation still to get through Congress," the chief executive reminded his host. Then, chiding Reuther for his frequent European trips, the president pointedly warned his supporter. "And Walter, if you could just forget the labor movement in Norway . . . long enough to help out, that would be fine. You fellows better get off your seats and work," said the president, "because if they elect a Republican House of Representatives it will do nothing but investigate for two years."[57]

The message to Reuther must have been clear—politically, labor had no choice but to stick with the Democrats and the president knew it and knew that Reuther knew it. Thus, with the adjournment of the Eighty-ninth Congress, the AFL-CIO's most serious, and most disappointing, national campaign against union security restrictions receded into history. Vietnam now pushed to the forefront of Democratic controversy and by 1968 had rent the party and helped elect Republican Richard Nixon over Democratic Vice-President Humphrey. Through a tenuous convergence of forces, in 1963 and 1964 the Democrats, organized labor, and civil rights groups had put together an effective electoral coalition. The extensive victory of liberal forces in 1964 presented labor's political strategists with the environment they had worked for for over two decades. Out of that environment, federation leaders expected that all members of the coalition would get, if not all the items on their legislative agenda, then at least their most important objective.

While that proved to be the case for civil rights lobbyists and non-labor liberals, AFL-CIO leaders were left with gains but not the victory dearest to their hearts. The president remained unconvinced—rightly or wrongly—that labor leaders wielded sufficient electoral influence to force him to go to great lengths on their behalf; keeping his legislative influence in Congress at full strength had been more essential to Johnson's objectives. The 14(b) repeal drive during the Eighty-ninth Congress showed that even when liberal Democrats wielded effective control of the legislative machinery, party leaders would only go so far in furthering the aspirations of its undeniably most important mobilizing force. The labor movement *could* move the party's leadership into an offensive stance regarding its special interest goals, but only to a limited degree and only after the party's agenda had been largely accomplished. Nevertheless, Democratic politicians never seemed bashful about seeking labor's political resources, no matter what the party's record was on labor legislation. As presidential hopeful Hubert Humphrey wrote Walter Reuther in November 1967, "I am worried and concerned, Walter, about putting together an effective combination of labor and the Democratic Party this coming year, and I would like to talk. I think," wrote the vice-president to his friend, "we ought to have a visit."[58]

NOTES

1. Archie Robinson, *George Meany*, p. 233.

2. AFL-CIO, *Proceedings*, 1963, pp. 283–285; Reed Larson to Senator Pat McNamara, 5 November 1963, Box 193, Senator Pat McNamara Collection, WPRL.

3. "Report on National Democratic Committee and AFL-CIO COPE Conference on Registration," Philip Weightman Papers, cited in Draper, "A Rope of Sand," pp. 216, 220.

4. In 1963, a poll had revealed that Oklahoma voters supported the proposed right-to-work referendum by a 4 to 1 margin. See Oklahoma AFL-CIO, *Special Convention Proceedings*, 21 March 1963, p. 16; *State Labor Proceedings*, microform, Center for Research Libraries.

5. Ibid., pp. 16–17.

6. H. S. Hank Brown to Roy Tillman, 14 January 1964, 33–2–5; Field Reports, Dorothy Hall, State Director WAD, January 1963–February 1964, 33–3–8; Field Reports, Walter Gray, Oklahoma, January 1963–October 1965, 33–3–5; all COPE Area 8 Collection, TLA.

7. Oklahoma AFL-CIO, *Special Convention Proceedings*, 18 July 1964, pp. 1–9, 20–25, *State Labor Proceedings*, microform, Center for Research Libraries; Alexander Barkan to all Presidents and Secretary-Treasurers, State Central Bodies, COPE

State Directors, COPE Operating Committee, 10 June 1964, 33–2–5, COPE Area 8 Collection, TLA. For a contemporary analysis of the problems involved in building the labor–civil rights coalition around the right-to-work issue, see A. H. Raskin, "Labor and Civil Rights," *New York Times*, 20 May 1964, p. 33.

8. H. S. Hank Brown and Roy Evans to C. J. Haggerty, 5 June 1964, 33–2–5, COPE Area 8 Collection, TLA.

9. COPE to the Executive Council, AFL-CIO, "Summary of Report on 1964 Elections," 15 May 1964, Box 315, UAW President's Office: Walter P. Reuther Files, WPRL; Davis quoted in Draper, "A Rope of Sand," p. 256. For evidence of the national AFL-CIO's continual monitoring of state right-to-work activity, see Circular Letters, Carl A. McPeak, Special Representative for State Legislation, to all Presidents, AFL-CIO State Organizations, AFL-CIO Regional Directors, AFL-CIO COPE Directors, 20 February 1964, 22 July 1964, 10 November 1964, 28 January 1965, 31 March 1965, 110–17–8–11, Texas AFL-CIO Collection, TLA.

10. Terry Catchpole, *How to Cope with COPE: The Political Operations of Organized Labor* (New Rochelle, N.Y.: Arlington House, 1968), p. 192; Al Barkan to Barney Weeks, Alabama AFL-CIO President, 24 August 1965, Daniel Powell Papers, quoted in Draper, pp. 227–230, 257.

11. George Meany Oral History Interview, p. 6, Lyndon B. Johnson Library, Austin, Texas (hereafter LBJL); Memo, Jacob Clayman to [Walter P. Reuther], 23 December 1963, Box 331, UAW President's Office: Walter P. Reuther Files, WPRL. More probably, Johnson understood that while labor organizations' ability to influence might be problematic, labor did have substantial union resources to contribute. At any rate, there was little doubt that official Democratic party organs neglected to define labor law reform as an issue of importance to the party. For example, a Democratic National Committee functionary failed to mention right to work, or labor law at all for that matter, in listing issues of importance for the Democrats. See John M. Bailey to Senator Paul H. Douglas, 25 February 1964, Box 266, Senator Paul H. Douglas Papers, Chicago Historical Society, Chicago, Illinois.

12. [Larry O'Brien], Memo to the President, Re: Georgia, 24 September 1964, "Walter Reuther," White House Central Files (hereafter WHCF), Name File; Joseph Keenan Oral History Interview, p. 8–9; both LBJL.

13. Lawrence F. O'Brien to Walter P. Reuther, 5 November 1964, Box 387, UAW President's Office: Walter P. Reuther Files, WPRL; Robert Axelrod, "Where the Votes Come From: An Analysis of Electoral Coalitions, 1952–1968," table 1, p. 388 in Charles M. Rehmus, Doris B. McLaughlin, and Frederick Nesbitt, eds., *Labor and American Politics: A Book of Readings*, rev. ed. (Ann Arbor: University of Michigan Press, 1978).

14. Alexander E. Barkan to Roy Tillman, 16 November 1964, 33–2–2, COPE Area 8 Collection, TLA.

15. Meany quoted in Robinson, *George Meany*, p. 219.

16. H. S. Hank Brown Oral History Interview, p. 6, LBJL; Foley, pp. 47–48.

17. Foley, *The New Senate*, pp. 52–53; Robert Oliver Oral History Interview, pp. 12, 22–23, 29, LBJL.

18. IUD, "Transcript of Proceedings, Industrial Union Department," Meeting of the Executive Board, 23, 25 November 1964, pp. 11–26, 52–59, Box 329, UAW President's Office: Walter P. Reuther Files, WPRL.

19. Joseph Rauh Oral History Interview, p. 19, LBJL.

20. W. Willard Wirtz, Memorandum for the President, 1 December 1964, Box 1, EX/LA, WHCF, Executive File, LBJL; Joseph Goulden, *Meany* (New York: Atheneum, 1972), pp. 344–345.

21. The information concerning Meany's telephone communications with the president in November 1964 comes from handwritten notes made by Walter Reuther during a conversation with Hubert Humphrey on December 5, 1964. The notes, which are cryptic, indicate LBJ's dismay at Meany's attempt to get a commitment from the president on 14(b) repeal. Clearly, Johnson would have preferred that the AFL-CIO chief not press him on the issue. See "WPR Notes," Conversation with Hubert Humphrey, 5 December 1964, Box 324, UAW President's Office: Walter P. Reuther Files, WPRL; President's Appointment File: Diary Backup, 17 December 1964, Box 12, LBJL. The chronology of AFL-CIO activities on 14(b) repeal in the House comes from AFL-CIO, "Summary of AFL-CIO Activities on H.R. 77," 1 December 1965, AFL-CIO Legislative Department, Box 48, GMMA, (hereafter AFL-CIO, "H.R. 77 Summary," GMMA).

22. Memo, "Taft-Hartley Act Amendments," filed 29 January 1965, Box 1, EX/LA, WHCF, Executive File, LBJL.

23. Andrew J. Biemiller to All National, International Unions, State and Local Central Bodies, 31 December 1964, Box 311, UAW President's Office: Walter P. Reuther Files, WPRL.

24. Memo, W. Willard Wirtz to the President, "Subject: Conference with Walter Reuther," 9 February 1965, Box 1, LA(EX/LA), WHCF, Subject File, LBJL. For the administration's testing of congressional sentiment regarding 14(b) repeal, see Memo, Larry O'Brien to the President, 7 January 1965, Box 31, LA, WHCF, Subject File, LBJL.

25. Memo, Dave Bunn to Larry O'Brien, 5 May 1964, Box 11, Files of Larry O'Brien, LBJL.

26. Memo, Very Confidential, W. Willard Wirtz to the President, 20 May 1965, Box 63, CF LE/LA3; Memo, W. Willard Wirtz to the President, "Subject: May 18 Labor Message to Congress," 20 May 1965, Box 88, CF; both WHCF, Confidential File, LBJL.

27. For the statements of various witnesses before the subcommittee, see U.S., Congress, House, Special Subcommittee on Labor of the Committee on Education and Labor, *Hearings on H.R. 77, H.R. 4350 and Similar Bill*, 89th Congress, lst sess., May-June, 1965, pts. 1 and 2.

28. Henry H. Wilson Oral History Interview, pp. 10–11, LBJL; Hubert Humphrey to Walter P. Reuther, 23 June 1965, Box 388, UAW President's Office: Walter P. Reuther Files, WPRL.

29. H. S. Hank Brown to Area Councils and State Associations, "Repeal of 14(b) Program," 11 June 1965; H. S. Hank Brown, Roy R. Evans to Area Council Officers, 13 July 1965; both 110–1–16–6, Texas AFL-CIO Collection, TLA. For an example of another state federation program, see Box 58, generally, Irwin L. DeShetler Collection, WPRL.

30. Memo, Henry Wilson to Larry O'Brien, 20, 22 July 1965, Files of Larry O'Brien, LBJL; Robinson, *George Meany*, p. 245; Henry H. Wilson Oral History Interview, p. 9; Memo, the Vice-President to Larry O'Brien, "Vote on Repeal of 14(b)," 30 July 1965, Box 8, Files of Henry Wilson, LBJL. Also see Memo, Democratic Study Group, "Outstanding Performance Record," December 1965, Box

221, Congressman James G. O'Hara Collection, Michigan Historical Collections, Bentley Library, University of Michigan, Ann Arbor, Michigan.

31. Alexander E. Barkan to Roy Tillman, 30 July 1965, 33–2–3, COPE Area 8 Collection, TLA.

32. For Biemiller's testimony, see U.S., Congress, Senate, Special Subcommittee of the Committee on Education and Labor, *Hearings, To Repeal Section 14(b) of the Nation Labor Relations Act*, 89th Congress, 1st sess., June 1965, pp. 83–113; AFL-CIO, "H.R. 77 Summary," GMMA.

33. Larson and Newton quoted in Lee Edwards and Anne Edwards, *You Can Make the Difference*, chapter 5 (New Rochelle, NY: Arlington House, 1968), reprinted by permission by the National Right to Work Committee as *The "Impossible" Victory: The Story of the National Right to Work Committee's Successful Battles Against Union Professionals Seeking Repeal of Section 14(b) of the Taft-Hartley Act* (Washington, D.C.: National Right to Work Committee, 1968), pp. 4, 13.

34. Ibid., p. 5.

35. Ibid., p. 6.

36. Reed Larson to Michael Wade, 14 September 1972, quoted in Wade, *The Bitter Issue*, p. 123.

37. Memo, Mike Manatos to Larry O'Brien, 23 August 1965, Box 2, Files of Mike Manatos, LBJL; Memo, Mike Manatos to Larry O'Brien, 2 September 1965, Box 26, Files of Larry O'Brien, LBJL.

38. Memo, "Meany-Biemiller Meeting with the President," 10 September 1965, Box 134, LE/LA, WHCF, Subject File, LBJL; Larry O'Brien to Mike Manatos, 14 September 1965, Box 8, Files of Mike Manatos, LBJL; Everett M. Dirksen Oral History Interview, p. 6, LBJL.

39. Mike Manatos Oral History Interview, pp. 16–20, LBJL.

40. Memo, Andrew Biemiller to Larry O'Brien, 21 September 1965, "Visits with Senators on 14(b)," Box 134, LE/LA, WHCF, General File, LBJL. The federation's Senate lobbying is outlined in AFL-CIO, "Summary of AFL-CIO Activities on Behalf of 14(b) Repeal in the Senate," [February 1966], AFL-CIO Legislative Department, Box 48, GMMA (hereafter AFL-CIO, "Senate Summary on 14(b)"), GMMA.

41. Memo, W. Willard Wirtz to the President, "AFL-CIO Executive Council Meeting," 24 September 1965, Box 31, EX/LA 7, WHCF, Subject File, LBJL; Memo, Andrew Biemiller to Larry O'Brien, 21 September 1965, "Visits with Senators on 14(b)," Box 134, LE/LA, WHCF, General File, LBJL; AFL-CIO, "Senate Summary on 14(b)," GMMA.

42. For accounts of the Meany-Dirksen meeting from Meany's perspective, see Goulden, *Meany*, pp. 347–348, and Robinson, *George Meany*, pp. 246–247. For the encounter from Dirksen's view, see Louella Dirksen with Norma Lee Browning, *The Honorable Mr. Marigold: My Life with Everett Dirksen* (New York: Doubleday, 1972), pp. 196–198, and Neil MacNeil, *Dirksen: Portrait of a Public Man* (New York: World Publishing, 1970), pp. 264–267.

43. George Meany to Walter P. Reuther, 8 October 1965, Box 311, UAW President's Office: Walter P. Reuther Files, WPRL; Robinson, *George Meany*, p. 247.

44. Memo, the Vice-President to the President, "A Report from the Vice-President," 12 October 1965, "George Meany," WHCF, Name File, LBJL. Meany's

public comments on the Democrats were harsher. See the *New York Times*, 13 October 1965, p. 30.

45. Goulden, *Meany*, p. 347; Lyndon Johnson to Walter P. Reuther, 16 November 1965, Box 387, UAW President's Office: Walter P. Reuther Files, WPRL; Memo, Cliff Carter to Marvin Watson, Democratic National Committee, 26 October 1965, "George Meany," WHCF, Name File, LBJL.

46. Memo, David E. Feller to Walter P. Reuther, 27 October 1965, Box 332, UAW President's Office: Walter P. Reuther Files, WPRL. Feller's position found support among some union leaders. As early as December 1964, for example, IBEW secretary Joseph Keenan informed Meany that in addition to 14(b) repeal "we should develop specific[,] moderate, and reasonable proposals which will help the labor movement carry forward its work of organizing and collective bargaining and which can be presented in such a manner as to secure public support." See Joseph Keenan to George Meany, 30 December 1964, Box 324, UAW President's Office, Walter P. Reuther Files, WPRL.

47. AFL-CIO, "Senate Summary on 14(b)," GMMA.

48. IUD, "Transcript of Proceedings of the Executive Board Minutes, IUD, AFL-CIO," 17 November 1965, Box 329; Hubert Humphrey to Walter P. Reuther, 6 December 1965, Box 324; both UAW President's Office: Walter P. Reuther Files, WPRL; Goulden, *Meany*, p. 348.

49. For examples of AFL-CIO public relations material see AFL-CIO, "Inside on 14(b) Repeal, No. 4," Box 58, Irwin L. DeShetler Collection, WPRL, and "Tell Congress: A 'Yes' Vote on 77 Will End 'Right-to-Work' Laws," n.d., Box 325, UAW President's Office: Walter P. Reuther Files, WPRL.

50. Bill Moyers to the President, 9 January 1966, Box 1, EX/LA, WHCF, Executive File, LBJL.

51. Everett M. Dirksen Oral History Interview, tape 2, p. 5, LBJL; George Meany Oral History Interview, p. 15, LBJL. Joseph L. Rauh, Jr., Oral History Interview, pp. 14–15, LBJL. Mansfield's reflections are especially revealing: "The pressure for repeal of 14(b) came almost entirely from organized labor. As far as the President was concerned, he did not pressure me." Ambassador Michael Mansfield to the author, 16 December 1986. Interestingly, Mansfield announced the next order of Senate business after recess for Lincoln's birthday was to be the president's construction and procurement authorization Bill for Vietnam. See AFL-CIO, "Senate Summary on 14(b)," GMMA.

52. Mike Manatos, Memorandum for the President, 3 February 1966, "Andrew J. Biemiller," WHCF, Name File, LBJL. Dirksen quoted in MacNeil, *Dirksen*, pp. 265–266.

53. H.S. Hank Brown to George Meany, 11 February 1966, Box 134, LE, WHCF, Subject File, LBJL; James A. Ferracc to George Meany, 15 February 1966, Box 311, UAW President's Office: Walter P. Reuther Files, WPRL. Some observers friendly to the labor movement felt that the cloture defeat was more the fault of the AFL-CIO than Senator Mansfield. Joseph Rauh, for example, pointed out that the federation had had an opportunity at the beginning of Congress to change the Senate's Rule XXII, which authorized unrestricted debate. This was a traditional liberal objective. Even in 1964, however, only the NAACP and the UAW lobbied to get majority rule. "By and large the rest of the labor movement has sat on its hands and watched," he reminded Reuther. As it applied to the 14(b) fight, this was

obviously the kind of controversial measure on which it was difficult to get public consensus and thereby force cloture. The AFL-CIO should not blame Mansfield, Rauh wrote, mainly because you could not get a 24-hour quorum when you only had 51 to 52 senators on your side to start. See Joseph L. Rauh, Jr., to Walter P. Reuther, 18 February 1966, Box 160, UAW President's Office: Walter P. Reuther Files, WPRL.

54. Joseph Keenan Oral History Interview, p. 16; Memo, Clifton C. Carter to Marvin Watson, 7 March 1966, Box 60, LA, WHCF, Confidential File; both LBJL.

55. Memo, Joseph Califano to the President, 16 February 1966, Box 1, WHCF, Subject File, LBJL; Memo, Marvin Watson to the President, 15 February 1966, "George Meany," WHCF, Name File, LBJL; Henry H. Wilson, Memorandum for the President, 24 March 1966, LE/LA, WHCF, Executive File, LBJL.

56. George Reedy to the President, Personal and Confidential, 23 March 1966, LA, WHCF, Confidential File, LBJL. Of the oral history interviews of labor leaders on file at the Lyndon B. Johnson Library, those of George Meany, David Dubinsky, and Joseph Keenan indicate that the president was successful in his efforts to prove he had done all he could to defeat Dirksen's filibuster. Only CWA president Joseph Beirne partially dissented. While agreeing that the administration's lobbyists worked hard to secure 14(b) repeal, he admitted that "on labor legislation . . . one strange failing that we could neither impress Kennedy or Johnson with" was the justice of labor's case. See Joseph Beirne Oral History Interview, pp. 23–24, LBJL.

57. Although Wirtz attributed the lack of enthusiasm to foreign policy, other statements in his memo redirect the thrust of his comments somewhat. For example, the secretary of labor only received "perfunctory" applause when listing Johnson administration domestic accomplishments. In addition, union speakers "said *almost nothing* about the gains of the past five years, the President, or the Democratic Party. They seem to be staying away from politics." See W. Willard Wirtz to the President, Confidential, 25 May 1966, Box 60, WHCF, Confidential File, LBJL; Memo, Gardner Ackley to the President, "Attitudes of Union Leaders," 2 May 1966, Box 31, EX/LA7, WHCF, LBJL; Memo, [Harry Wilkinson] to Marvin Watson, 30 August 1966, "Walter Reuther," WHCF, Name File, LBJL; Bud Vestal, "Johnson Upset with Detroit Reception," *Jackson [Michigan] Citizen Patriot*, 9 September 1966, copy in Box 387, UAW President's Office: Walter P. Reuther Files, WPRL.

58. Hubert Humphrey to Walter P. Reuther, 10 November 1967, Box 388, UAW President's Office: Walter P. Reuther Files, WPRL.

7

Union Security in the 1970s

We are not running away from the issue [of 14b repeal] ... but we do not want to give our enemies an opportunity to use it as a basis for denying justice to workers who seek to organize a union.
—Lane Kirkland, then Secretary-Treasurer of the AFL-CIO, on Labor Law Reform, 1977[1]

Predictably, organized labor's failure to repeal section 14(b) once again only temporarily dampened controversy over union security legislation. The debates continued on into the 1970s, exhibiting both a continuity with the past and an increasing tendency of the parties to divide more cohesively on opposite sides of the issue. After organized labor had recovered sufficiently from the 14(b) defeat, several state labor movements went on the offensive in the mid–1970s seeking repeal or favorable amendment, but the political climate turned less hospitable after 1976. For the Democrats, how a potential presidential aspirant stood on the question of repeal loomed ever larger in intra-party wrangling during primary season. Disputes over right to work persisted, both in national party politics and in the state legislatures, with the defeat of the Labor Law Reform bill in 1978 seeming to mark the inauguration of an even more conservative period. It was in the area of presidential politics that the issue attracted the most attention after the defeat of the section 14(b) campaign.

RIGHT TO WORK AND PARTY POLITICS, 1968–1975

The presidential election of 1968 gave the first indication of how the matter would play out for the Democrats in coming years. Fighting desperately to solidify a badly factionalized party after a traumatic convention in Chicago, vice-presidential candidate Edmund Muskie (ME) utilized the right-to-work issue in an effort to counter the perceptible sentiment among more conservative unionists for the independent presidential campaign of George Wallace (D-GA). The Alabama governor, trying to cut deeply into the labor vote, had publicly claimed that he did not favor right-to-work laws. Speaking to an Iron Workers convention, Muskie derided Wallace's position, pointing out that the governor had led a state with an anti–union security statute for years but had not seen fit to attempt to do away with it. If labor had meant what it said about opposition to right to work being one of the primary litmus tests for organized labor's political endorsement, the comparison between the Humphrey-Muskie ticket and Wallace on this question was clear. "What is your choice?" the Maine Democrat rhetorically asked the delegates.[2]

While the bulk of labor voters' support did finally go to Hubert Humphrey in his narrow loss to Republican Richard Nixon, the next Democratic presidential nominee did not do as well. It became clear by 1972 that the labor-oriented wing of the party would use the right-to-work issue whenever possible to undercut any sign of popularity for non-labor-oriented Democrats. For example, in the primaries and in the convention both Edmund Muskie, now a presidential nomination seeker, and Senator Henry "Scoop" Jackson of Washington, used Senator George McGovern's (SD) vote against repeal of section 14(b) in 1966 to stiffen labor's opposition to the rising support for McGovern. While George Meany's intense dislike of the McGovern candidacy also stemmed from the South Dakota senator's anti-Vietnam stand, McGovern's failure to vote "right" on 14(b) repeal had led to a "deep distrust" of him in top AFL-CIO circles. "I have heard union presidents here who have never in years talked of anything but support of the Democratic party," reported a veteran federation political operative during the convention in July, "saying that maybe now is the time to have a labor party." However, when McGovern won the nomination, instead of trying to found a labor party AFL-CIO chieftains largely sat out the presidential election. Withholding campaign funds from the top of the ticket, they then concentrated COPE's activities on an attempt to keep the control of Congress in friendlier Democratic hands.[3]

Never one to miss the political potentialities inherent in a situation, President Nixon shrewdly avoided any national Republican advocacy of right-to-work legislation. The president, sensing the possibility of a mandate-type win over McGovern in November, hoped to garner a significant portion of the working-class vote on social issues, and visible Republican backing of union security strictures at the national level would subvert this attempt. Therefore, Nixon White House staffers lobbied heavily against the endeavors of ardent party right-to-workers pushing for a platform plank opposing section 14(b) repeal. The president, of course, won, but according to platform committee chairman Congressman John J. Rhodes of Arizona, the debate between Nixon supporters and anti–union security advocates caused more intra-party controversy than any other issue.[4]

Thus, while the Democrats, because of the fracturing of their governing coalition, had a tendency to inject the right-to-work issue into their contests for the highest office in the land, the Republicans at the same level struggled to keep from becoming too closely identified with anti–union security proposals. Richard Nixon's subsequent landslide victory over McGovern once again allowed national interest in the subject to wane, and shifted the focus to the state legislatures. And there, organized labor had started to show a rising combativeness.

In a span of six years, from 1969 to 1975, state labor leaders took the initiative in five of the seven state legislative campaigns that reached floor votes, attempting outright repeal in two states and amendment to allow the agency shop in three others. After a 1969 gubernatorial veto prevented the Kansas legislature from enacting an enabling statute to their 1958 state constitutional amendment, Nebraska laborites tried to obtain an agency shop amendment in 1973, with Alabama and Utah following in 1975. In the same year, both Wyoming and South Dakota's labor movements pushed for repeal of the state laws, while Louisiana labor fended off the most serious right-to-work agitation since 1954. Only in Kansas did anti–union security backers finally win with an enabling statute in 1975.[5]

Indeed, shortly after the defeat of 14(b) repeal, much of the activity surrounding union security restrictions focused on the state legislatures rather than the referendum route. In the opinion of Frank Emig, national AFL-CIO state and local central organization representative, this was due to the inability of National Right to Work Committee (NRTWC) operatives to take advantage of the congressional defeat. According to Emig, after the unsuccessful 14(b) repeal campaign, Oklahoma right-to-workers, believing the public still favored their position and that labor had become demoralized, once again cranked up an initiative drive. Oklahoma unionists, not relishing the idea of facing yet another expensive electoral fight, responded by aggressively confronting petition distributors in public places as well as paying for a good deal of preventive informational advertising, which ultimately resulted in the failure of right-to-workers to obtain the required number of signatures to put the question on the ballot. Afterward, Emig believed, disheartened NRTWC strategists concentrated on less visible lobbying efforts where any defeats would not have as great a public relations consequence. And even there, they did not do especially well.[6]

In fact, in the late 1960s, as Tables 6.2, 7.1, and 7.2 show, the only floor votes on right-to-work measures were in Wyoming in 1967 and Kansas in 1969. In both of these states, party cohesion followed the usual patterns. Wyoming labor's drive to secure passage of a repeal bill actually won in that state's House in 1967, only to lose when the measure did not come up

7.1
Rice Index of Cohesion of Democratic Party, in All State Legislatures, on Right-to-Work Measures, 1969–1979

STATE/YEAR	TOTAL	INDEXES SENATE	HOUSE	BALLOTS CAST SENATE	HOUSE
Wyoming 1975	-	-100	NV	15	NV
Vermont 1976	-	-82	NV	11	NV
Maine 1979	-79	-100	-76	12	74
Kansas 1969	-77	-100	-71	8	35
Idaho 1977	-73	-73	-73	15	22
New Hampshire 1979	-65	-85	-63	13	112
Wyoming 1977	-63	-100	-43	15	28
Louisiana 1975	-	-60	NV	35	NV
New Mexico 1977	-37	-13	-53	32	47
South Dakota 1975	-	-33	NV	18	NV
Utah 1975	-	NV	-30	NV	40
Delaware 1979	-	NV	-30	NV	20
New Mexico 1979	-29	-13	-41	32	41
Kansas 1975	-5	-100	20	13	50
Alabama 1975	-	NV	4	NV	100
Louisiana 1976	14	26	10	38	102
Nebraska 1973	NP	NP	NP	NP	NP

Source: Appendix A
Key: NV-No Vote, VV-Voice Vote, NP-Non-Partisan Legislature
Index: +100(Totally Cohesive in Favor of Right to Work)
           -100(Totally Cohesive Against Right to Work)

for a vote in the senate. Twenty-eight Democrats voted solidly for repeal, scoring a perfect − 100 Rice Index of Cohesion. Wyoming's 25 house Republicans, on the other hand, scored a pro-right-to-work 68. Similarly, the 43 Kansas Democrats' combined index of cohesion was a pro-labor − 77 (− 100 in the senate and −71 in the house). Their more numerous Republican colleagues tallied a total anti-labor percentage of 78, with an index of 86 in the senate and 75 in the house.

After the start of the new decade, state-level labor leaders increasingly contemplated taking the initiative. For example, in 1971, the Arkansas AFL-CIO began to study the feasibility of repealing or amending the state's 1944 right-to-work constitutional amendment. The State federation's executive committee authorized an opinion survey to determine

7.2
Rice Index of Cohesion of Republican Party, in All State Legislatures, on Right-to-
Work Measures, 1969–1979

STATE/YEAR	TOTAL	INDEXES SENATE	HOUSE	BALLOTS CAST SENATE	HOUSE
South Dakota 1975	–	100	NV	16	NV
Utah 1975	–	NV	100	NV	32
Louisiana 1976	100	100	100	1	3
New Mexico 1977	93	75	100	8	20
Wyoming 1977	92	87	94	15	33
New Mexico 1979	89	78	93	9	29
Wyoming 1975	–	87	NV	15	NV
Kansas 1975	85	59	94	26	67
Kansas 1969	78	86	75	29	81
New Hampshire 1979	62	20	64	10	201
Idaho 1977	62	60	63	20	48
Maine 1979	33	0	41	18	71
Delaware 1979	–	NV	25	NV	16
Vermont 1976	–	-67	NV	18	NV
Alabama 1975	–	NV	NR	NV	NR
Louisiana 1975	–	NR	NV	NR	NV
Nebraska 1973	NP	NP	NP	NP	NP

Source: Appendix A
Key: NV-No Vote, VV-Voice Vote, NP-Non-Partisan Legislature
          NR-No Republicans
Index: +100(Totally Cohesive in Favor of Right to Work)
          -100(Totally Cohesive Against Right to Work)

public attitudes both toward labor in general and union security in particular. In short, while the poll revealed mixed results in the public's attitude toward labor (favorable toward labor as an "institution" and
negative toward "labor leaders"), on the right-to-work question Arkansas citizens were apparently highly confused as to exactly what the concept meant. Nevertheless, the analyst did conclude from answers to one
of the questions that if the state's labor leaders could publicly define the
union security issue without using the words "right to work" "it would
be highly possible that the citizens of Arkansas would accept" changes
allowing companies and unions to negotiate on the subject. And in addition to Arkansas, in 1972 the Kansas State Federation of Labor, which

had recently struggled against the attempted imposition of an enabling statute, considered trying a ballot repeal in 1974. In a political atmosphere that included a sympathetic governor and attorney general, as well as a newly formed progressive political coalition including labor, teacher, youth, and farmer organizations, the state organization targeted as potential converts over 400,000 new voters, aged 18 to 24, who would be able to vote in the 1974 election. The officers of both the Arkansas and Kansas state organizations requested the counsel and assistance of the national office in their endeavors.[7]

In the mid-1970s, other state labor movements pushed forward with repeal or amendment campaigns. Nebraska's unicameral, nonpartisan legislature just narrowly refused to pass an agency shop modification to the state's right-to-work law by a vote of 22 to 19 (for a cohesion score of 7). These efforts peaked in 1975, when six state legislatures cast floor votes on some form of union security proposal. The results are shown in Tables 7.1 and 7.2. Democratic cohesion scores stretched from an anti-labor 4 for the Alabama house (agency shop) to a perfectly pro-labor −100 for the Wyoming senate (repeal). In between, in descending order of support for labor came Louisiana's senate with −60 (proposed statute), South Dakota's senate with −33 (agency shop), Utah's house with −30 (agency shop), and Kansas with a combined −5 (−100 in the senate and 20 in the house, on an enabling statute). The available Republican indexes (Alabama and Louisiana had no Republican votes) ranged more narrowly from an aggregate 85 for Kansas (59 in the senate and 94 in the house) to 100 for South Dakota's senate. In ascending order of backing for right to work were Wyoming's senate and Utah's house, with 87 and 100, respectively. The Democrats' wider span and low to moderate cohesion (except for Wyoming) no doubt resulted from the offensive nature of most of the proposals—while Democrats would at times vote cohesively to protect labor from unfavorable proposals, they usually did not respond as solidly when voting to advance favorable propositions. Only in the Kansas house, where legislators considered an enabling statute, did Democratic representatives abandon a pro-labor stance in a defensive fight.

These legislative forays signified that even in right-to-work states with moderate to small union populations, the labor movement intended not only to continue the struggle to prevent the further extension of restrictions, but also to win relief where possible. By early 1976, the Watergate scandal had considerably eroded public confidence in Republican leadership, and the AFL-CIO's political and legislative strategists began to give thought once again to the workabilty of a broader national labor law reform package—which presumably would contain 14(b) modifications—should the Democrats emerge victorious. Thus, the focus began to shift back to the national legislative arena once more.

UNION SECURITY AND LABOR LAW REFORM, 1976–1979

By the time of the Wisconsin primary in March 1976, Democratic presidential contenders had resurrected the intra-party right-to-work scuffle of 1972 and made it even more prominent than it had been four years earlier. Senator "Scoop" Jackson of Washington, an exemplar of the pro-labor wing of the party, found this tactic especially useful in putting opponents Morris Udall (AZ) and former Georgia governor Jimmy Carter on the defensive. Speaking before labor audiences in the early stages of the Wisconsin primary, he chastised the Arizona congressman and Carter for their sins of commission and omission on the union security question. Congressman Udall, in particular, received the brunt of Jackson's attack for he—like George McGovern—had actually voted against repeal of section 14(b) in the 1960s due to the political pressures he faced in his state. Jackson also pointed out that Carter had not only accepted Georgia's law during his tenure as the state's chief executive, but he had recently stated that if elected president he would not work for repeal.[8]

Carter quickly realized the growing importance of the controversy. While organized labor in Georgia might not have been a major political power broker, in national Democratic politics the situation was a bit different. Several days after Jackson's charges, Carter answered a Milwaukee union member's question about right-to-work laws by stating that he thought section 14(b) should be repealed—quite a contrast to one month previously when he had said he did not care one way or the other about the issue. In the judgement of a *New York Times* political reporter, Carter was beginning to make gestures of accommodation. The relative unknown who did not have any support base in the national Democratic party, was "now reaching out to organize blocs in the Democratic coalition and finding many established leaders reaching back."[9]

As Carter's candidacy grew in popularity through the spring, "Scoop" Jackson continued to hit on the right-to-work theme in an effort to derail the Georgian's drive for the Democratic nomination. In recession-plagued Pennsylvania, speaking to 60 laid-off workers from the back of a flatbed truck, the Washington senator used the recent move of a local sporting goods plant to Alabama to emphasize the job-eroding competition of right-to-work states. Carter, he insisted, had only changed his stand on the issue after northern unionists voiced their opposition to the former Georgia governor. In late April, Jackson replayed this scene to a much larger audience on ABC's *Issues and Answers*, a public affairs television program. During the discussion, Carter's "usual calm seemed disturbed" as Jackson accused him of surreptitious anti-labor bias and "less than full enthusiasm" for repeal of section 14(b), according to a *New York Times* political analyst. This prompted a heated Jackson-Carter exchange that, for whatever its effects on the right-to-work debate, marked the emergence of Carter as the ac-knowledged front-runner.[10]

By the time Jimmy Carter secured the nomination in the summer of 1976, he was well educated on the electoral significance of the union security issue. In an effort to solidify the ranks, he chose Senator Walter Mondale (MN), a Hubert Humphrey protege and close legislative ally of labor, as his vice-presidential running mate. This, as well as his willingness to make some movement on his right-to-work position, eventually brought organized la-bor's political resources into his fall campaign, providing important assist-ance in his close victory over President Gerald Ford. Now, of course, the AFL-CIO expected some sort of legislative acknowledgment of its contri-bution as the Carter administration planned its assumption of power.

As always, repeal of section 14(b) remained near and dear to the hearts of AFL-CIO officials. Recent events at the state level, however, signaled that some circumspection would be in order. Vermont laborites easily defeated an anti–union security measure in that state's 1976 legislative session, but in July an unfortunate turn of events saddled Louisiana unionists with a right-to-work statute for the second time. More importantly, in November Arkansas labor failed in its electoral attempt to improve the state's union security situation.

Early in the year Vermont's state senators disposed of a right-to-work proposal on a non-partisan basis. As Tables 7.1 and 7.2 indicate, the indexes of cohesion between Republican and Democratic senators were only mar-ginally different: eighteen Republicans scored a pro-labor percentage of − 67 and eleven Democrats a slightly higher − 82. In Louisiana, though, a violent incident at a Lake Charles chemical plant construction site—involving the death of one worker and the wounding of four others and ostensibly related to a contractor's use of non-AFL-CIO affiliated union workers—played into the hands of right-to-work backers. In 1975 35 Louisiana Democratic state senators had voted against an anti–union security proposal with a cohesion index of − 60; in July 1976, 38 senators scored an anti–labor 26 and 102 of their house counterparts a 10, for a total, pro-right-to-work index of 14 and the passage of an anti–union security statute.[11]

Even more significant for any national labor law reform movement en-compassing repeal of section 14(b) was Arkansas's 1976 union security referendum. The state AFL-CIO organization had been considering a cam-paign to repeal or amend the state's right-to-work constitutional amendment since the public opinion survey it had taken in 1971. That survey had indicated that Arkansas's electorate consisted of a substantially different generation of voters from the one that had passed the 1944 constitutional amendment. There was a distinct chance, the study argued, that organized labor could persuade these voters on the union security question. After some deliberation, the state organization's executive council decided that the amendment approach would have the most public support and eventually collected enough voter signatures to put the question on the 1976 ballot. Arkansas's labor federation then set up a steering committee to direct the effort and employed the public relations talents of Charles Baker, who had masterminded the 1958 Ohio victory, to design their media campaign. Funding for the drive came from a special $10 per member assessment. In addition, with advice and counsel from the national office, the state central helped put together the type of citizen coalition committees that had proved effective in other right-to-work elections. The state's one million plus registered voters, commented a *New York Times* reporter, would thus provide a "clue" for 1977 in the "most exciting contest" of the 1976 election in Arkansas.[12]

Unfortunately, the results of the election, as revealed in Table 7.3, disheartened Arkansas's labor leaders. The amendment failed to carry in any of the state's 75 counties. In popular votes it lost by 257,111 to 466,243, a 36 to 64 percent margin. Moreover, the defeat of the proposal was quite broad, for 94 percent of those voters who voted for the highest office in the election also cast ballots on this amendment to the state constitution. The defeat on the initiative vote underlined the difficulty Arkansas labor had in advancing change in a conservative political environment. Though Arkansas labor had a respectable percentage of the work force organized (17.6 percent, or approximatley 113,000 members), the reaction of the state's political establishment and general lack of access to media channels severely hamstrung their efforts to clarify and change opinions. According to Arkansas AFL-CIO president J. Bill Becker, numerous offers to debate were simply ignored by the media; radio stations, in particular, seemed unified in their desire to keep the subject off the airwaves. Additionally, prominent politicians either became enemies or remained neutral. Support for the amendment came largely from black areas and those regions of the state that had a strong union presence. Labor's funding of the campaign, Becker acknowledged, had been spotty, but even with more money it might not have been successful. In retrospect, the Arkansas AFL-CIO president judged, in his state it would take more than one electoral campaign to educate and change the climate of opinion on right to work.[13]

Thus, in the face of recent events in Louisiana and Arkansas, organized labor would have difficulty raising the union security issue once again at the national level—particularly with a southern president. Apparently, top AFL-CIO strategists realized this, for A. H. Raskin, labor reporter for the *New York Times*, wrote shortly after the election that the federation would adopt a "go slow" policy on repeal of section 14(b). "No single domestic issue could have embarrassed the President-elect" more than an AFL-CIO demand to repeal that provision, according to Raskin. Carter, who had "walked a tight-rope" on right to work during the election, had taken ten southern states, and the recent right-to-work election results in Arkansas demonstrated that public opinion, at least in the South, still favored union

7.3
Public Right-to-Work Elections, 1976–1978

STATE AND YEAR	YES RTW	NO RTW	TOTAL	%RATIO	COUNTY Y/N RATIO	# MARGINAL COUNTIES	% OF VOTE FOR HIGHEST OFFICE IN ELECTION	APPROXIMATE UNION MEMBERSHIP
Arkansas 1976	466243	257111	723354	64/36	75/0	7	94	113000(17.6%)
Missouri 1978	630764	944071	1574840	40/60	48/66	45	78	570840(27.6%)

Source: Appendix B, Cox, and Troy. See explanation in Appendix B as to the derivation of percent of state vote and union membership.

security restrictions. On top of that, the closeness of the presidential contest, combined with the divisiveness of the 14(b) issue, convinced federation policy makers that a repeal drive at the opening of Congress would split the country and prevent and endanger the desired administration initiatives on full employment and the economy. Added to these considerations was the claim of the National Right to Work Committee that it could muster enough votes to block any repeal attempt. So, even though many COPE-endorsed Democrats had won, there would be no immediate pressure from labor. "Given the emotion that always attaches to the issue," Raskin concluded, "most of the victorious Democrats hope they will not have to choose sides in a hurry."[14]

Shortly after the start of the Carter presidency, however, the AFL-CIO began to question the ultimate goals of the administration. In particular, federation executives' hopes that they would be satisfied with the performance of the Carter administration on economic policy issues eroded over the first six months of 1977. Since little progress had been made on this front, AFL-CIO legislative strategists moved forward with a broad, labor law reform package and contemplated seeking repeal of section 14(b) separately. President Carter, in order to win back labor's legislative support, agreed to back a reform package in return for abandonment of any 14(b) repealer.[15]

Arguably this was a favorable arrangement, for most observers believed that NRTWC allies in the Senate had enough votes to defeat any section 14(b) repeal bill with a filibuster. Nevertheless, strong right-to-work agitation in both New Mexico and Idaho in early 1977 drove home the continued importance of that section of the Taft-Hartley Act. In fact, in Idaho an anti–union security measure actually passed both chambers but did not make it out of the conference committee. In New Mexico, a similar proposal passed the senate but narrowly failed in the house. Only in Wyoming, where a repealer succeeded in the senate but not in the house, did labor find itself not on the defensive. In all three of these states, as Tables 7.1 and 7.2 record, the parties divided along the usual lines. Democratic, pro–labor cohesion scores ranged from − 37 in New Mexico, to − 63 in Wyoming, to − 73 in Idaho. Republicans in each state tallied anti-labor cohesion indexes. New Mexico's GOP members came first with a 93 followed closely by Wyoming's with a 92. Idaho Republicans compiled the lowest pro-right-to-work cohesion with a 62. The near misses in New Mexico and Idaho, though, insured that AFL-CIO abandonment of 14(b) repeal was tactical and not strategic.

Mindful of these events, AFL-CIO decision makers would evaluate their chances to improve the union security situation in relation to the success of the labor law reform package. With the president's approval, a House bill combining a number of administrative and substantive labor law changes moved steadily through the lower chamber. Included in the legislation were revisions to increase the National Labor Relations Board's efficiency through

7.4

Rice Index of Cohesion of Congressional Parties, on the Labor Law Reform Act, 1977–1978

LEGISLATION/YEAR	AGAINST LABOR	FOR LABOR	TOTAL	PERCENT YES	PERCENT NO	RICE INDEX
H.R. 8410 1977						
House						
D						
Northern	6	184	190	3	97	-94
Southern	53	37	90	59	41	18
Total	59	221	280	21	79	-58
R	104	36	140	74	26	49
Senate 1978						
D Cloture						
Northern	2	41	43	5	95	-91
Southern	15	3	18	83	17	67
Total	17	44	61	28	72	-44
R	22	14	36	61	39	22
Both Chambers						
D	76	265	341	22	78	-55
R	126	50	176	72	28	43
Total	202	315	517	39	61	-22

Source: Congressional Quarterly, Congressional Quarterly Almanac, 1977, 1978 (Washington, DC: Congressional Quarterly, 1977, 1978).
Index: +100(Totally Cohesive Against Labor)
          -100(Totally Cohesive in Favor of Labor)
          Rice Index Rounded to Nearest Integer
Note: Of the 5 Cloture Votes in 1978, Vote 4 Was Chosen As The Point of Maximum Labor Influence.

administrative restructuring as well as by setting strict time limits for representation elections. The proposal also sought more effective protections for workers subjected to anti–union discrimination by their employers. Allied to this was a grant of greater power to the NLRB to fashion punitive remedies against repeated labor law violators. Probably the most controversial modification mandated equal access to workers on company time during organizational campaigns. By October 1977 this labor law reform bill, H.R. 8410, passed easily by a vote of 257 to 163. Table 7.4 presents the party cohesion indexes on that vote and shows that Democrats and Republicans divided on opposite sides of the issue with about the same amount of solidity. The House's 280 Democratic representatives compiled a pro-labor − 58 in contrast to the 140 Republicans who scored a 49 in opposition.[16]

In the Senate, however, the reform measures did not fare as well when the bill came up for passage in June 1978. Opponents of revision had mounted an intense grass roots lobbying campaign during the interim that meted out a "stinging humiliation" to organized labor, according to the *Congressional Quarterly*. Legions of business lobbyists—in the main small businesspeople who rarely lobbied an issue at the national level—aroused sufficient notice to convince a number of senators to filibuster. Conse-

7.5

Rice Index of Cohesion of Congressional Parties, by Geographic Areas, on the Labor Law Reform Act, 1977–1978

LEGISLATION	EAST	SOUTH	MID-WEST	WEST
House				
H.R. 8410 1977				
D	-100	-2	-94	-96
R	-20	100	64	48
Senate				
H.R. 8410 1978				
D	-100	45	-88	-80
R	-80	100	50	40

Source: Congressional Quarterly, Congressional Quarterly Almanac, 1977, 1978 (Washington, DC: Congressional Quarterly, 1977, 1978).

Index: +100(Totally Cohesive Against Labor)
        -100(Totally Cohesive in Favor of Labor)
        Rice Index Rounded to Nearest Integer

quently, Senate Majority Leader Robert Byrd (D-WV) and AFL-CIO allies found their first two attempts blocked by filibuster leaders Orrin Hatch (R-UT) and Richard Lugar (R-IN), who had also attracted a number of conservative southern Democrats to their cause. Unlike the failed 14(b) repeal attempt in 1966, though, the Democratic leadership of the Senate under Byrd strove energetically to engineer passage during the next four votes on invoking cloture. A compromise proposal put together by Senator Harrison Williams (D-NJ) and Senator Jacob Javits (R-NY) gained some additional support. Nevertheless, shortly afterward, on June 15, the Democrats lost the battle for cloture by two votes. Though Byrd tried to resurrect some type of reform legislation later, the issue proved to be a dead one.[17]

As Table 7.4 indicates, the indexes of cohesion for the vote totaled a pro–labor −44 for Democratic senators and an anti-labor 22 for their Republican counterparts. Table 7.5 is more revealing, however, for it breaks down the cohesion scores for each party in each chamber by geographic regions. In the House, all four areas produced pro-labor indexes: −100 in the East, −96 in the West, −94 in the Midwest, and a nearly insignificant −2 in the South. Except for the eastern region of the country, where GOP members scored a mildly pro-labor −20, Republicans opposed the revision with 100 in the South, 64 in the Midwest, and 48 in the West. In the Senate, Democrats from the East, West, and Midwest again strongly supported organized labor on cloture, with cohesion tallies of −100, −88, and −80, respectively. Southern Democrats, on the other hand, went in the reverse direction with an anti-labor 45. With scores similar to their House brethren, Republican senators—again with the exception of eastern lawmakers who compiled a strong pro-labor −80—voted against cloture. Southern Republicans were the most cohesive in opposition with 100, followed by 50 for midwesterners, and 40 for westerners. Thus, the majority of the Republican party, in tandem with southern Democrats, once more forestalled the efforts of the AFL-CIO to effect favorable labor law revision.

The defeat of this relatively mild set of proposals for national labor law reform outraged many important union leaders. This time, however, they first directed their anger at the American business community. UAW president Douglas Fraser, for example, resigned from the elite Labor-Management Committee in protest over the solidarity the business community showed in defeating the changes. It was evidence, he charged, that American business had declared class war on organized labor while it hypocritically preached cooperation and mutuality of interests.[18]

While labor law reform did not explicitly deal with union security, the apostles of right to work—hoping to seize the advantage emanating from probable union demoralization—redoubled their activity in the wake of the June 1978 labor loss. The first battleground was Missouri where anti–union security backers, who had been previously thwarted in the legislature, succeeded in obtaining a ballot for the November 1978 election. Missouri labor, with the assistance of the national AFL-CIO office and virtually the entire progressive community, came together to wholeheartedly defend union security in particular and unionism in general. And in this industrialized midwestern state, the labor movement—comprising 571,000 members or 27.6 percent of the labor force—had the resources to put up a good fight. Table 7.3 shows that it accomplished its goal without question. Out of the nearly 1.6 million votes cast, the referendum lost by a 60 to 40 percent margin (944,071 no to 630,764 yes).[19]

The substantial Missouri victory picked up the spirits of AFL-CIO legislative leaders somewhat. It proved once more that in industrialized areas, when aroused and in possession of sufficient resources (in numbers and dollars), labor could normally defend its union security prerogatives at the ballot box. At the February 1979 meeting of the AFL-CIO executive council in Bal Harbour, Florida, labor executives, stimulated by the events in Washington and Missouri, discussed possible tactical changes in legislative initiatives. Perhaps organized labor should focus much more action on local efforts, they speculated, for recent experiences in Congress and in Missouri seemed to suggest that labor would do better at that level. One important goal for such a change in orientation would be a trial federation program aimed at repealing a right-to-work law in a single state. While broad national labor law reform had failed, AFL-CIO lobbyists could certainly continue their efforts for revision on a piecemeal basis.[20]

Despite the confident talk, in early 1979 organized labor was again on the defensive in the state legislatures. While Maine legislators rejected a right-to-work bill by a comfortable margin, floor votes in Delaware, New Hampshire, and New Mexico did not go well. In Delaware, a bill failed to pass the senate by only two votes. In New Hampshire, the house gave its approval to a measure which then lost in the senate. And in New Mexico, perennially under the threat of such legislation, only a gubernatorial veto prevented a right-to-work statute from being inscribed in the state's *Public Acts* for 1979.[21]

For Democratic legislators in these states, cohesion scores in favor of labor ranged from a low of − 29 in New Mexico to a high of − 79 in Maine, as shown in Table 7.1. In between fell New Hampshire with a − 65 and Delaware's senate with a − 30. Parallel Republican indexes are listed in Table 7.2. New Mexico Republicans had the most cohesive pro-right-to-work index with an 89, followed by New Hampshire's with a 62. Maine and Delaware GOP legislators found themselves less united with scores of 33 and 25, respectively.

Thus, by 1979 regular patterns of political support for and against right to work had developed as well as a pattern of continual oscillation between national and state levels. As the decade closed, anti–union security forces claimed they had gained the upper hand once more when Louisiana elected its first Republican governor since Reconstruction. The state's 1976 right-to-work law became a salient part of the campaign, with Republican governor-elect David C. Treen promising to veto any repeal effort and Democrat Louis Lambert pledging to strike it from the statute books. With over 1.4 million ballots cast, Treen won by a scant 9,557 votes which, while hardly impressive, was a great victory for the National Right to Work Committee, claimed its public relations representative Carter Clews. That campaign had been a pivotal election, according to Clews, as victory for the NRTWC's labor-endorsed opponent would have given steam to repeal drives not only in Louisiana but in Arizona and Iowa as well. Now, Treen's election would reinvigorate the anti–union security group's efforts in a number of areas.[22]

And so, predictably, it appeared the skirmishing would continue into the 1980s. As long as section 14(b) of the Taft-Hartley Act gave states the right to legislate in this area, anti–union security supporters would continue to proselytize and organized labor would continue to defend itself and occasionally even try to strike back. Though dim, it was an outlook the AFL-CIO had, of course, faced many times before in the 36-year history of its struggle over the right to work.

NOTES

1. A. H. Raskin, "Labor May Sidetrack 'Right-to-Work' Plea," *New York Times*, 2 June 1977, p. 5.

2. Warren Weaver, Jr., "Muskie Heckled on Syracuse Campus," *New York Times*, 8 October 1968, p. 34.

3. Ben A. Franklin, "McGovern's Gain Embitters Labor," *New York Times*, 12 July 1972, p. 20. For evidence of the intensity of labor feeling against McGovern for his first 14(b) vote, see the senator's somewhat apologetic explanation to George

Meany in George McGovern to George Meany, 29 November 1965, Box 48, AFL-CIO Legislative Department Files, GMMA.

4. John Hebers, "Platform Hails G.O.P. Tax Record of 'Sound Reform,' " *New York Times*, 20 August 1972, p. 1.

5. The agency shop is a modification of the union shop wherein individuals within the bargaining unit are not required to *join* a labor organization, but are required to pay an *agency* fee of some type for collective bargaining representation. Under the interpretation of some state attorney generals, some of the state right-to-work statutes (depending on the wording) did not foreclose an agency shop arrangement.

6. Interview with Frank Emig, former national AFL-CIO State and Central Organization Representative, April 1985. Emig was Carl McPeak's successor in the responsibility of monitoring state right-to-work developments.

7. J. Bill Becker, President, Arkansas State AFL-CIO to George Meany, 16 June 1971, with attachments, "*Confidential,* Labor Survey," by Jim Ranchino, Box 81; Carl Courter, President, H. J. Yount, Executive Vice-President, and Ralph McGee, Executive Secretary, Kansas State Federation of Labor, to Frank Emig, Representative, AFL-CIO State and Local Central Bodies, 17 May 1972, Box 82; both in AFL-CIO Legislative Department Files, GMMA.

8. Udall protested he had had the consent of the Arizona AFL-CIO to cast a negative ballot and promised he would lead a fight for repeal as president. Carter did state he would sign a repeal bill if Congress saw fit to pass one. See "Jackson, in Wisconsin, Assails Carter and Udall Records on Right-to-Work Legislation," *New York Times*, 31 March 1976, p. 21.

9. Christopher Lydon, "Some Leaders Are Responding to Carter," *New York Times*, 2 April 1976, p. 9.

10. John Hebers, "Jackson Hedging on Pennsylvania," *New York Times*, 22 April 1976, p. 24; Charles Mohr, "Two Rivals Attack Carter on Labor and Black Issues," *New York Times*, 26 April 1976, p. 1.

11. *New York Times*, 16 January 1976, p. 34, and 9 July 1976, p. 12. The Kansas legislature had passed a bill in 1969 but the governor vetoed the legislation.

12. Interview with J. Bill Becker, President, Arkansas AFL-CIO, June 1986; Edward Cowan, "Arkansas Weighing Repeal of 'Right-to-Work' Law," *New York Times*, 28 October 1976, p. 50.

13. Cowan, "Arkansas Weighing Repeal," p. 50.

14. A. H. Raskin, "The Labor Scene," *New York Times*, 8 November 1976, p. 49.

15. Raskin, "Labor May Sidetrack 'Right-to-Work' Plea."

16. For the legislative history of the labor law reform bill of 1977–1978, see Congressional Quarterly, *Congressional Quarterly Almanac, 1977* (Washington, D.C.: Congressional Quarterly, 1977) and *Congressional Quarterly Almanac, 1978* (Washington, D.C.: Congressional Quarterly, 1978).

17. Congressional Quarterly, *Congressional Quarterly Almanac, 1978* (Washington, D.C.: Congressional Quarterly, 1978), pp. 284–287.

18. For the reaction of organized labor to the defeat see David Brody, "Industrial Relations, Part II: The Political Battleground," in David Brody, *Workers in Industrial America: Essays on the Twentieth Century Struggle* (New York: Oxford University Press, 1980), p. 249.

19. Frank Emig interview, April 1985.

20. Jerry Flint, "Legislative Tactics Modified By Labor," *New York Times*, 24 February 1979, p. 8.

21. See Appendix A for the actual vote counts.

22. Philip Shabecoff, "Backers of 'Right to Work' Laws Hail Treen's Victory in Louisiana," *New York Times*, 14 December 1979, p. 27.

8

Right to Work in Perspective

> [National Right to Work Committee president Reed] Larson also ex-
> pressed deep satisfaction with the GOP's continued support for Section
> 14(b)....
>
> This year...Rep. Jack Kemp (R-NY) made several strong, if lonely,
> efforts to scuttle the [party's platform plank on] Right to Work pro-
> tections....
>
> On each occasion, however, the discarded vice presidential hopeful
> was soundly rebuffed by Republican Party leaders....
> —*National Right to Work Newsletter*, August 1980[1]

This examination of organized labor's response to the right-to-work problem over four decades aimed at accomplishing two tasks. First, it sought to
supply a general narrative history of the issue from the early 1940s through
the late 1970s at both the state and national levels; and relatedly, at the
same time to present, in microcosm, an accessible account of labor politics
for most of the post–World War II era. Second, and more importantly, a
survey of the AFL's, CIO's, and AFL-CIO's efforts to grapple with this
legislative onslaught afforded an opportunity to define with some specific-
ness the nature of organized labor's "special interest" influence within the
context of modern American party politics. More particularly, a comparison
of the responses of both parties vis-à-vis the labor federations' attempts to
influence them provided a methodology to analyze and evaluate the effectiveness of labor's political alliance with the Democratic party on institutional issues of special interest to labor. Given the respective aggregate
responses of the parties, a fair conclusion is that, although beset by numerous
difficulties, the alliance between organized labor and the Democratic party
provided an important channel through which the American union leaders
could wield a respectable amount of special interest influence. While this
influence apparently was not strong enough to allow the labor movement's

political directors to push back inroads made in geographic areas of weakness and during times of strong public dismay over union activity, it did consistently and successfully function on a day-to-day basis as a means of protection. Before going into this evaluation in some quantitative detail, it would be useful first to summarize the main outlines of the politics of right to work.

The years from 1943 to 1949 encompassed both the gestation period and the first flowering of the right-to-work movement, as well as organized labor's initial reaction to the problem. During World War II, organized labor lobbied for union security in exchange for wage restraint and succeeded in obtaining it by government decree. In a move calculated to circumvent pro-labor policy makers at the federal level, conservative forces launched a movement at the state level to limit, and hopefully push back, these union security gains. After generally unsuccessful efforts in several state legislatures, anti–union security proponents established their first credibility by winning public right-to-work referendums in Arkansas and Florida in 1944, and subsequently in South Dakota, Nebraska, and Arizona in 1946. Now claiming public support, like-minded lawmakers in nine other states, responding either to concern over widespread labor militancy after the war or the potential targeting of their region for union organizing drives, argued that the citizenry wanted such legislation and managed to place similar restraints on their respective state's statute books in 1947. In the main, right-to-workers found their greatest acceptance in the South, the Southwest, and in the Plains states, notably in North Carolina, Georgia, Virginia, Tennessee, Texas, Iowa, and North Dakota. They also won an occasional victory in the more conservative and rural parts of the North and East, as in Delaware and New Hampshire. These events had a parallel impact at the national level, for when Congress considered broad reform of national labor relations policy during the Taft-Hartley debates in 1947, the conservative authors of the revisions considered it important to protect state anti–union security restrictions by explicitly ceding jurisdiction over the subject to the states.

During the course of these developments, a divided labor movement struggled to respond effectively. True to its decentralized organizational traditions, the AFL's national office preferred that its state organizations deal with the electoral aspect of the battle largely on their own, while it concentrated on a legal challenge. Conversely, top CIO executives ardently tried to galvanize their state-level counterparts into electoral action, believing it the only realistic way to protect industrial unionism from onerous legislative constraints. Neither mode of resistance worked especially well, however. While conceivably the national AFL could have made a difference in the close electoral contests of 1944, the subsequent protection afforded by section 14(b) of the Taft-Hartley Act undercut the basis of the older federation's protest of federal preemption and left only feeble claims of unconstitutionality. And the CIO's recognition that the outcome would ultimately be won or lost in the electoral arena fared little better, for its economic weakness in just those areas most prone to pass the restraints had meant it exerted little political influence.

In this formative period of the right-to-work struggle, both the breadth of the attack at the state level and the related national events that culminated in the Taft-Hartley Act forced union leaders to reassess their commitments to electoral activity and confront their relationship to the two major political parties. In this analysis the CIO led the way with significant portions of the AFL following after 1947. Upon reviewing organized labor's political activity during the discussions surrounding the formation of the Political Action Committee (PAC), CIO strategists concluded there was little chance that unions would ever exercise much influence within the Republican party. They argued that with very few exceptions Republicans at all levels of government voted against labor in a fairly unified fashion. On the other hand, Democrats from most two-party areas supported labor's position on a wide range of issues and thus deserved the movement's partisan political commitments on a regular and continuing basis. The major problem of course—and it was a *major* one—was that the sizeable faction of the party comprising the conservative wing dissented consistently and cohesively from pro-labor New Deal propositions, especially on labor legislation. Top CIO policy makers realized this but believed that a combination of sufficient electoral activism from labor, increased union organization in conservative areas, and a political coalition of progressive forces would eventually break the power of reactionary Democrats. In the context of the 1940s, with the labor reforms of the New Deal still fresh in their minds, this seemed an obtainable goal to many union leaders. This position received additional validity after the AFL's and CIO's electoral contributions helped tip the scales in President Truman's favor in the 1948 election, for labor then won administration support for an attack on the hated Taft-Hartley Act and nearly emerged victorious. Moreover, in 1948 an aroused labor movement won right-to-work elections in Maine, Massachussetts, and New Mexico, and tried an unsuccessful ballot repeal in Arizona. It also stopped a bill cold in the Massachusetts legislature. Only in North Dakota, where voters approved the 1947 action of their legislature, did labor lose badly. In addition to the Taft-Hartley campaign in 1949, unionists reclaimed two states by achieving legislative repeal of anti–union security statutes in Delaware and New Hampshire. Thus, with labor's surge of electoral activity and the resultant legislative offensives, in the late 1940s it seemed as though a liberal, pro-labor reinvigoration of the Democratic party through partisan commitment would not be as difficult to achieve as it ultimately proved to be.

If the decade of the 1940s produced an anti-labor legislative atmosphere that aroused labor's partisan political consciousness, continuing widespread anti–union security agitation during the 1950s transformed that consciousness into expanding electoral commitments and a progressively intimate but troubled alliance with the Democratic party. In the early years of the decade, some segments of organized labor still explored non-partisan lobbying from time to time in an attempt to deal with union security questions, but without much success at the national level due to the election of Republican Dwight Eisenhower to the White House who was well aware of the intense Democratic affinity of large parts of organized labor. While it was true that four Democratic-dominated southern states—Alabama, South Carolina, Louisiana, and Mississippi—passed right-to-work laws by 1954, southern Democrats were less cohesive in adopting anti-labor positions than they had been in the 1940s. Moreover, in other areas of the country experiencing agitation, Republicans provided a strong base of votes for proposed restrictions, although they only succeeded in Nevada and Utah, the first two western states to pass the legislation. By 1955 the state-level drives beyond the South and the visible affiliation of prominent Republicans with national right-to-work schemes helped bring both the AFL's and CIO's political impulses into sufficient congruence to facilitate merger. And without question, George Meany, the president of the new federation, came to the conclusion shortly after the unification convention that the new federation had to continue, and indeed even expand, labor's political operations. His experience at attempting rapprochement with the National Association of Manufacturers (NAM) convinced him that only by committing substantial organizational resources to electoral activities would labor be able to protect itself against further right-to-work incursions fomented by single-issue groups like the National Right to Work Committee, and supported by solidly pro-Republican business associations such as NAM and the U.S. Chamber of Commerce.

After 1955, then, there was no question that labor's short-range focus would be on state-level politics. In 1956 key victories in the Louisiana legislature, where a united statewide movement repealed the 1954 law, and in Washington state, where well-organized unions trounced an initiative proposal, foreshadowed future success for grass roots labor politics. In 1957, however, an unexpected legislative victory for the Indiana Right to Work Committee, in a highly unionized state, signaled that anti–union security forces would continue to wage a desperately fought struggle. The Indiana defeat also clearly solidified the evolving perception among labor leaders that despite periodic talk of resolving the problem through national legislation, it was too dangerous to rest on the supposition that anything would be done soon. When right-to-work supporters succeeded in obtaining referendums in six more states for the 1958 elections—thrusting the issue into the national political limelight—it only underlined the necessity that all levels of organized labor had to respond in a unified fashion to a challenge that was at once both local and national.

And respond it did. The Indiana defeat had aroused the interest and wholehearted commitment of top industrial union leaders in the 1958 elections. Previously spared from experiencing the full impact of union security restrictions due to the geographic distribution of the laws, industrial union chiefs such as Walter Reuther observed that not only had Indiana joined the ranks of right-to-work states, but now the important industrial union areas of California and Ohio—in addition to Washington State, Kansas, Colorado, and Idaho—were under threat. Reuther prodded the AFL-CIO's national office into deeper involvement, and with craft and industrial leaders thus unified, the labor movement put together an impressive electoral response to the challenge to union security. In these six elections, as well as in several earlier ones during the 1950s, many of organized labor's state-level activists began developing expertise and sophistication in special issue campaigning, in addition to important experience in practical politics. Collaterally, COPE's campaign in Ohio tapped into an unexpected source of opposition to right to work among the Buckeye State's black citizens, supplying an important trade union rationale and justification for future efforts to build electoral coalitions. Clearly misreading the level of voter support for their cause, the National Right to Work Committee and its associated state groups lost five of the six proposals, succeeding only in Kansas. More significantly, the AFL-CIO's Committee on Political Education (COPE) could rightfully claim that the intensity of the union security controversy in 1958 had envigorated labor's electoral response nationwide, resulting in parallel liberal Democratic victories in many parts of the country. And with those victories, union executives hoped, would finally come a concomitant realization by the congressional Democratic party of the need to end the right-to-work dispute by repealing section 14(b) of the Taft-Hartley Act.

Indeed, the inability to move the Democratic party into an offensive stance on labor legislation had exasperated labor's legislative strategists throughout the 1950s. While labor lost seven states to right-to-work forces by legislative votes from 1951 to 1957, four of those states were in the one-party Democratic South. And unfortunately, many leaders of the congressional party hailed from that conservative area. Since organized labor was not a major political force in those states, AFL-CIO functionaries always operated at a disadvantage in their efforts to participate in agenda setting. Therefore, during a period in which the Republicans controlled the executive branch of the government and "legislating by consensus" became the watchwords in Congress, legislative generals Sam Rayburn (D-TX) and Lyndon Johnson (D-TX) remained adamant in their refusal to advance measures that would reinforce the Democrats' factionalization—and repeal of section 14(b) was certainly foremost among those types of proposals. In many ways and for many reasons, then, the erosion of the power of the conservative bloc of the party—envisioned by labor leaders in the 1940s—had been put on hold in the 1950s.

Initially, the 1958 electoral gains for liberals seemed to establish the most favorable legislative outlook for labor in nearly a decade. Despite overheated rhetoric about repealing section 14(b) in the immediate aftermath of the elections, AFL-CIO straw polls in late 1958 caused the federation's legislative directors to realize that they had engaged in a bit of wishful thinking, and that their overall margin was not wide enough, realistically, to put together a meaningful offensive. As it turned out, it mattered little, for the long-running congressional investigations into alleged union racketeering dominated the legislative agenda in early 1959. Not long after the start of the first session, members of Congress perceived strong public opinion favoring legislation that would provide financial safeguards for union funds as well as some guarantees of democratic procedures. In the debates surrounding the passage of what came to be the Landrum-Griffin Act, the obstructionist stance of segments of organized labor frayed the relationship between union lobbyists and important liberals. Subsequently, while labor fought six right-to-work battles, three of them repeal efforts, at the state level from 1959 to 1961, by the end of the latter year there existed even less support than usual within Congress for any contentious labor law change. Even the election of a Democratic president did not improve the situation, for John F. Kennedy opportunistically backtracked on his promise to seek repeal of section 14(b) as soon as the party's conservative icons threatened active opposition to his candidacy in the South. Afterward, the president-elect's narrow party majorities shifted the balance of power further in the Dixiecrats' direction. By 1963, when right-to-work backers captured Wyoming and secured a future referendum in Oklahoma, the federation's legislative directors appeared especially dejected over their lack of success at transforming electoral activity into trade-union-oriented legislative gains.

In relatively short order, however, this dejection turned into elation as a fortuitous convergence of developments produced an outstanding electoral triumph for reform-minded Democrats. After President Kennedy's assassination and Lyndon Johnson's accession to power, the growing civil rights crisis fused and energized the elements of a progressive political coalition that included organized labor, civil rights groups, and middle-class liberals. The potential of this coalition became visible first in Oklahoma, where labor's unanticipated defeat of a proposed right-to-work constitutional amendment drew critical support from the state's black voters in mid-1964. When President Johnson won his landslide victory over Republican Barry Goldwater (AZ), an ardent right-to-work promoter and longtime nemesis of organized labor, Democratic leaders at last had the numbers necessary for broad reforms in a number of areas, and these seemed to include labor law. Top AFL-CIO executives realized this, and events in Indiana, where state labor leaders finally achieved repeal of the detested 1957 law in early 1965, only stiffened federation leaders' insistence that the national Democratic party finally repay its cumulative electoral debts to labor by repealing section 14(b). It was at this point that the limitations inherent in organized labor's special interest influence in a partisan context finally came into sharper focus.

Labor's campaign to repeal section 14(b) in the first session of the Eighty-ninth Congress revealed that while partisanism led the large majority of Democrats to ultimately vote with labor—indicative of one important type of special interest influence—it also diluted the power to impose believable negative sanctions against the party's lackluster leadership. At the height of Democratic power and control, the AFL-CIO *could* demand that the Johnson administration propose and back repeal, and that House and Senate leaders do basically the same, but it *could not* set the timing and method of battle, nor the intensity with which the measure would be pursued by party chieftains. Thus, repeal moved along at a pace determined by the White House and congressional leaders, with only modest support from the administration, until the opposition had organized sufficiently to raise the price of success. At that point, despite growing labor pressure, the AFL-CIO's special interest influence passed its peak. To mollify AFL-CIO executives, the president ordered his aides to undertake superficial actions and he himself made shallow promises to appease union executives. Nevertheless, mindful of his upcoming foreign policy proposals in the Senate, Johnson refused to allow the repeal contest to disrupt his relationship with any of his former colleagues. The president and several other critically placed Democrats judged that labor's political ties to the party had grown so strong that there was little chance of abandonment in any truly destructive way. And predictably they were correct, for although labor responded lethargically in the mid-term 1966 elections, in part due to the disappointment engendered by the 14(b) defeat, over the long run AFL-CIO leaders swallowed their embarrassment and continued their partisan commitments.

Unionists' concern over right-to-work agitation did not disappear with the defeat of 1966, however. Despite the Democrats' failure to deliver relief, implying that party officials might be better off not raising the subject, union security legislation continued to play a role within national Democratic party politics throughout the 1970s. Right-to-work proposals cropped up in various state legislatures from time to time, with the momentum seeming to run in organized labor's favor through 1975, before turning in the opposite direction in 1976. During these years, party voting lines appeared sharper in contrast; Republicans more consistently backed restrictions or opposed labor-sponsored improvements in the laws, and Democrats, with a few exceptions, voted the labor position on union security measures.

Perhaps this moderate increase in cohesion occurred because the Democratic party fractionalized even further in the wake of the Vietnam War, and consequently many candidates strove harder not to alienate any traditonal bases of support. At any rate, the divisions within the party were most clearly apparent in Democratic presidential politics, where labor-oriented cold war liberals such as Senator Edmund Muskie (D-ME) and Senator

Henry Jackson (D-WA) used the issue in the 1972 and 1976 primaries to put non-labor-oriented liberals like Senator George McGovern (D-SD), or moderate-conservative Democrats such as former governor Jimmy Carter (D-GA) on the defensive. The accumulative effect of these attacks did lead to a positive development for the AFL-CIO in 1976; the intra-party debate moved candidate Jimmy Carter from a position of opposition disinterest to labor law reform, to a position, upon being elected president, of supporting pro-labor revisions in national labor policy.

Meanwhile, at the state level, through 1975 organized labor went on the offensive in at least five right-to-work states, and lost only one defensive battle in Kansas, where an enabling statute was passed. In 1976, however, the Louisiana legislature reinstituted a full-blown anti–union security statute and the Arkansas labor movement failed to amend the state's constitutional restriction in a referendum. These events marked a reversal and damaged the AFL-CIO's hope that it would be able to persuade president-elect Jimmy Carter to sponsor or include an offensive against section 14(b) in any administration-backed reform package. There were other labor law subjects of importance, though, and federation executives finally won administration approval for other types of revisions in exchange for dropping its ideas about repeal.

In 1977 and 1978, in what came to be the last attempt to amend national labor policy in a pro-labor direction, the AFL-CIO received strong Democratic support in all geographic areas except the South, and this time also obtained substantial commitment from the party's congressional leadership. Republicans were a bit less cohesive than usual in opposing the general reform proposals known informally as the Labor Law Reform Act, and this should have led to victory. The peculiar rule allowing unlimited debate in the Senate, however, once again enabled a minority of Republican and southern Democratic arch-conservatives to scuttle the reform package. After the final filibuster defeat in mid–1978, the labor movement placed the blame squarely on the shoulders of American business leaders, whose sponsorship of a massive, anti-reform lobbying effort hardened the resolution of the filibustering senators.

Emboldened by the conservatives' victory, the National Right to Work Committee and its allies resolved to take advantage of unionists' anticipated legislative disarray. In 1977, organized labor tried another repeal campaign in Wyoming, fought off strong agitation in New Mexico, and barely escaped the imposition of a statute in Idaho. Then, in 1979, right-to-work measures succeeded in Delaware's house, New Hampshire's lower chamber, and the entire New Mexico legislature, where ultimate passage failed due to a gubernatorial veto. Only in Maine, where a bill lost in both chambers, was there a state drive that was not closely contested. Though right-to-work evangelists did not emerge with a single victory, when Louisiana voters elected a Republican governor pledged to keep the state's new law on the

books in late 1979, NRTWC officials claimed the momentum would continue to flow in their direction. With no conceivable possibility of resur-
recting the section 14(b) issue nationally, as organized labor headed into
what appeared to be an even more conservative decade, the AFL-CIO's
outlook narrowed once more to a rearguard action, defending union security
on a piecemeal basis wherever and whenever it could.

While the above discussion qualitatively summarizes organized labor's
response to the right-to-work controversy, its interactions with both political
parties in relation to it, and the broad outlines of labor's alliance with the
Democratic party on a paradigmatic special interest issue, a deeper analytical
evaluation is possible by comparing the aggregate party reactions quantitatively from the early 1940s through the late 1970s. Such a comparison
yields the conclusion that organized labor's political activity during this
period was marked by substantial, though not controlling, influence on the
party structure on even so blatant a trade-union special interest issue as
right to work. In attempting to wield this influence, the AFL-CIO was most
consistently successful in invoking a pro-labor response within the Democratic party, but this basically beneficial relationship suffered, and continues
to suffer, from circumscriptions due to a number of factors. And it was
these circumscriptions, some of which were beyond labor's direct or immediate control though others were not, that resulted in right-to-work legislation in the Democratic South and repeatedly defeated labor's national
legislative offensives. Nevertheless, the quantitative analysis reveals clearly
divergent responses between the parties as a whole: Republican legislators
from all regions of the country except the East, at both the state and national
levels, voted fairly cohesively for right-to-work restrictions, and this cohe-
siveness intensified over time at the state level; Democrats, in all areas save
the South, cast their ballots, with a similar growing solidarity, for the labor
position, with the anti-labor South becoming less cohesive on the question
over time. Before contrasting each party further, it would be useful to
characterize Republican and Democratic aggregate quantitative responses
in more detail.

Table 8.1 lists the Rice Index of Cohesion for the Republican party on
right-to-work measures at the state level, from 1943 through 1979. Most
notable is the lack of any negative, pro-labor index score for any decade in
any region of the country. Republican state legislators' tallies, in the total
index column, ranged from a low of 15 in the 1940s in the East to a high
of 91 for the South in the 1970s. The bulk of GOP right-to-work voting
took place in two regions. The East accounted for nearly 33 percent of
union security ballots and the Midwest for almost 45 percent (with the West
contributing 16 percent and the South 6 percent). And, examining all chambers, senate and house, for all states experiencing floor votes from the early
1940s through the late 1970s, only three times did the index of cohesion,
in aggregate terms, tip in a pro-labor direction. Each time this occurred in

8.1

Rice Index of Cohesion of Republican State Legislators, Aggregate, by Region and Decade, on Right-to-Work Measures, 1943–1979

REGION/DECADE	TOTAL	INDEXES SENATE	HOUSE	BALLOTS CAST SENATE	HOUSE
East					
1940s	15	-21	17	38	519
1950s	-	NV	-4	NV	211
1960s	NV	NV	NV	NV	NV
1970s	46	-22	56	46	288
Total	20	-21	24	84	1018
Midwest					
1940s	60	67	58	181	400
1950s	70	69	71	130	346
1960s	80	82	79	68	103
1970s	87	76	94	42	67
Total	69	74	67	461	916
West					
1940s	NV	NV	NV	NV	NV
1950s	72	81	69	42	144
1960s	66	88	62	16	95
1970s	80	76	82	50	113
Total	73	80	71	108	350
South					
1940s	57	40	64	20	50
1950s	14	8	25	13	8
1960s	NV	NV	NV	NV	NV
1970s	91	78	96	18	52
Total	66	45	76	51	110
Totals, By Region					
East	20	-21	24	84	1018
Midwest	69	74	67	461	916
West	73	80	71	108	350
South	66	45	76	51	110
Totals, By Decade					
1940s	39	51	36	239	969
1950S	52	68	47	185	707
1960S	74	83	71	84	198
1970S	65	47	71	156	520

Source: Appendix A
Key: NV–No Vote
Index: +100(Totally Cohesive in Favor of Right to Work)
          -100(Totally Cohesive Against Right to Work)

the East, the least anti-labor Republican region, where senates in the 1940s and 1970s compiled − 21 and − 22 indexes, respectively, and in the 1950s where house chambers totaled an even weaker − 4. Other than that, all cohesion indicators for GOP state legislators across these decades and regions indicated significant anti-labor solidity.

In fact, except for the East, Republicans in all other regions of the country backed union security restrictions strongly with almost no exceptions. A review of the aggregate Totals, By Region section (found toward the bottom of Table 8.1), shows the depth of the party's support for the legislation. Even in the East—where organized labor could be intermittently effective in influencing Republican state legislators due to a higher degree of urbanization, industrialization, and unionization—over the long run the cohesion scores ended up in favor of right to work. For example, the total column in the region summary, which combines both senate and house scores, indicates that over these four decades eastern GOP state lawmakers accumulated an index of 20 in support of restricting union security. In the Midwest, West, and South, however, the solidarity of Republicans was much stronger. Western legislators scored the highest cohesion with a 73, followed by their midwestern colleagues with 68, and a much smaller number of southern Republicans with a 66. All regions, though, adopted anti-labor positions in the aggregate.

Perhaps even more significantly, a chronological analysis shows a pattern of growing anti-labor cohesion on union security by Republicans. The Totals, By Decade section at the bottom of Table 8.1 puts all regions of the country into a time series. And as this section outlines, in both senate and house chambers (with the exception of GOP senates in the 1970s), the party's state legislators progressively increased their cohesion in favor of right-to-work legislation. In house chambers, for instance, Republican scores went from 36 in the 1940s, to 47 in the 1950s, to 71 in the 1960s and 1970s. In senates, the party's lawmakers started at a base index of 51 in the 1940s, moved to 68 in the 1950s, and then on to 83 in the 1960s, before dropping sharply to 47 in the 1970s. In combination, the total index scores advanced similarly, with the 1940s yielding a 39, the 1950s a 52, the 1960s a 74, and the 1970s a 65 (the falling off due to the decline in cohesion of Republican senates in the 1970s).

In contrast to these aggregate measures of generally solid Republican cohesion favoring right-to-work legislation at the state level, Democratic state legislators in all regions, with the exception of the South, substantially backed organized labor with their votes. Table 8.2 profiles the Rice Index of Cohesion of Democrats for these four decades. Immediately noticeable are the large number of negative pro-labor index scores, dominant in every part of the country except one. As charted in the total column, however, Democratic indexes spanned a much greater range because of southern Democrats' desire for right-to-work legislation. At the anti-labor end of the spectrum was the South in the 1960s with a 71 index. In comparison, the highest pro-labor tallies of −93 appeared in the East in the 1940s and the Midwest in the 1960s. And predictably, the lion's share of right-to-work voting on the part of Democrats took place in the South, which accounted for a full 69 percent of all ballots cast (followed by the East with 13 percent, the Midwest with 10 percent, and the West with 8 percent). Outside of the South the only positive, anti-labor index score, a 20, befell trade unionists in Midwest house chambers in the 1970s.

8.2
Rice Index of Cohesion of Democratic State Legislators, Aggregate, by Region and
Decade, on Right-to-Work Measures, 1943–1979

REGION/DECADE	TOTAL	INDEXES SENATE	HOUSE	BALLOTS CAST SENATE	HOUSE
East					
1940s	-93	-100	-93	26	243
1950s	-	NV	-49	NV	129
1960s	NV	NV	NV	NV	NV
1970s	-68	-89	-64	36	206
Total	-75	-94	-73	62	578
Midwest					
1940s	-45	-14	-55	7	22
1950s	-61	-70	-59	33	158
1960s	-93	-97	-91	69	108
1970s	-11	-61	20	33	50
Total	-64	-79	-57	140	338
West					
1940s	NV	NV	NV	NV	NV
1950s	-48	-68	-44	37	143
1960s	-84	-82	-86	11	82
1970s	-60	-92	-44	45	90
Total	-60	-80	-54	93	315
South					
1940s	48	52	46	406	1353
1950s	22	4	26	203	767
1960s	71	63	73	38	126
1970s	-10	-12	-10	169	290
Total	33	28	35	816	2536
Totals, By Region					
East	-75	-94	-73	62	587
Midwest	-64	-79	-57	140	338
West	-60	-80	-64	93	315
South	34	31	35	783	2536
Totals, By Decade					
1940s	28	42	24	439	1618
1950S	-4	-13	-2	273	1197
1960S	-29	-44	-24	118	316
1970S	-33	-40	-30	281	636

Source: Appendix A
Key: NV-No Vote
Index: +100(Totally Cohesive in Favor of Right to Work)
         -100(Totally Cohesive Against Right to Work)

The southern Democrats' record on the issue at the state level deserves some further attention. Even at the height of right-to-work agitation in the region in the 1940s, organized labor wielded some influence, as the total aggregate index of cohesion for the decade ended up at 48, a definitely pro-right-to-work, but not overwhelming, score. Furthermore, this anti-labor cohesion eroded a bit in the following decade; in the 1950s southern Democrats compiled an index of 22—still in favor of restricting union security but by a significantly lower margin. Approximately 81 percent of all southern Democrats' votes on the issue came during these two decades, and those ballots also accounted for 56 percent of *all* state Democratic voting over the four decades. While there was a fairly steep increase in anti–labor cohesion in the 1960s, in the 1970s the South's Democrats actually tipped into a pro-labor column in the aggregate. Overall, from the early 1940s through the late 1970s, 90 percent of all Democratic votes in favor of right-to-work measures came from the southern region of the country.

Thus, from the perspective of organized labor, if there was any betrayal by the Democratic party on the union security issue it was confined almost exclusively to the South. This is further confirmed by examining the Totals, By Region section of Table 8.2. Eastern Democrats evidenced the strongest support of labor on right to work with a −75, followed by midwestern representatives with −64, and western lawmakers with −60, all respectable indexes of party cohesion considering a span of 36 years. Again, the South was the only region that fell into the anti-labor column with a positive 34 score, a definite, though not unquestioning, endorsement of right-to-work legislation.

Even so, when viewed chronologically, the Democrats' performance as a party improved on the union security question. A review of the Totals, By Decade portion at the bottom of Table 8.2 indicates an increasing tendency to vote more cohesively in support of labor's position on right-to-work proposals. With the inclusion of the large number of southern Democratic states voting for these measures during the 1940s and 1950s, though, the cumulative cohesion was weak. Nevertheless, a progression is clearly discernible. Lower chambers in all states went from an index of 24 in the 1940s, to −2 in the 1950s, to −24 in the 1960s, and finally to −30 in the 1970s. Senate bodies likewise went from a 42 index in the 1940s, to −13 in the 1950s, to −44 in the 1960s, and to −40 in the 1970s. With both chambers combined, state Democrats compiled a score of 28 in the 1940s, −4 in the 1950s, −29 in the 1960s, and −33 in the 1970s. In light of the foregoing aggregate regional and chronological analysis, there seems little doubt that the center of pro-right-to-work legislative voting behavior on the part of Democrats was, is, and most probably will continue to be in the South.

Similar party responses are found at the national level on legislation affecting, or attempting to affect, major national labor policy revisions. Table 8.3 conveniently summarizes both Republican and Democratic cohesion indexes from the passage of the Taft-Hartley Act in 1947 through the failure of organized labor to win passage of the labor law reform bill in 1978. Three of these episodes explicitly involved union security questions: the amendment of the Railway Labor Act, the excision of the union shop election requirements from Taft-Hartley, and the repeal of section 14(b). Only one of these, the repeal vote, produced opposing party reactions. Both the amendment of the Railway Labor Act and the union shop election

8.3
Rice Index of Cohesion of Congressional Parties, Aggregate, on National Labor Law Reform Measures, 1947–1978

LEGISLATION/YEAR	TOTAL	INDEXES SENATE	HOUSE	BALLOTS CAST SENATE	HOUSE
TH, 1947					
D	15	-5	20	42	177
R	90	88	91	51	236
THR, 1949					
D	-45	-12	-51	52	255
R	71	43	78	42	165
RLA USA, 1951					
D	-58	-38	-61	42	218
R	-76	-50	-84	40	125
THA USA, 1951					
D	–	VV	-84	VV	167
R	–	VV	-94	VV	157
THA, 1954					
D	–	-100	NV	46	NV
R	–	87	NV	45	NV
LG, 1959					
D	-35	-49	-32	59	279
R	79	88	77	34	151
THR 14(b), 1965-1966					
D	-38	-34	-40	67	286
R	69	63	70	32	138
LLR, 1977-1978					
D	-55	-44	-58	61	280
R	43	22	49	36	140

Source: Tables 2.5, 3.1, 5.1, 6.3, 7.4
Key: TH-Taft-Hartley, R-Repeal, A-Amendment, RLA-Railway
          Labor Act, USA-Union Security Amendment, LG-Landrum-
          Griffin, LLR-Labor Law Reform, VV-Voice Vote,
          NV-No Vote
Index: +100(Totally Cohesive Against Labor)
          -100(Totally Cohesive in Favor of Labor)

provision evoked little opposition from Republicans, primarily due to a lack of unified business antagonism. In every other instance of potential or actual labor law change, the parties disagreed. Discounting the two 1951 votes, the perceived public concern over post-war labor militancy caused Democratic cohesion to reach its nadir with an index of 15 during the passage of the Taft-Hartley Act in 1947; it climbed to its apex of − 100 (in the Senate) during the vote to recommit anti-labor amendments to Taft-Hartley in 1954. The rest of the party's scores fell into the − 35 to − 55 range. Republicans, on the other hand, tended to be more cohesive in voting against pro-labor changes and backing disadvantageous ones. Again, excluding the two non-opposed votes, GOP cohesion indicators ranged from a low of 43 during the labor law reform bill debates in 1978 to a high of 90 during the passage of Taft-Hartley in 1947. The rest of their cohesion indexes were superior to the Democrats': 69 on the attempt to repeal section 14(b) in 1966, 71 on the attempt to repeal Taft-Hartley in 1949, 79 on passage of Landrum-Griffin, and 87 on the vote to recommit anti-labor Taft-Hartley changes in 1954. In sum, then, both parties at the national level normally responded divergently to efforts to change the country's labor policy. Republicans usually evidenced substantial cohesion against the labor position on an issue; the Democrats, because of the inclusion of the conservative southern congressional contingent, which by and large was more anti-labor than eastern Republicans were pro-labor, did not unite as effectively. Still, under typical conditions each party ultimately came down on opposite sides of the fence.

In light of the foregoing analysis, a much more nuanced evaluation of labor's political effectiveness on special interest issues is possible. Modern labor politics, some observers have argued, has been distinguished by a de facto abandonment of organized labor's previous approach of non-partisanism in political matters—the political expression of the "voluntarism" espoused by AFL president Samuel Gompers. Voluntarism was the idea that organized labor could accomplish its objectives best in American society if it concentrated on the economic sphere of action—collective bargaining, strikes, boycotts—and only engaged in politics when necessary to protect labor's freedom to use its self-help measures. A major principle derived from this was the view that since "partisanism" would endanger labor when the party it supported periodically lost power, unionists should "reward their friends and punish their enemies" in both parties. Gompers' concept, however, lost applicability over the course of the first third of the twentieth century, finally breaking down altogether as a result of the Great Depression and the Democrats' adoption of the New Deal. Subsequently, in the place of non-partisanism the labor movement chose to ally itself primarily with one political party—the Democratic party—and attempts to shape legislative policy through partisan electoral activity as well as traditional lobbying. A major development stemming directly from this transformation has been an increase in organized labor's electoral commitments, most clearly exemplified by the creation of a continuing organizational political apparatus that often performs a good deal of the voting work normally conducted by political parties. For the most part the legislative results of labor's partisan relationship with the Democratic party have been problematic. And while the CIO, the AFL, and later the AFL-CIO eventually succeeded on many social-welfare issues that they advanced on behalf of broader coalitions when the Democrats were at their peak of power, on strictly trade-union-related special interest questions they have failed more than once in their efforts to secure favorable legislation, block unfavorable proposals, and roll back unwanted restrictions.[2] Therefore, a full acceptance of this viewpoint might well lead one to speculate that either a return to non-partisanism (for those laborites on the right) or a drive toward building a labor party (for those unionists of the left) could have more effectively advanced labor's immediate interests during this era.[3]

Had the labor movement adopted either position, however, the immediate probable results would have been much worse than problematic. This study has used the right-to-work issue at both the state and national levels as an analytical tool to examine the dynamics of organized labor's special interest influence in the context of modern American politics, and more particularly, to attempt a balanced evaluation, based upon both qualitative and quantitative evidence, of the overall effectiveness of labor's partisan alliance with the Democratic party. The union security issue was especially well suited to this task because it is a subject that provokes intense reactions from both labor and business. Consequently, each group's efforts to influence the political structure and their relative ability to do so are thrown into sharp relief. Additionally, though there were fluctuations in the intensity of right-to-work agitation, the issue spanned the entire period under consideration with some continuity.

In summary, the qualitative and quantitative research points to the following conclusions. Insofar as the willingness of a legislator to vote with or against labor's position on right-to-work is an accurate and meaningful measure of the political influence of a group, and the commitment of a political party to it, organized labor must be credited with wielding a respectable level of influence in American politics, even on issues that are almost completely of a special interest nature. However, this influence, centered basically within the Democratic party, has been marked by limitations arising primarily from the yawning ideological chasm between southern and non-southern Democrats. Notwithstanding these difficulties, given the nature of the GOP's unified anti-labor response on the right-to-work question, unionists operated out of a partisan context almost by necessity, engaging themselves in politics as much to defend their unions against unwanted economic restrictions as to promote advantageous legislation, and aligning themselves programmatically with the largest segment of the body politic in which they perceived they had support.

In terms of an influence range on special interest questions, union politicians did best during these years when the issue was a question of non-public administrative decision making, or when special conditions necessitated winning labor's cooperation. From this high point through a middle range, the labor movement's legislative influence appeared generally effective within the party when the proposal involved protecting a status quo position that favored labor, with the pro-labor cohesion span dependent on such particular factors as the labor relations opinion climate, the regional political and social structure, and the degree of urbanization, industrialization and unionization. At the lower end of the influence spectrum, Democrats often did not to vote cohesively on behalf of labor when events caused a significant number of representatives to believe that public opinion favored restrictive action—as in the passage of the Taft-Hartley Act, for instance. Nevertheless, while partisanism may have contributed to an inability to sway many Republican lawmakers, and collaterally weakened labor's capacity to impose political costs on the Democratic leadership at critical points, in every region of the country outside of the South and across all time periods the labor federations did receive a return on their electoral investments from the Democrats.[4]

This is not to de-emphasize the fact that organized labor has had major problems with the party. Two areas of special note were the assaults of the southern Democrats during the 1940s and 1950s and the pallid legislative leadership exercised at the national level throughout the entire period. Dixiecrats, inflamed by the specter of large-scale union organizing drives in the South after World War II, were the earliest disciples of the right-to-work movement (although their conservative philosophical brethren in midwestern Republican areas quickly followed their lead). For this state of affairs— the existence of a powerful ideologically conservative wing within the Democratic party—organized labor obviously bore no responsibility since it was a product of historical circumstances. At least some of labor's legislative strategists realized this from the beginning but believed that politicized southern workers could remake the country's pluralist political parties. Union executives' efforts in this endeavor were only minimally successful; first, because politicizing workers meant labor had to first organize them into unions in large numbers, a task which was never done and for which the labor movement carries some responsibility; and second, because a restructuring of this magnitude in such a short time requires historical disruptions of great proportions—something that the labor federations' intermittently efficacious electoral activism obviously was not.

The second and more troubling problem in the alliance between organized labor and the Democratic party was the poor quality of leadership shown by the congressional contingent, although this too was in some ways connected with the entrenched power of the southern members. The lack of vigor with which the party's legislative directors attempted to translate party promises to labor into party actions was substantial. For much of this period, however, the leadership came from the southern section of the party, and consequently it was perhaps not surprising that little progress was made. And, in addition to this difficulty, when southerners were not in control, moderate, non-labor-oriented politicians occupied the positions of leadership, showing a proclivity to abandon labor causes that they perceived had little public support.

Even so, one cannot ignore the fact that the AFL, CIO, and AFL-CIO pushed three reluctant Democratic presidents (Truman, Johnson, and Carter) into supporting and working for major changes in national labor policy—and two of those chief executives hailed from the South. This in itself implies influence of significant dimensions. And while labor lost a good deal of territory to right-to-work forces, it did protect many areas through its political activity—about 38 percent of the floor votes on union security proposals during the period (in 30 states) favored unionists. Quantifiably, the primary reason for the inroads made by anti–union security advocates lay not in any defect within organized labor's political alliance that it was not aware of in originally contemplating the tie, but in the periodic ability of business conservatives to marshall their political resources within the body politic, and, once having done that, to win legislative restrictions at times when the labor movement was inattentive or weakened. Once having won those restrictions, business leaders generally proved capable of protecting legislation such as right-to-work statutes from assaults by labor lobbyists. It was the relative balance of economic power between business and labor in American society that ultimately determined the legislative outcome—as it always has.

NOTES

1. NRTWC, *National Right to Work Newsletter*, 29 August 1980.

2. The classic statement reflecting this view is found in J. David Greenstone, *Labor in American Politics* (New York: Alfred A. Knopf, 1969). It has been seconded to some degree by David Brody in *Workers in Industrial America: Essays on the Twentieth Century Struggle* (New York: Oxford University Press, 1980), chapter 6, "The Uses of Power II: Political Action," pp. 215–255. Brody extends the discussion of labor politics into the 1970s by discussing some of the political forces operating to reduce organized labor's effectiveness at performing an aggregative role for the Democratic party. In particular, Brody makes the point that issues such as the environmental movement, the foreign policy divisions brought about by Vietnam, the tax rebellion, and the decline of party politics all worked to erode the influence of labor within the Democratic party even further. The "breakdown of party politics meant that a partisan effort no longer translated into the kind of ongoing, predictable influence the unions had exerted within the Democratic party for the twenty years after World War II"(p. 245). While Brody's arguments are perceptive and well grounded, the quantitative analysis of the right-to-work issue in the 1970s at the state level, as well as the cohesion evidenced by Democrats during the labor law reform votes, indicates that his arguments on the decline of union influence within the party are at least premature, if not a bit overdrawn. The number of Democratic defections on the attempted labor law revision was hardly unprecedented.

3. The left-leaning position is implicit in Mike Davis, "The Barren Marriage of American Labour and the Democratic Party," *New Left Review* (November-December 1980):43–84. Although Davis's article deals mainly with the 1930s and 1940s, he touches briefly on the 1960s in his concluding paragraphs. Exactly how dominant the "voluntaristic" political philosophy of the AFL was at lower levels in earlier years is a subject open to debate. See Gary M Fink, *Labor's Search for Political Order: The Political Behavior of the Missouri Labor Movement, 1890–1940* (Co-

lumbia: University of Missouri Press, 1973) and Fink, "The Rejection of Voluntarism," in Rehmus, et al., *Labor and American Politics*, pp. 108–132.

4. A study containing a broad quantitative analysis of organized labor's legislative record in the post-war era is Richard B. Freeman and James L. Medoff, *What Do Unions Do?* (New York: Basic Books, 1984), chapter 13, "Union Political Power: Myth or Reality?", pp. 191–206. Freeman and Medoff focus, however, on labor's overall success rate in the legislative arena at the national level. "The key issue in evaluating labor's success is not whether unionization influences voting," they write, "but whether the influence is sufficient to pass the requisite legislation over the opposition it engenders" (p. 196) Their findings implicitly support this study's analysis in that they conclude that the union lobby at the national level is more effective in passing general social legislation and protecting beneficial status quo arrangements than in advancing special interest changes. In Freeman and Medoff's estimation, while unions cannot obtain legislation designed to strengthen labor's economic power without general public assent, they do have considerable political power in some areas.

Appendix A: The Rice Index of Cohesion

The Rice Index of Cohesion is a widely used method of legislative roll call analysis first developed by political sociologist Stuart Rice. Its main use has been to enable descriptive quantitative comparisons of legislative voting across groups. Those groups can be members of a political party, members from a certain type of socio-economic constituency, members from districts with certain demographic characteristics, or members from certain regions or areas within a political entity—virtually any type of group that can be identified as existing within a legislative body. By analyzing and comparing the idea of cohesion, or how solidly a group coheres together in legislative voting, inferences can be drawn regarding the impact of certain variables such as party membership, particularly by comparing the reactions of two identifiable groups to the same issue or types of issues.

For a study that was attempting to assess the success of organized labor in influencing party voting on a trade union issue, the Rice Index was an especially appropriate technique for comparing the parties' records. In fact, because the indexes derived focused on one specific type of labor legislation and incorporated a measure of internal conflict, their meaning was more easily comprehensible than other fairly complicated quantitative methods. And, by analyzing the variable of party across geographic regions, time, and to a lesser degree, levels of government (state and national), it was hoped that any patterns emerging would yield a basically accurate portrayal of labor's ability to influence party structures on this special interest question. This is doubly true because virtually no other group besides organized labor had a vested interest in trying to prevent this type of legislation from being enacted, or seeing it repealed where it had passed.

The logic behind the index of cohesion is as follows. In a group of 100 legislators, if all forces influencing their voting operated in a totally random manner, 50 would vote one way and 50 another on any given issue. Therefore, there would be no "cohesion" in this group and their index score would be 0. If, on the other hand, all 100 voted in one direction on a proposal—either yea or nay—the group would be evidencing perfect cohesion and hence compile an index of 100. Where a group falls between 0 and 100 depends on how much their vote, which again can go either way, departs from the 50/50 random level. The index is calculated by determining the percentages of the vote and subtracting them to express the absolute difference. For example, if a group of 100 Democrats in a given state legislature voted 75 against a right-to-work measure and 25 for it, their index of cohesion would be computed in this way:

Percent yeas: 75 yeas / 100 total Democratic votes * 100 = 75%
Percent nays: 25 nays / 100 total Democratic votes * 100 = 25%
Rice Index of Cohesion: 75% − 25% = 50

Thus, when three-quarters of a group of 100 vote in a given direction, their Rice Index of Cohesion would be 50. The higher the index the more likely it is that some variable, in our case the variable of party, is influencing the response of the legislators. In drawing these inferences, though, one must be careful to have a valid reason for believing that the variable chosen for examination is the most important one, and also one must be cognizant of the fact that variables other than the one being examined could be having some effect. In addition, party cohesion in one-party states, whether Democratic or Republican, tends to be lower than in two-party states. For a discussion of the Rice Index, its derivation, and its usefulness, see Lee F. Anderson, Meredith W. Watts, Jr., and Allen R. Wilcox, *Legislative Roll-Call Analysis* (Evanston, Ill.: Northwestern University Press, 1966).

Before going on to discuss how this study identified potential right-to-work floor votes for inclusion, mention must be made of a modification of the Rice Index of Cohesion as used in this work. Normally, indexes are expressed, as explained above, in absolute terms, whether two groups agreed or disagreed on a specific issue. In order to avoid the problem of constantly having to specify that an index of Democrats was 75 in favor of labor's position on a union security proposal, and that an index of Republicans was 75 against the labor stance, the computation of the index was adapted to include a negative dimension to facilitate quick comprehension in comparing indexes. Therefore, when calculating the index this study does not reverse the subtraction order to get the absolute difference when two groups disagreed. Instead, it substracts percent in favor of right-to-work legislation from percent against in both cases, resulting in a negative index for *pro-labor* positions on anti–union security proposals. At a glance, then, the reader can quickly determine from the tables whether the index of cohesion was in favor of the labor position (a negative score) or against it (a positive value). This change does not affect the concept of cohesion: the higher the score (going in the direction of 100) the greater the cohesion. It simply specifies in a convenient way which direction (pro or anti right to work) the vote went. As a final example, in a group of 100 Democrats, an index tally of − 100 would mean that all of them voted *for* the labor position on a union security bill. Conversely, a score of 100 would mean that they all voted *against* the labor movement (which sometimes happened in the South, for instance).

All state-level votes on right-to-work measures found in tables throughout the study were computed from the actual votes listed in Table A.1 of this appendix, and these floor votes were obtained from official house and senate journals or legislative records of the various states, except for North Carolina's, which came from newspaper accounts. In general, the vote counts used were those that followed what is normally the most significant legislative expression of sentiment, the third and final reading of the bills. In a few instances where third readings were not available the votes are those that followed a second reading, an amendment attempt, or a motion to recommit. While these are less meaningful than the final readings on the question to pass, they still have validity as indicators of party cohesion. Two caveats are in order: first, there is little doubt that there were floor votes throughout these decades that have been missed because of the difficulty in searching through the legislative journals of 50 states over 36 years without first having identified the year and state in which there was a floor vote of some type, even assuming the journals were themselves indexed well enough to enable a researcher to uncover a vote on a right-to-work measure. Even so, it seems that the research identified a sufficient number of votes to enable meaningful generalizations. Second, in evaluating legislative voting one should always be careful to remember that an actual vote at any stage of the legislative process may not be as it seems. That is, representatives sometimes wait to see the trend in the roll call, and, if it looks like a measure is going to pass or fail without their vote, will cast their ballot more to reflect a public relations position than their actual sentiment. But despite all the difficulties that can arise in using roll call voting cohesion as an indicator of party response, when patterns emerge from a large number of states over a fairly long span of years, the effects of quirks in the legislative process can be discounted.

States that had union security roll call votes from the 1940s through the late 1970s were located using the following methods. Those states that have, or at one time had and repealed, a right-to-work law were obviously the most quickly identifiable grouping, and the years of their passage or repeal were widely available and listed in both Paul Sultan, *Right-to-Work Laws: A Study in Conflict* (Los Angeles: University of California Institute of Industrial Relations, 1958) and Joseph R. Dempsey, *The Operation of the Right-to-Work Laws* (Milwaukee, Wis.: Marquette University Press, 1961). In addition, in several cases monographic studies referred to floor votes on earlier attempts to pass laws in several of the right-to-work states prior to the time they actually did pass and those years were also added to the list. A second grouping of states and years came from tables in both Sultan and Dempsey that listed the status of right-to-work agitation in various states through the late 1950s. Many times these proposals did not pass through the legislature but floor votes in one or both chambers were taken and hence were valuable indicators of party cohesion. A third source of identification that went beyond the late 1950s was the *New York Times Index*, which has a "Union Security" sublisting under its "U.S. Labor" subject index. This provided the names and years of many of the states that had votes in the 1950s, 1960s, and 1970s. And a final group of state floor votes during the 1970s was brought to my attention through correspondence with Frank Emig, former national AFL-CIO representative for state legislation. Included in this group was virtually *any* type of measure having to do with union security: a bill to pass a law, a bill to repeal one, a resolution to submit a referendum to the public, an amendment in either a pro– or anti–labor direction, or, in more recent years, an agency shop proposal. All measures applying to the labor movement *in general* were included (an agency shop for teachers only, for example, was not included because it seemed a less valid indicator of general party support or opposition to the labor movement as a whole). All measures were carefully reviewed to determine whether a yea or nay was a vote in favor of the concept of right-to-work restrictions (and thus an anti–labor position) or against legislative restrictions on union security (a

A.1
Floor Votes in State Legislatures on Right-to-Work Measures, Alphabetical, by State and Year, 1943–1979

STATE/YEAR	DEMOCRATS		REPUBLICANS		RESULTS
	Y/RTW SEN/HSE	N/RTW SEN/HSE	Y/RTW SEN/HSE	N/RTW SEN/HSE	
Alabama 1953	VV/67	VV/24	NR/NR	NR/NR	SP
Alabama 1955	NV/47	NV/38	NR/NR	NR/NR	SRF
Alabama 1975	NV/52	NV/48	NR/NR	NR/NR	ASF
Alabama 1979	15/NV	17/NV	NR/NV	NR/NV	CAF
Arizona 1947	14/33	05/16	NR/05	NR/00	SP
Arkansas 1947	25/72	08/16	NR/03	NR/00	SP
Delaware 1947	00/03	04/10	09/20	00/00	SP
Delaware 1949	00/00	08/17	06/04	01/14	SRP
Delaware 1979	NV/07	NV/13	NV/10	NV/06	SF
Florida 1943	23/67	11/24	NR/NR	NR/NR	CAP
Georgia 1947					
Bill 1	34/156	00/28	01/01	00/00	SP
Bill 2	39/146	00/16	01/01	00/00	SP
Idaho 1955	NV/05	NV/18	NV/23	NV/13	SF
Idaho 1957	02/05	23/22	17/28	02/04	SF
Idaho 1977	02/03	13/19	16/39	04/09	SFCC
Indiana 1957	02/03	15/20	25/51	08/22	SP
Indiana 1961	01/NV	25/NV	23/NV	01/NV	SRF
Indiana 1965	00/00	35/73	12/21	03/01	SRP
Iowa 1947	01/00	03/10	35/74	09/21	SP
Iowa 1959	NV/15	NV/33	NV/59	NV/00	SRF
Kansas 1955	01/05	03/30	31/61	04/16	SFV
Kansas 1957	00/08	06/30	30/76	03/06	CAP
Kansas 1969	00/05	08/30	27/71	02/10	SFV
Kansas 1975	00/30	13/20	21/65	05/02	SP
Kentucky 1956	NV/09	NV/30	NV/05	NV/03	SF
Louisiana 1946	23/55	15/43	NR/NR	NR/NR	SFV
Louisiana 1954	22/58	14/41	NR/NR	NR/NR	SP
Louisiana 1956	18/44	21/57	NR/NR	NR/NR	SRP
Louisiana 1957	08/NV	25/NV	NR/NR	NR/NR	SF
Louisiana 1975	07/NV	28/NV	NR/NV	NR/NV	SF
Louisiana 1976	24/56	14/46	01/03	00/00	SP
Maine 1947	DV/00	DV/21	DV/87	DV/28	SF
Maine 1979	00/09	12/65	09/50	09/21	SF
Maryland 1955	VV/31	VV/59	VV/10	VV/11	SF
Massachusetts 1948	00/00	14/80	00/05	22/123	SF
Mississippi 1954	34/92	11/42	NR/NR	NR/NR	SP
Mississippi 1960	31/109	07/17	NR/NR	NR/NR	CAP

STATE/YEAR	DEMOCRATS		REPUBLICANS		RESULTS
	Y/RTW SEN/HSE	N/RTW SEN/HSE	Y/RTW SEN/HSE	N/RTW SEN/HSE	
Nebraska 1947	NP (28Y/10N)	Unicameral	NP (28Y/10N)		SP
Nebraska 1973	NP (22Y/19N)	Unicameral	NP (22Y/19N)		ASF
New Hampshire 1947	DV/06	DV/106	DV/188	DV/50	SP
New Hampshire 1949	VV/DV	VV/DV	VV/DV	VV/DV	SRP
New Hampshire 1979	01/21	12/91	06/165	04/36	SF
Nevada 1951	04/14	02/10	08/16	02/04	SP
New Mexico 1947	10/18	08/12	05/15	01/03	CAP
New Mexico 1959	13/NV	12/NV	04/NV	04/NV	SF
New Mexico 1977	14/11	18/36	07/20	01/00	SF
New Mexico 1979	14/12	18/29	08/28	01/01	SFV
North Carolina 1947	32/108	14/10	NA/NA	NA/NA	SP
North Dakota 1947	02/02	01/00	28/63	14/45	SP
South Carolina 1954	VV/80	VV/28	NR/NR	NR/NR	SP
South Carolina 1955	NV/85	NV/28	NR/NR	NR/NR	SRF
South Dakota 1945	ND/01	ND/02	33/66	00/05	SP
South Dakota 1945	ND/01	ND/02	31/64	02/07	CAP
South Dakota 1947	ND/01	ND/03	32/55	00/15	SP
South Dakota 1955	02/01	04/13	24/48	05/07	AP
South Dakota 1975	06/NV	12/NV	16/NV	00/NV	SRF
Tennessee 1947	24/53	04/21	02/11	03/05	SP
Tennessee 1949	15/NV	13/NV	02/NV	02/NV	SRF
Tennessee 1955	13/NV	12/NV	03/NV	02/NV	AF
Texas 1945					
Bill 1	17/68	10/63	NR/NR	NR/NR	SF
Bill 2	NV/60	NV/53	NR/NR	NR/NR	CAF
Texas 1947	23/82	04/42	NR/NR	NR/NR	SP
Utah 1955	00/00	06/27	13/33	00/00	SP
Utah 1959	NV/16	NV/26	NV/20	NV/01	SRF
Utah 1975	NV/14	NV/26	NV/32	NV/00	ASF
Vermont 1959	NV/02	NV/37	NV/91	NV/99	SF
Vermont 1976	01/NV	10/NV	03/NV	15/NV	SF
Virginia 1947	29/72	06/19	03/05	00/01	SP
Wyoming 1963	01/04	10/15	15/29	01/08	SP
Wyoming 1965	NV/02	NV/33	NV/21	NV/04	SRF
Wyoming 1967	NV/00	NV/28	NV/27	NV/06	SRF
Wyoming 1975	00/NV	15/NV	14/NV	01/NV	SRF
Wyoming 1977	00/08	15/20	14/32	01/01	SRF

Source: Official Legislative Records, Various States
Key: S-Statute, R-Repeal, P-Passed, F-Failed, V-Veto, A-Amendment,
CA-Constitutional Amendment, AS-Agency Shop, NV-No Vote,
CC-Conference Committee, NA-Not Available, NR-No Republicans,
ND-No Democrats, NP-Non-Partisan, DV-Division, VV-Voice Vote

pro–labor ballot). The tables throughout the text give the total index of cohesion and the indexes for each respective chamber, when available. They also provide the number of legislators voting on the issue. A pro–labor index of − 100 for the small number of Democrats in the South Dakota legislature in 1940s, for example, somewhat strains the idea that there is a party vote at all. Nevertheless, in the interests of completeness it is included.

In addition to the state data, party indexes of cohesion were tabulated for all major measures of labor relations legislation at the national level—several of which had explicit or implicit union security ramifications—in order to provide some depth of comparison between what was occurring at the state level and how national party structures were responding. These votes, of course, are much more readily available in the *Congressional Quarterly Almanac*, which was the source for all of them. The aggregate table for national legislation in Chapter 8 is simply a compilation of the "total" indexes for both parties on these issues conveniently put into one table. When, in a few cases, national indexes based upon regional divisions are given, the states were arbitrarily grouped as follows: EAST—Connecticut, Delaware, Maine, Maryland, Massachusetts, New Hampshire, New Jersey, New York, Pennsylvania, Rhode Island, Vermont, and West Virginia; MIDWEST—Illinois, Indiana, Iowa, Kansas, Michigan, Minnesota, Missouri, Nebraska, North Dakota, Ohio, South Dakota, and Wisconsin; WEST—Alaska, California, Colorado, Hawaii, Idaho, Montana, Nevada, Oregon, Utah, Washington, and Wyoming; SOUTH—Alabama, Arizona, Arkansas, Florida, Georgia, Kentucky, Louisiana, Mississippi, New Mexico, North Carolina, Oklahoma, South Carolina, Tennessee, Texas, and Virginia.

Finally, the aggregate state tables in Chapter 8 were derived by taking the states that had floor roll call votes and dividing the country into four regions thusly: EAST—Delaware, Maine, Maryland, Massachusetts, New Hampshire, and Vermont; MIDWEST—Indiana, Iowa, Kansas, Nebraska, North Dakota and South Dakota; WEST—Idaho, Nevada, Utah, and Wyoming; SOUTH—Alabama, Arizona, Arkansas, Florida, Georgia, Kentucky, Louisiana, Mississippi, New Mexico, North Carolina, South Carolina, Tennessee, Texas, and Virginia. Then all votes from these states during the decades of the 1940s, 1950s, 1960s, and 1970s were summed up into pro- and anti-right-to-work totals and indexes of cohesion for the regions by decades were calculated for each party. Lastly, all regions were grouped into a decade time series in order to see more clearly the overall chronological patterns in party responses. The above procedure rendered a weighted index rather than a simple average of the previously computed indexes for the various states.

Appendix B: State Right-to-Work Elections

While the main focus of quantitative analysis in this study is on legislative roll call voting, nineteen separate states had a public referendum on the union security question at one time or another from 1944 through 1978, and five of those had more than one referendum. Thus, in order to put the actions of the legislators from these states in a constituent context, it was desirable to include some basic descriptive statistics about the right-to-work elections in those states. The aggregate voting statistics for these elections are listed alphabetically in Table B.1. In all instances, these are the official voting statistics for that election, as provided by the official election record keeper for that state (usually the secretary of state's office, but in one or two instances a special state election board). The election records from these states listed yes/no votes in each county of the state. The total tabulations for each county in each case matched the official cumulative total in the official state records except for California in 1944 and 1958, Ohio in 1958, and Arkansas in 1976. This was probably due to the unlisted inclusion of absentee ballots or calculation errors in the official tabulations. At any rate, both California's and Ohio's differences were less than 50 votes and Arkansas's less than 900; in none of the three cases did this discrepancy affect the percentage distributions because of the large numbers of voters involved.

The tables throughout the work try to give a somewhat deeper analysis than the broad aggregate picture by including county-level, percent of vote, and union membership data. Percentages on county yes/no votes were computed to give a basic county-level yes/no ratio, and the number of counties that fell into a marginal range (45 to 55 percent in either direction) were compiled as well. In combination, these give a better picture of how "broad" a victory or defeat was in a given state. Additionally, by taking the total votes on the union security measure, and determining what their percentage was of the total votes cast for the highest office in that particular election (president, governor, senator, and in few instances, total votes in the primary in which the election was held or total votes for all house representatives), one gets a better idea of how much of the voting public cared to cast ballots on the issue. Normally, unlike the voter participation on referendums

B.1
Public Right-to-Work Elections, 1944–1978

STATE/YEAR	YES RTW	NO RTW	TOTAL	% RATIO
Arizona 1946	61875	49557	111432	56/44
Arizona 1948	86866	60295	147161	59/41
Arizona 1952	115389	67036	182425	63/37
Arkansas 1944	105300	87652	192952	55/45
Arkansas 1976	466243	257111	723354	64/36
California 1944	1304430	1893630	3198060	41/59
California 1958	2080020	3070870	5150890	40/60
Colorado 1958	200319	318480	518799	39/61
Florida 1944	147860	122770	270630	55/45
Idaho 1958	118718	121790	240508	49/51
Kansas 1958	395839	307176	703015	56/44
Maine 1948	60485	126285	186770	23/68
Massachusetts 1948	505575	1290310	1795890	28/72
Mississippi 1960	105724	47461	153185	69/31
Missouri 1978	630764	944071	1574840	40/60
Nebraska 1946	212465	142702	355167	60/40
Nevada 1952	38823	37789	76612	51/49
Nevada 1954	38480	36434	74914	51/49
Nevada 1956	49585	42337	91922	54/46
New Mexico 1948	43229	60865	104094	42/58
North Dakota 1948	105192	53515	158707	66/34
Ohio 1958	1160320	2001530	3161850	37/63
Oklahoma 1964	352267	376555	728822	48/52
South Dakota 1946	93035	39257	132292	70/30
Washington 1956	329653	704903	1034560	32/68
Washington 1958	339742	596949	936691	36/64

in general, it appears that a good many citizens did have opinions about union security restrictions, for the percentages for right-to-work referendums are typically a fairly high proportion of the total voters for that election. The voting statistics for the highest offices are from Edward F. Cox, *State and National Voting in Federal Elections, 1910–1970* (Hamden, Conn.: Archon Books, 1972). For 1976 and 1978 they are from Richard M. Scammon, *America Votes: A Handbook of Contemporary American Election Statistics, 1976 and 1978* (New York: Macmillan, 1956–).

Finally, an attempt was made to give a fair estimate of approximately how many union members a given state had at the time of the right-to-work election. These statistics were derived from Leo Troy and Neil Sheflin, *U.S. Union Sourcebook: Membership, Finances, Structure, Directory* (West Orange, N.J.: Industrial Relations Data and Information Services, 1985). Unfortunately, Troy and Sheflin's membership data for various states were periodic and in many instances did not include those years in which the right-to-work election was held. Therefore, probable union membership was prorated by taking the membership as listed prior to and after the election, either in an increasing or decreasing direction, determining the difference, dividing that difference by the years between the periods to get a yearly figure of actual and percentage increase or decrease, and then adding or subtracting those numbers from the earlier period up to the year of the election. While this is obviously an imperfect method, since an increase or decline in membership within a state may not occur in an evenly paced manner such as this, it seemed the only logical way to derive an approximation of union membership in a state at the time it had a union security election.

Bibliographical Essay

ARCHIVAL AND MANUSCRIPT REPOSITORIES

Labor Collections and Proceedings

No examination of organized labor's involvement in legislative affairs can ignore the official AFL-CIO records recently opened in the George Meany Memorial Archives at the George Meany Center for Labor Studies in Silver Spring, Maryland. While currently the main relevant sources open without restriction are the records of the federation's legislative department and the office of the president (William Green and George Meany Files), the minutes and notes of executive council meetings, primarily found in the records of the secretary-treasurer's office (William Schnitzler Files), at this time closed, promise to be much more revealing on union executives' perceptions of the right-to-work problem at the highest levels of the labor movement than are either of the previously mentioned collections.

For the time being, though, the various labor collections housed at the Walter P. Reuther Library of Labor and Urban Affairs at Wayne State University in Detroit continues to be the most valuable repository for a fairly high-level view of the conflict over most of its development. The *Proceedings of the Meetings of the International Executive Board, CIO* provides good coverage of that federation's response during the 1940s (balanced for that period, of course, by the AFL's State Legislation Files, housed at the State Historical Society of Wisconsin in Madison, Wisconsin). The archival collections of the CIO's president and secretary-treasurer's office are especially useful for legislative matters for the early 1950s, as are the official UAW records of the president's office (Walter P. Reuther Files), the Washington office, and the citizenship department for the rest of the 1950s and early 1960s. In addition, the Reuther Library also has three other collections having important right-to-work materials: the papers of Charles Baker, the public relations consultant who orchestrated the 1958 Ohio Right-to-Work battle for that state's labor movement, the Irwin L. DeShetler Collection, which documents the struggle in California in that same year, and the fascinating records of John W. Edelman, longtime Washington lobbyist for the Textile Workers.

Other archival records of high quality were somewhat harder to come by for the state-level activities of organized labor. Both the Texas Labor Archives at the University of Texas, Arlington and the Southern Labor Archives at Georgia State University in Atlanta have state-level collections of AFL-CIO documents, encompassing both state federation records as well as regional office files for regions 4, 6, 8, and 17, collectively covering most of the prime right-to-work territory in the south and southwest. Moreover, the COPE Area 8 Collection at the Texas Labor Archives documents the Oklahoma fight of 1963–1964 in some detail. Finally, the microform edition of the AFL-CIO's *State Labor Proceedings* (available from the Center for Research Libraries) yielded significant information, although the uneven comprehensiveness of the proceedings from state to state and lack of individualized indexing hampered their use.

Political Collections

For a view of the right-to-work contest from the perspective of the politicians involved, particularly at the national level, the presidential libraries of Dwight D. Eisenhower (Papers as President, Ann Whitman Files and Records as President, White House Central Files) and Lyndon B. Johnson (Presidential Papers) were extremely valuable. They provided both differing party perspectives and a means for conceptualizing a narrative analysis of the two primary periods when union security legislation surfaced as a national issue. In addition to those central sources, each institution has on file subsidiary collections of administration aides who were actively involved with the subject as well as a number of oral histories of various officials both in and outside of government. The very recent opening of the Jimmy Carter Presidential Library may offer some insights into the controversies surrounding the battle over Labor Law Reform in the late 1970s, although the right-to-work controversy was somewhat peripheral to that struggle and adequately covered in the press.

The papers of national political figures outside of the presidential libraries were voluminous but contributed relatively little insight. In the modern era the vagaries of the legislative process seem to result in politicians below the top executive levels leaving little in the way of written documentation. Thus the papers of Senator Patrick McNamara (D-MI) at the Reuther Library, Senator Paul H. Douglas (D-IL) at the Chicago Historical Society, and Representative James G. O'Hara (D-MI) at the Michigan Historical Collections in the Bentley Library at the University of Michigan in Ann Arbor added little except a review of the constituent context impinging on legislative decision-making.

Pro-Right-to-Work Collections

The papers of two right-to-work advocates, Charles Sligh, Jr. (in The Sligh Family Collection at the Bentley Library) and state-level activist Ira Latimer (located at the Chicago Historical Society), provided needed perspective on the strength of organized right-to-work proponents. In the future, perhaps the records of the National Right-to-Work Committee will become available for scholarly research and they would potentially provide the most solidly grounded source for study of the political forces arrayed against organized labor on this issue, and their impact on both political parties in different areas of the country.

LEGISLATIVE DATA

Public Documents and Quantitative Data

Virtually all of the hearing transcripts of various emergency boards, government agencies, state and congressional legislative committees charged with dealing with some aspect of the union security issue since the 1940s provide a public record of the rationales on both sides of the debate. They of course tend to be self-serving and thus often remain superficial because of this polemical posturing. Nonetheless, they are useful records for they can inspire related lines of inquiry while conveniently periodizing ebbs and flows of political influence.

In the long run, however, a more worthwhile exploration of the legislative dimensions of the union security controversy developed out of an examination of quantitative legislative data, both at the national and state levels. National information on legislative roll calls is readily available, usually in the *Congressional Quarterly* almanacs. Similar information at the state level is available as well, but much more difficult to obtain for it generally requires identifying widely dispersed state legislative libraries that contain the appropriate House and Senate *Journals* (or other official daily legislative activity log) listing roll call voting on the measures and the party affiliations of the representatives. Then, through correspondence, the roll calls must be located through a bill number (not often available at first), a subject index in the *Journal* (sometimes omitted), or a date of passage. Nevertheless, diligence and patience brought most of this quantitative information under purview. Similarly, the records of the public right-to-work referendums over three decades are dispersed. In almost all states the secretary of state is the official that keeps the historical county-level voting statistics on right-to-work elections, and they are normally obtainable through correspondence if the date of the election can be identified.

Index

About the Author

GILBERT J. GALL is Assistant Professor of Labor Studies at the Pennsylvania State University. He has published articles in *The Historian, Labor
Studies Journal,* and *Labor History.*